Supply Chain Security

Supply Chain Security

International Practices and Innovations in Moving Goods Safely and Efficiently

VOLUME 2

EMERGING ISSUES IN SUPPLY CHAIN SECURITY

Andrew R. Thomas, Editor

Praeger Security International

 PRAEGER

AN IMPRINT OF ABC-CLIO, LLC
Santa Barbara, California • Denver, Colorado • Oxford, England

Copyright © 2010 by Andrew R. Thomas

All rights reserved. No part of this publication may be reproduced, stored in a
retrieval system, or transmitted, in any form or by any means, electronic,
mechanical, photocopying, recording, or otherwise, except for the inclusion of brief
quotations in a review, without prior permission in writing from the publisher.

Library of Congress Cataloging-in-Publication Data is available at www.loc.gov

ISBN: 978-0-313-36420-4
EISBN: 978-0-313-36421-1

14 13 12 11 10   1 2 3 4 5

This book is also available on the World Wide Web as an eBook.
Visit www.abc-clio.com for details.

Praeger
An Imprint of ABC-CLIO, LLC

ABC-CLIO, LLC
130 Cremona Drive, P.O. Box 1911
Santa Barbara, California 93116-1911

This book is printed on acid-free paper ∞
Manufactured in the United States of America

Contents

Preface

Since the inception of transportation networks, security has always played a role in planning and execution, albeit mostly a tertiary one to increased efficiencies and reduced costs. On September 12, 2001, leaders of organizations of all sizes woke up to a set of realities that were as formidable as many of them had ever faced. Some of the realities were subtle: government agencies increasingly scrutinized the content of telecommunications and financial transactions. Others were stark and in your face: mind-numbing security lines at airports and new import/export regulations.

As the post-9/11 era has evolved, it is clear that newly acquired friction would be around for as long as we could foresee. Organizations that had once been accustomed to a steady devolution of the non-revenue generating aspects of their enterprise like security were now thrust into the need to somehow deal with these realities.

The spectacular nature of the 9/11 attacks, and later suicide assaults on transport networks in India, Russia, England, and Spain, have altered the ways that supply chain security is viewed by governments, industry, and researchers around the world. Protecting the physical infrastructure of the supply chain along with cargo, passengers, and personnel is now held as both a national security priority and an organizational necessity around the world. Melding two very different objectives—security for the nation and efficiency for stakeholders who use the networks—is posing a new challenge to researchers who seek to understand the changing dynamics of the global supply chain.

In the United States, the creation by the federal government of the Transportation Security Administration in 2002 threw down the gauntlet as to the importance of the issue from both a public policy and management point of view. New governmental mandates and compliance requirements have forced supply chain security to become a priority for all firms, whether they agree with it or not.

Moreover, in the hypersensitive, media-obsessed world of today, international and even domestic terrorists recognize the impact an attack against the global supply chain can have. As a result, much of the interest in transportation security is being driven by the actions of those who seek harm to the system, including the criminal element: individuals and groups who have shown remarkable resilience and no sign of backing away from the multiple targets of opportunity they perceive that the supply chain provides them.

Finally, as globalization takes stronger root around the world, the exponential expansion of the supply chain in the coming decades will ensure that the security component remains front and center.

The purpose of this volume is to look at cutting-edge supply chain security practices and innovations. Frances Edwards and Daniel Goodrich start off making the compelling case for the need for continuous assessment when it comes to supply chain security. Next, G. Tom Gehani of Target Corporation and R. Ray Gehani of the University of Akron provide an innovative risk management approach to reinforce supply chain security.

In another great contribution, Mary Schiavo looks at how supply chain security management impacts shareholder value. Dr. Yuko Nakanishi provides critical performance metrics for the field.

Dimitrios Tsamboulas and Panayota Moraiti detail a formula for the identification of potential targets for terrorists. Hector Guerrero, David Murray, and Richard Flood put forth a model for restoration in the event of a catastrophic port closure. Staying with the maritime theme, a U.S. Government Accountability Office (GAO) analysis of vessel tracking systems is also found here.

From Canada, A.O. Abd El Halim and Mohamed Elshafey highlight a reliable and effective detection, protection, and repair system for the oil/gas pipeline system. Jarrett Brachman of Center for Transportation Security at the Upper Great Plains Transportation Institute, housed at North Dakota State University, reveals some recent innovations in trucking security.

Two persuasive chapters on developments within air cargo are presented. From Mauritius, Mohammed Karimbocus shows how airport operations can be integrated into the global supply chain. And Marie Buzdugan and Triant Flouris explore the regulation of air cargo security at the international level. A GAO report on a risk-based approach to commercial vehicle security follows, and finally, award-winning artist and writer Ross Harley presents a photo essay on supply chain security.

On behalf of the contributors, the publisher, and myself, I thank you for taking a look at this two-volume set. Please feel to share any ideas or recommendations you may have in the spirit of collaboration with which this publication was assembled.

Andrew R. Thomas, University of Akron
Editor
art@uakron.edu

Acknowledgments

A project of this scope and magnitude is the effort of many people whose confidence and hard work must be mentioned here. First and foremost, I wish to thank my editor, Jeff Olson. He believed in this project from the beginning. Jeff is a tough and fair critic of my work, something I am always grateful for. Each of the contributors to this volume set worked on faith to deliver the world-class chapters you are reading here. Their dedication to advancing the global knowledge of supply chain security is to be highly commended.

At the University of Akron, I have been blessed to work with some great colleagues who have supported my desire to explore this research stream. Doug Hausknecht, Deborah Owens, Todd Finkle, Karen Nelsen, Jim Barnett, and Jim Emore were always willing to listen and offer a constructive opinion when needed. In addition, it has been my distinct pleasure to work with the team at the world-class Taylor Institute for Direct Marketing at UA: Dale Lewison, Bill Hauser, Mike Kormushoff, and Steve Brubaker. Thanks to each of you—and Go Zips!

My wife, Jacqueline, and my children, Paul Bryan and Alana, always believe in me. Their unconditional love carries me though.

CHAPTER 1

Supply Chain Security and the Need for Continuous Assessment

Frances L. Edwards and Daniel C. Goodrich

On April 8, 2009, the first act of piracy against an American flag vessel in over 200 years occurred in the Indian Ocean. The Maersk Line's *MV Alabama* was boarded by pirates who took the captain for ransom. The well-trained crew, many of them former Marines, prevented the pirates from capturing the ship by disabling it, leaving the pirates the choice of facing off with the U.S. Navy in a ship dead in the water, or departing in a lifeboat. The crew even managed to take a pirate captive for twelve hours and later tried to trade him for the captain, without success. Naval vessels of the 5th Fleet responded, along with FBI hostage negotiators and other military assets. The ship was carrying only about half of its potential load of containers, all of which were filled with food products being donated by a United Nations agency for refugee relief in Africa.[1]

Supply chain security managers have not been planning for piracy attacks to interrupt their operations, but shippers in the Horn of Africa area have had to plan for piracy for several years. At the time the *Alabama* was attacked there were sixteen ships and 200 crew members being held for ransom by pirates. In 2008, pirates attacked 122 vessels and seized 42 of them, demanding ransoms of $1–3 million for their release.[2] While professional merchant marine crews have received training in dealing with pirates, they are not permitted to be armed. The American crew is the first to successfully retake a ship after a pirate attack.[3]

Arming crews seems to be a logical response to the lawlessness at sea, but ship owners and insurers have concerns about the impact of armed crews on piracy. In the past, crews have used "Molotov cocktails, crates of rubbish and oil drums. They've electrified handrails, sprayed attackers with high-pressure fire hoses and simply kicked the pirates' rickety ladders overboard."[4]

Owners fear that weapons on board ships would escalate the violence when pirates arrive. They are also afraid that volatile cargoes would combust during gun fire. Worse yet, if the crew had weapons, the company might be liable for deaths and injuries sustained on board the ship. British insurers and owners are concerned over the lack of rules of engagement for dealing with pirates. While the pirates have not routinely killed hostages, the sinking of a Thai pirate mother ship by the Indian Navy resulted in the rescue of only one of fifteen hostages.[5] On April 10, 2009, the French Navy retook a French sailboat from pirates off the coast of Somalia, but two pirates and one hostage were killed.[6]

The ships being taken by pirates are all freighters, part of the international supply chain of goods. They sail into many different ports on one trip. An intelligence expert noted that armed ships could be denied entry into certain ports. Weapons held by the crew would have to meet firearms regulations of both the flag nation and the cargo port, making it unlikely that effective long-range weapons able to pose a threat to pirates could be employed on cargo ships.[7]

Piracy has myriad impacts on the security of the supply chain. Later in this chapter, some of the specific impacts will be discussed. But the most obvious is the loss of time to delivery when ships are held to random for months. Another is the escalating cost of ransoming vessels and crews. In 2008, pirates extorted $40 million from shipping companies.[8]

The example of one emerging threat, piracy, makes it clear that management must embrace the concept that the threat environment is constantly evolving, and that there is an ongoing need to respond to these changes in an iterative manner. Supply chain security is no longer the responsibility of a single company. "Globalization and business fragmentation create the need for tackling the issue from the point of view of the entire supply chain."[9] Viewed in terms of return on investment, security can be structured as a high net return element within the supply chain, but all the corporate stakeholders must collaborate to ensure that the benefits of coordinated security are realized. Continuously assessing the threat and operational environment is key to obtaining the maximum benefits from supply chain security.

DYNAMIC ENVIRONMENT

The environment in which supply chain security operates is dynamic. While some threats are permanent, others evolve, disappear, and are replaced by new threats. A thorough threat assessment must underlie any supply chain security plan, and frequent reviews and updates will be required. Natural hazards and technological hazards may be relatively static. For example, San Francisco Bay area companies have to plan for earthquake-based disruption to their supply chain and operational capability, while Miami area companies must plan for hurricanes. Every region of the world has the potential for accidental power blackouts, as well as for denial of service attacks by criminals and terrorists against power networks.

For example, some threats against critical infrastructure may be systemwide. On April 8, 2009, *The Wall Street Journal* carried a front-page article on the cyberattack against the SCADA software controls for the nation's power grid. The attacks were only discovered by the U.S. intelligence agencies that worry about foreign intrusion into the operation of nuclear plants or the electrical grid.[10]

Other attacks on critical infrastructure may be localized but highly disruptive to business in the area. On April 9, 2009, AT&T telephone fiber cable was cut in four locations in a denial-of-service attack, apparently by vandals with intimate knowledge of the system. Although the cable was underground and protected by manhole covers with unique removal requirements, knowledgeable criminals entered vaults in south Santa Clara County, San Jose and San Carlos, California and cut through fiber optic cables containing 48–360 strands, each of which serves 300–400 calls.[11] The damage took most of the day to repair, denying critical emergency and business services to Gilroy, Morgan Hill, San Martin, and parts of southern San Jose, San Benito, and Santa Cruz counties for 23.5 hours. Disruptions included lack of cell phone service and ATM services. Banks locked their doors and admitted one customer at a time, provided handwritten deposit receipts, and could not guarantee that funds would be deposited into checking accounts in time to cover automatic payments due at midnight. Stores could not accept checks, credit cards, or debit cards, and many closed for the day. Fifty-two thousand households in Gilroy and Morgan Hill served by Verizon lost their land line services, while 911 services to the effected areas were also lost. Emergency services personnel were stationed on mountainsides to scan for fires, and extra ambulances were positioned in the outage area.[12]

At the end of the outage, AT&T, which had initially offered a $100,000 reward, upped the ante to $250,000 for information leading to the arrest and conviction of the vandals, a measure of the disruption to its service supply chain to its residential and business customers.[13] While AT&T customers were eligible for "credits for the day of lost service . . . businesses that suffered due to lack of communication should not expect to recoup their losses." But Verizon's 52,000 customers will get nothing because the outage lasted less than 24 hours.[14]

Some threats are unique to time and place. Ecoterrorist attacks are more common against animal testing facilities, large motor vehicle dealerships, and developments in wildland areas,[15] while politically motivated terrorist attacks are more likely in high-profile cities and among large groups of people. Industrial espionage and sabotage are possible in any company, but especially in companies with cutting-edge technologies and large research and development operations.

Planning for disasters, whether large or small, requires anticipating impacts on the supply chain. Customers may demand increased supplies to replace items lost in the disaster.[16] The ability to "surge" capacity to meet immediate disaster needs may both increase sales and benefit the company's public image.

For example, as Hurricane Katrina was developing from a tropical depression into a hurricane, Wal-Mart staff tracked the storm and modified their shipments to stores in the hurricane area to include extra supplies of batteries, bottled water, and other items subject to "panic buying" when hurricane landfalls are predicted. After Hurricane Katrina struck, Wal-Mart greatly increased the supply of household cleaning products being sent to its stores in the disaster area, which both met the disaster recovery needs of the consumers and boosted the sales tax revenues of impacted jurisdictions. Wal-Mart was able to respond rapidly, even though its stores were also victims of the hurricane, because a disaster plan was in place. Wal-Mart decided to "play to its strength"—which is logistics—and mobilized its supply chain to meet the needs of damaged communities for water, cleaning products, and baby supplies.[17] Wal-Mart's response was only possible because it had prearranged agreements with its suppliers for surge capacity. It also had fallback sources for essential goods. It had agreements with employees to report to work, and storm response teams ready to augment employees in damaged areas.

The Department of Homeland Security and the Transportation Security Administration, in cooperation with the Federal Bureau of Investigation, identify specific threats against air transportation, banking facilities, and federal buildings. However, analyses of rails, buses and trucks, and the commercial vehicle sector are incomplete. Although the 9/11 Commission Act (Public Law 110-053) required an analysis of commercial vehicle vulnerabilities, no report has been created. House Homeland Security Committee Chairman Bennie Thompson (D-MS) stated, "the security of the nation's trucking industry is vital to our economy . . . . we must do a better job of ensuring that commercial vehicle security initiatives follow a risk based strategy."[18]

The Government Accountability Office agreed, issuing a report entitled, "Commercial Vehicle Security: Risk-Based Approach Needed to Secure the Commercial Vehicle Sector." GAO pointed out that the risk assessment needs to be backed up with performance measures for the effectiveness of strategies employed to improve commercial vehicle safety and to identify the roles of all stakeholders.[19] Considering the critical role trucking plays in the supply chain, such a security assessment is crucial for the development of appropriate security strategies to protect goods in the supply line.

Economic

Economic conditions and pressures also contribute to the dynamic environment in which supply chains are operated. Commodity prices fluctuate with supply and demand. Later in the chapter, the impact on criminal behavior of fluctuating prices for commodities like copper will be detailed, demonstrating how supply chain security plans must change based on new threats.

Hurricane Katrina damaged the Port of New Orleans, blocking Midwest soy beans and corn from their international markets.[20] This changed the distribution routes of Midwest farm goods from river-based transportation to road-based transportation and changed their destinations from international ports to American processors like Archer Daniels Midland. Supply chain security plans for these changes would have been developed based on the continuous assessment of the commercial conditions in the effected industries.

International food-growing and distribution practices are changing based on water supplies, global warming, fuel prices, and currency fluctuations. For example, in India and Pakistan, groundwater use in agriculture is depleting future supplies, while deserts are encroaching on former fields. Although food is more readily available in the globalized marketplace, transportation costs for food are being driven up by diesel fuel costs, changing consumption and distribution patterns. Supply chain security managers need to be aware of the dynamic marketplace for agricultural goods as sustainable agricultural practices replace petroleum-based fertilizers, causing local food production to increase and replace imports.[21]

April 2009 saw a dramatic drop in American food exports, a crucial part of many farmers' income streams, leading to a projection of up to a one-third drop in the agricultural sector's income. Factors contributing to this change were financial, social, and economic. Better growing conditions in Australia and food import cutbacks in developing markets in China and India caused part of the drop. Better domestic yields in Morocco, India, Mexico, and Bangladesh have led to lowered food imports by those nations, and even increased exports of some foods at lower prices than U.S. farmers can accept. Rice, wheat, corn, and sorghum all dropped from October 2008 to January 2009. The strengthening dollar was also bad for agriculture. For example, the Euro traded at $1.62 in 2008 but only at $1.32 in 2009. The British pound traded at over $2 in 2007 but only at $1.47 in April 2009.[22] With exports accounting for 20 percent of overall farm income, such drops will reverberate through the supply chain, affecting packing houses, warehouses, cargo handlers, and shippers in the United States and abroad.

Political

Political aspects of the supply chain are affected by American and foreign elections, trade agreements, UN actions, and bilateral agreements. International standards such as those promulgated by the ISO are adopted by some nations, changing their profile for receiving goods from other nations. Internal food and drug regulations evolve, limiting access to formerly open markets. For example, Japan has strict requirements for imported cosmetics and hair products.

Another challenge for supply chain security is foreign business practices. In some nations, bribes are an accepted method of opening trade negotiations, but American law prohibits American companies from giving bribes. Recently the World Bank has begun a campaign against bribes in business transactions, noting that corruption is the "single greatest obstacle to economic and social development."[23] The World Bank Institute says bribes constitute a 20 percent tax on international business.[24] In a dynamic environment where bribes are being withheld, supply chain security dynamics will also change, requiring guards for goods and personal security for negotiators.

Within the United States, the 9/11 terrorist attacks had a major impact on supply chain security. In addition, attacks on transit systems in Madrid and London led to the realization that surface transportation has long been a target for terrorists. In response to these concerns, the federal government began a Transportation Security Grant Program in 2003, including a Regional Transit Security Strategy requirement in 2005. This money passed through the states to the eligible transportation systems, including $8.4 million for the Bay Area and $4.0 million for the Los Angeles area of California.[25] These grants were followed by $445 million in critical infrastructure grants, including $201.2 million for port security, $171.8 million for the Transit Grant Security Program, $11.6 million for the Intercity Bus Security Grant Program, and $11.6 million for the Trucking Security Grant Program.[26] By 2009, $25.5 million was set aside for Bay area ports, and $36.3 million for Los Angeles area ports.[27] But because of California's state budget problems the port security money was not passed through to the intended recipients,[28] creating stress for supply chain security plans dependent on enhancements to be funded through these grants, which covered physical security enhancements.

Finally, political unrest in other nations can impact the supply chain. As discussed earlier, Somali pirates have become the scourge of the Gulf of Aden and the Horn of Africa shipping lanes. Such piracy is only possible because Somalia is a failed state. The nation has lacked a working central government since 1991. The pirates, who have extorted millions of dollars from shipping companies, use the coast of Somalia with impunity for their criminal operations. They launch their mother ships from Somali ports and hold ships for ransom in Somali coastal waters because there is no functioning government that is accountable to the international community.

An American-led coalition of warships from the European Union, Japan, Iran, Russia, India, China, and other polities patrols the Gulf of Aden, but fifteen to twenty warships in over 1 million square miles of open sea is not necessarily effective in stopping such attacks. U.S. Navy experts estimate that sixty-one ships would be needed to protect the shipping lanes in the gulf alone.[29] During the same week as the attack on the *Alabama*, the U.S. Office of Naval Intelligence held a meeting of the Horn of Africa Piracy Conference in Maryland with 300 representatives of the shipping industry, academia, and military services,[30] seeking solutions to the disruption of trade.

Somalia's new government has agreed to antipiracy actions, but it lacks the resources to patrol Africa's longest coast—1,900 miles. Improved stability in Somalia might lure young men away from their lucrative crime spree, but after twenty years of rebellion and instability, that will be difficult.[31]

While supply chain security managers may see their role as protecting the logistics function, the dynamic environment makes it essential that they constantly scan for political, social, and economic changes that will transform the threat matrix in which logistics operates. Close cooperation with all elements of corporate planning is essential to ensure that the threat assessment is current and the security measures effective.

Trends in Criminal Behavior

Security managers must maintain a heightened awareness of the trends in criminal behavior. Smuggling, drug trafficking, and human trafficking all impact the security of the supply chain. A continuous assessment of criminal activity requires close cooperation with intelligence fusion centers, local police departments, and appropriate federal law enforcement entities such as the Coast Guard and Federal Bureau of Investigation. Interpol also investigates international criminal behavior. Stratfor.com and open-source news reporting may provide important sources of information on trends in supply chain–related crime.

The Transported Asset Protection Association (TAPA) reports an epidemic of cargo thefts in the Netherlands, for example. In 2007, "theft of load" losses amounted to $450 million, causing shippers to consider rerouting cargoes to avoid the Netherlands, long a major distribution center for Europe. TAPA noted that "for every Euro of loss there are five Euros of consequential damages, such as investigation of the theft, replace[ment of] the stolen goods, and mak[ing] up for the lost production or delivery cycle."[32] Across Europe, supply chain theft amounted to $11.5 billion. As a result of this threat to its port business, the government "engaged in an action agenda with manufacturers, transport and logistics providers, law enforcement agencies and trade associations to support this vigilance, especially at Schiphol Airport and Port of Rotterdam."[33]

Gilad Solnik of TAPA noted that heightened internal security has pushed commercial crime to the supply chain, "the weakest link."[34] This led to the establishment of TAPA by Intel, Compaq, Sun, and other security managers, with the goal of exchanging information with law enforcement agencies to encourage enforcement of laws against cargo crime, and to focus on supply chain security through certifications and best practices. TAPA offers an incidents information services database that tracks crimes against supply chains. The database covers 8,166 incidents with a value of €603 million.

This database is an important part of the continuous assessment of supply chain security issues that can lead to the development of effective countermeasures. The database shows, for example, that thefts from vehicles accounted for 1,000 of the incidents, while thefts of vehicles with loads accounted for over 300 incidents from January to October 2008. Data also shows that consumer electronics accounted for over 250 events in 2007 and 2008, while tobacco and pharmaceuticals accounted for less than 50 events each. Services also include a recovered goods database, IIS alerts regarding insecure parking areas and bogus police, alerts regarding false identity documents, and incident trends. Such information can direct scarce security resources toward developing strategies to address the most significant vulnerabilities in the supply chain for businesses operating in or receiving cargo from or through Europe, Africa, or the Middle East.[35]

International Relations

One of the most challenging aspects of security is the impact of international relations and terrorism on the supply chain. Security can be compromised through a variety of attacks, work stoppages, and piracy. Security managers need to be aware of international relations issues that have the potential to spill over into supply chain security. For example, the American involvement in the Iraq war has destabilized some Middle Eastern trade routes as insurgents attack convoys and pipelines.[36] European efforts to encourage moderation in the conservative elements of the Muslin community may have the desired effect of eliminating radicalization of British citizens by imams of extremist sects. However, while Britain has taken the lead in developing outreach programs to create positive relations among the Muslim community, especially young people, it is still unclear whether this will stop radicalization or merely push it underground.[37]

The oil crisis of 2008 created a change in the consumer profile of gasoline in the United States and other industrialized nations. This has led to a drop in foreign currency for many Middle Eastern nations. While the drop in income is expected to deprive the Iranians of the funding needed for their nuclear research, it is depriving other oil producers of funding used to educate their people, provide health care, and offer social services. A drop in national income could result in a backlash against the West.[38] Transportation of goods is being affected by the rise in diesel fuel costs, most notably affecting "food in the globalized market place."[39] Environmental concerns are driving a number of groups to interfere with production and distribution of products that deplete the earth, pollute the air, or create greenhouse gases. Environmental terrorism in the United States has led to attacks on Hummer dealerships in California and ski resorts in the West.[40] Such actions could be turned against other industries not perceived as environmentally responsible.

Most recently, the Chinese have signaled that they will not tolerate a devaluation of the dollar because of their extensive investments in U.S. treasury bills and other instruments.[41] Destabilization of the trade relationship between American consumers and Chinese producers could impact global commerce directly and indirectly. A Western depression could lessen the demand for luxury goods[42] while increasing the demand for basic goods bought at Wal-Mart and made in China.[43]

But a downturn in overall consumption of Chinese-made goods could result in radical changes in shipping routes, impacting the amount of trade passing through West Coast ports, whose trade mostly comes from Asia. In 2009, an 18.1 percent downturn in deliveries was noted in the Port of Long

Beach, forcing the port to lower its cargo rates by 10 percent for each container, and as much as 50 percent for new customers.[44] Ships are idle around the world, putting crews out of work and impacting the entire supply chain. This one port alone employs 280,000 people in Los Angeles County and handles $357 billion in goods, with the downturn also impacting inland warehouse and distribution areas.

The Port of Oakland was down 22 percent because of the downturn in consumer spending and the reluctance of companies to develop inventories. Seattle and Tacoma experienced downturns of around 39 percent and 29 percent, respectively. East Coast ports, with a mix of trade sources, have seen lower downturns, with 6.8 percent for New York and 29.5 percent for Charleston. One oceangoing container freight company estimated a drop of one-third in its revenues, or $68 billion.[45]

STRUCTURE

The supply chain has multiple facets, beginning with the manufacturer and its facility, including quality control to prevent substandard or sabotaged items from entering commerce. The second layer is local transportation from the manufacturer to the national or international transportation facility. Threats include hijacking, internal theft, mislabeling of the item for deliberate redirection of the goods, and substitution of the manufactured item with another item. The third layer of the supply chain is international transportation, which may be by air, rail, road, or water. At this level, the normally accepted practice is using a shipping container for ease of transition among the modes of transportation, and to provide inventory tracking. Incidents that can occur at this level include hijacking, piracy, substitution of goods, destruction through transportation accident, or deliberate destruction, including derailments and attacks on ships, trucks, and planes. The fourth layer is domestic transportation at the receiving point, which is subject to the same threats as transportation at the sending source. The final level is movement of goods after the company or company subcontractor has accepted the goods. Items are subject to theft, diversion, and destruction before they are incorporated into the manufacturing process. Some aspects of the goods management system offer enhanced opportunities for security surveillance and oversight.

The International Organization for Standardization (ISO) has created the ISO 28000 series, the standard for supply chain management aimed at reducing the risk of terrorism, piracy, and fraud. "With an internationally recognized security management system, stakeholders in the supply chain can ensure the safety of cargo and people, while facilitating international trade, thus contributing to the welfare of society as a whole."[46] The focus is on manufacturers, shippers, and all others in the supply chain working closely with customs organizations to ensure the security of goods from manufacturing to delivery.

Just-in-Time Supply

The just-in-time supply strategy was created to minimize overhead in an effort to maximize profit. In effect, anything in storage is considered a drain on profits—capital tied up in unused goods and storage space. As a result, when using just-in-time, there are fewer redundant assets available for immediate use. Any disruptions to the supply chain when using the just-in-time model start a domino effect through the rest of the company. Under normal circumstances, extra materials can be acquired quickly to fill the gap and maintain operations. But just-in-time management is not perfect, with its own inevitable gaps between purchased materials and finished products, which may provide a small measure of redundancy.

Just-in-time is really focused on a reduction in investment in stock, creating vulnerability when other sections of the supply chain cannot increase production or shipping to meet increased needs. For example, during the evacuations in advance of Hurricane Rita in Houston, Texas, drivers were stranded without gasoline because the gas stations received gas supplies based on normal usage by day of the week and day of the month. The sudden flight of almost 1 million people on the same day and over the same route overwhelmed the just-in-time supplies.

Internal just-in-time procedures are overlaid by international trade agreements. Because of the constant search in just-in-time management for the cheapest items available that meet the manufacturing criteria, components suppliers around the globe are accessed. The total cost is considered, from manufacturing through the cost of transportation to time of delivery. That means that the route of goods bought one month may be entirely different than the route of goods bought another month, making security arrangements challenging. Security issues in different nations, different ports, and different modes of transportation demand reassessment of the systems in place to ensure that the assets arrive intact and when needed. Cost factors include not only the cost of the finished product, but also the cost of local transportation, port costs and fees, and the need for local payments to officials. Trade agreements such as most favored nation status and embargos may result in the purchase of goods with a higher initial cost but lower final cost because of favorable trade agreements, while the cheapest production item may become more expensive through tariffs and trade restrictions.

Department of Homeland Security Cargo Security Programs

The terrorist attacks on 9/11 created demand for heightened inspection of goods entering the United States through ports. One program designed to do this is the Transportation Worker Identification Credential (TWIC), which provides a commercial background check for multimodal transportation workers and results in issuing identification cards that include biometric identification methods. The Transportation Security Administration (TSA) is responsible for enrolling the workers, while the Coast Guard is responsible for enforcing the enrollment requirement in the ports. Lockheed Martin produces the system that enrolls the workers and issues the cards to those who pass the background check. The system enrolls not only the port workers but also the delivery mode workers, such as train and truck crews, recognizing that cargo tampering may occur at any point in the supply chain.[47]

Cargo surveillance is a second aspect of American port security. Out of concern that radiological materials or other weapons of mass destruction might be introduced into the country in cargo containers, the Department of Homeland Security began a program to inspect cargos before they are sent into the supply chain. The Coast Guard uses cameras and radar to identify ships whose cargo might pose a threat. U.S. Customs and Border Patrol surveys cargo it once in port using radiological detectors and both traditional and backscatter X-ray devices to search for drugs and human cargo.[48]

To maximize the benefit of the inspection protocols, the Coast Guard has created Command 21 to gather information from all surveillance sources and make it available to key security stakeholders. It is part of the mandate for information fusion centers at ports under the Security and Accountability For Every (SAFE) Port Act of 2006.[49] The most innovative aspect of Command 21 is Watchkeeper, which integrates the streams of data and then displays critical information. This system helps overcome the "stovepipe" systems of the past with first responders, shipping companies, manufacturers, transportation workers, and others in the supply chain now linked for security assessment.[50]

Overseas Container Certification

In an effort to create balance between perceived vulnerability and accessibility, the Department of Homeland Security began a program to secure cargo in foreign ports. The intent is to create a buffer between the United States and the country of origin through a layered surveillance process. Seven million cargo containers enter American ports each year.[51] The U.S. Bureau of Customs and Border Protection introduced the Container Security Initiative, which operates in fifty-eight ports in thirty-three countries, employing several hundred officers.[52] High-risk containers are identified and prescreened before they are shipped. Cargo is inspected at the port of origin "using large scale X-ray and gamma ray machines and radiation detection devices."[53] In addition, smart containers that easily reveal tampering are preferred for U.S. destinations.[54]

In the international corridor, there is unsurpassed access to examining the cargo, because there is no presumption of confidentiality or privacy. Search warrants, probable cause, or specific suspicion are not required for a thorough search. Virtually any cargo can be inspected by customs officials of the sending and receiving nations. The volume of cargo traveling through the corridor prevents inspection of most containers, so effective targeting of the highest-risk items is essential.[55]

However, once the cargo is underway, its control generally falls under the country of registry of the vessel, so jurisdiction while at sea is less clear. Thus, reinspection in U.S. ports may still be prudent.

Another predelivery security initiative is the voluntary public–private partnership C-TPAT. Private companies agree with the Customs and Border Patrol to enhance the security of their cargos in their country of origin, including by requiring their foreign partners to adhere to C-TPAT regulations. Companies benefit by experiencing a lowered incidence of loss, damage, and theft while denying terrorists easy access to the international supply chain.[56] Partners include importers, customs brokers, terminal operators, carriers, and foreign manufacturers.[57] The Free And Secure Trade (FAST) program at Canadian and Mexican ports of entry provides for expedited cargo inspections, allowing registered C-TPAT members to use the "green lane."[58]

Borderless European Union

International regional treaties have also impacted security of goods in transit. For example, goods shipped across the European Union are not subject to inspection at borders or ports. The loss of border-based inspections means that goods in transit internationally are vulnerable to tampering, demanding higher levels of security measures for their cargos. In cases where loads of goods are augmented during transportation, opportunities for theft, smuggling, and even human trafficking are substantial, making traditional locks and bond tags ineffective.

The European Union is developing a trusted agent program for companies in international trade. Known as Authorized Economic Operators (AEO), the program was defined by the European Commission.[59] Participants include "manufacturer, exporter, forwarder, warehouse-keeper, customs agent, carrier and importer."[60] They abide by security and safety standards based on the concepts of C-TPAT and the World Customs Organization's Framework of Standards to Secure and Facilitate Global Trade (SAF Framework).[61] Members can grant AEO status to any international trade component company that abides by the security criteria based on a risk management model.[62] AEOs are encouraged to get compliance agreements with their business partners outside the AEO group.[63]

Drawbacks of Standardization

Standardization of customs inspection processes eliminates security's greatest asset, randomness. By creating minimum international standards, with the intent of maximizing through-put of cargo, a reduction in the number of potential security checks is created. Because the process is more standardized, it is potentially easier to breach the security systems by developing countermeasures to the known barriers. The concept of randomness in security creates apprehension in potential criminals about what security systems and protocols may be used to inspect the container holding their contraband goods. Standardization works against this very concept. If the variety of customs checks is limited, the difficulty of developing countermeasures by perpetrators is reduced.

Supplier Security

Companies may heighten cargo security by marking containers with a seal or indelible marking designed to be difficult to forge. Individual packaging can also be sealed or marked to make product tampering difficult. Inspections of products at the delivery point will reveal whether the shipment has been compromised, thereby enhancing confidence in the materials. Radio frequency identification tags or GPS technology can ensure that the product that was shipped from the manufacturer is what has been received by the customer. Such systems, while not tamperproof, will provide an additional level of assurance for both international imports and domestic transportation of goods.

Critical Junctures of Security

The supply chain involves multiple modes of transportation, which themselves must be protected to ensure its safety. One breach of the supply chain transportation assets may result in a denial of service for multiple customers, causing cascading events for other transportation mechanisms. Rail or highway bridges to ports can become single points of failure for the supply chain in a region. For example, a single bridge connects the freight staging yards along the Alameda Corridor Transportation Agency's rail system to the port of Long Beach, after trains pass through the heart of Los Angeles.[64] Similarly, the loss of the Hanshin Expressway in the Kobe Earthquake cut off the Port of Kobe from the rest of Japan for weeks, interrupting the global supply chain of LEDs.[65]

Technological failures in one infrastructure may adversely impact others. For example, the August 14, 2003, Eastern United States and Canada power outage left thousands of communities without traffic lights, computer control for bridges, and power for railroads.[66] Ports lacked communications systems, lights, and power for cranes drawing up to two megawatts of electricity[67]—a serious compromise in the production of the port.

Deliberate attacks on key facilities, such as ports, could take a facility out of service for months. Sinking a ship at a dock would require a lengthy salvage process to restore the facility. Homeland Security analysts have planned against the use of a propane tanker as a bomb in an urban port facility.[68]

The interconnectedness of transportation and other critical infrastructures means that supply chain security relies on tamper prevention protocols for all the elements. Loss of one element may result in the inability to deliver process or protect goods in transit.

Bottlenecks and Vulnerabilities

Bottlenecks are locations where the flow of traffic is constricted by an immovable object, or a process such as Customs Inspection. As a result, a special set of vulnerabilities exist, depending on the nature of the bottleneck. For example, a hijacked ship in the Straits of Malacca could be used to block the shipping lanes, compromising the delivery of oil to the Pacific coast ports.[69] Brush fires in Sumatra have caused the closure of the harbor in Port Kelang, affecting shipping in the Straits of Malacca.[70] This narrow channel carries 50,000 cargo ships each year—20 percent of international trade. Experts worry that terrorists could blow up a tanker in one of the ports along the straits, blocking shipping in the area.[71] Other bottlenecks for international trade include the Strait of Hormuz (in the oil-rich Persian Gulf) and the Suez Canal (which is considered a potential target for Islamic terrorists).[72]

CONTINUOUS ASSESSMENT

Security personnel can either conduct periodic or continuous assessments of the threat and operational environments. The value of continuous assessment is being able to monitor, on an ongoing basis, the continually changing environment in which security must operate. Changes in regulations, political sensitivity, economic factors, and motivations for criminal behavior all impact elements of the supply chain, from raw materials to transportation of the finished product to the consumer. Changes in any one of these parameters affect the others.

The reaction time between these elements can be instantaneous or extremely slow. There is often no clear way of determining what changes will have pronounced effects or negligible impacts, and in what areas they will appear. Because of this, a strategy of ongoing environmental and operational evaluation must be in place at all times by all the different participants in the supply chain. This information needs to be shared among the security, manufacturing, and shipping elements of the supply chain. Security is often reluctant to reveal information to other stakeholders, but across-the-board participation in supply chain security analysis is critical for ensuring the accuracy and reliability of the information.

Evaluate the Environment

With multimodal systems in use, and the complexities of each system, transportation supply chains are more vulnerable than ever before. With multiple sources in a single supply chain, accountability for product composition, purity, and conformity with regulations is diffuse. Security leaders must be aware of changing dynamics along the entire supply chain, from the original source of raw materials through to the delivered finished product.

Political unrest, labor relations problems, criminal actions, and new regulations at any point in the supply chain may lead to unexpected changes to the supply chain condition with detrimental effects. For example, in May 1984, Mexico created 600 tons of radioactive steel, requiring the U.S. Border Patrol to install Geiger counters at every border crossing. The radioactive steel was inadvertently manufactured after being contaminated with Cobalt 60 through recycled materials stolen from a hospital. The border patrol seized and buried all the contaminated steel, disrupting the supply chain for numerous U.S. companies and changing the economics of the international recycled steel industry.[73]

In April 2009, imported Chinese wallboard was implicated in damage to copper pipes and toxic fumes in homes in the American southeast. Heat and humidity appear to cause wallboard components to break down more quickly, resulting in the release of some chemicals, causing odor and damage. More than 500 million pounds of the potentially contaminated wallboard has been installed in over 100,000 homes between 2004 and 2008, including some rebuilt after Hurricane Katrina damaged the originals.[74]

Political and Economic Influences on Criminal Behavior

Actions of governments and the conditions in the economy can also change the security of a supply chain. For example, when the United States passed the RICO Act in 1970,[75] it changed the structure of organized crime to a more disbursed model to avoid criminal convictions, making it more difficult for police and security personnel to track thefts and diversions.

When the price of gasoline rose to $4 a gallon in the United States in 2008, theft of fuel increased.[76] In Hawaii, fleets of trucks parked unattended overnight with 20–30-gallon gas tanks were the focus of thieves who cut the plastic fuel lines to circumvent the locking gas caps.[77] The losses included not only the gasoline but damage to the vehicles and time out of service for repairs. The cost benefit of enhanced security for the fleets became clear only after the losses were incurred.

During the economic boom of the 2000s, the theft of copper from transformers in the United States and overseas[78] posed a problem for supply chain security. The international price of copper rose 500 percent from 2001 to 2008, creating a market for illicit copper. The FBI notes that sites where copper was pilfered included "electrical substations, railroads, security and emergency services, and other sensitive sites. Already, copper thefts have been responsible for shutting down railway systems and even 911 emergency systems." Tornado sirens and an FAA tower have been targets of thieves.[79]

Not only power and energy are affected—agriculture is, as well. In Arizona, the theft of copper wire impacted irrigation systems for field crops, resulting not only in lost crops and replacement costs, but also in lost opportunity costs as farmers are now hesitant to install electrical irrigation systems in new fields. "Other and more extensive property damage is created as a result of the theft. Fences are cut for the thieves to obtain access. Sturdy chain link fences are cut or backed over. Motors must be rewound, panels are stripped, bearings and transformers pulled down and stripped, oil drip lines cut and removed. Debris is scattered." But the theft of a few hundred dollars' worth of copper can result in overall damages many times that value. "Secondly, the stripping causes much ancillary damage. In mid-January a neighbor had $12,000 damage caused to a single well, motor and pump, while the thieves made off with a couple of hundred dollars worth of copper wire."[80] Not just copper is being stolen. "The Phoenix police department actually has four metal-theft detectives on staff. They report 12,000 transactions per month of copper and nonferrous metals being sold in Phoenix alone. Because of current law, there's no way of telling whether a metals transaction is legitimate or not."[81]

These are just a few examples of the ways that supply chains are being disrupted by copper theft alone. A continuous awareness of crime trends is crucial in combating and responding to new and changing threats. At present, the theft of copper is classified as simple larceny, so even when criminals are caught, their bail is a few thousand dollars and the charges carry light sentences. The law does not take into account the value of the ancillary damages and losses incident to their crimes.[82] The federal Copper Theft Prevention Act of 2008 was proposed to cut criminal copper transactions by requiring recycled metals buyers to document their purchases by collecting drivers' license information from sellers and paying transactions of more than $250 by check.[83] This act has not yet become law.

Lack of government control of coastlines has led to a change in the incidence and severity of piracy in certain shipping lanes. As discussed earlier in the chapter, in recent years pirates have hijacked ships, demanding ransom and resorting to violence. Merchant seamen have not been routinely armed, nor have large ships had protective weapons. In 2008 alone, $150 million has been paid to ransom ships and crews involved in 293 pirate attacks across the shipping lanes. While attention has been paid to hijackings in the Gulf of Aden, experts believe that these figures represent only 20 percent of actual attacks worldwide.[84]

A return of piracy has changed the security profile for all unarmed ships. As demonstrated by the successful repulsion of pirates by the *Alabama*, crews must have heightened situational awareness of the safety issues in the sea lanes they use, as well as in their immediate area of operation. Technology such as long-range cameras and surface-search radar can enhance awareness, while access control systems can provide better security for personnel and cargo. However, these techniques require different training for merchant crew members on technology operation, threat recognition, and appropriate response to pirate sightings. Emergency plans for dealing with attempted attacks must be developed, and crews must be trained on using them.[85] Captain Shane Murphy, the second-in-command of the *Alabama*, had received antipiracy training at the Massachusetts Maritime Academy,[86] but maritime security experts point out that most crews are poorly trained and low-paid, working for ship owners who tell them not to resist pirates for fear of loss of life.[87]

While Thomas Jefferson sent the U.S. Marines to fight the Barbary pirates on the shores of Tripoli, today's piracy is a law enforcement problem, with no "rules of engagement" for navies and pirates. A recent agreement between the United States and an unnamed country in the Gulf of Aden area will permit the U.S. Navy to pursue and arrest pirates there.[88] However, 5th Fleet officials point out that there are over 1 million square miles of sea lanes in the Horn of Africa and Indian Ocean area off Africa. The lawless Somali coast is as long as the east coast of the United States,[89] yet the NATO antipiracy fleet has only fifteen vessels, of which three are American warships. At the time of the attack, the closest American war ship was 300 miles away.[90]

Again, it is the ancillary costs of piracy that are having the greatest impact on the global supply chain. Increased insurance costs, increased operating costs for avoiding areas with known piracy problems, and higher security costs will change the economic profile for imported goods in the supply chain.[91] Experts note that bypassing the Gulf of Aden for travel between Asia and Europe can add two weeks to the trip, as well as significant additional costs.[92] Regardless of this fact, two major companies, including Maersk, have chosen to send their slower-moving ships around the Cape of Good Hope to avoid pirate attacks, lengthening voyages by 40 percent,[93] which represents lost time and money in the supply chain. Crews need training on effective techniques for avoiding boarding by pirates while working unarmed against pirates using automatic weapons. The pirates also take advantage of modern technology, using satellite phones to negotiate the ransoms and GPS and maritime databases to plan the attacks. As noted above, international efforts to combat piracy are under way, but the political and economic forces are against a swift solution.

Synchronize Security with Management

Spot analysis conducted periodically will not allow the security element of a company to keep up with the emerging trends in supply chain management that could be leveraged to enhance supply chain security. The just-in-time environment makes the dual use of technologies more urgent. Emerging technologies such as radio frequency identification (RFID) chips, GPS, and bar code scanning can have dual use in tracking and securing goods. When security officials partner with staff managing the supply chain, opportunities for dual use can be identified and implemented quickly. Security may also evaluate functionalities of technologies that reveal gaps in supply chain security that can be remedied through protocol changes. For example, access to tracking information may expose the supply chain to theft, while a change in protocol could enhance security.

By leveraging the product tracking technologies and changes in supply chain management, security can create a positive cost–benefit relationship between its role and the manufacturing and shipping roles. By incorporating security into proposed managerial changes, a clearer picture of the costs of security is created, revealing security's role as a participant in creating a positive financial result for technology applications. For example, better training of merchant ship crews in situational awareness technology can lead to reductions in insurance cost increases. RFID, originally introduced to identify military aircraft in flight, became an antitheft device for commercial goods, as well as a tracking device used in transportation and logistics. Wal-Mart and the U.S. Department of Defense have both required RFID tags to improve supply chain management.[94]

Appreciate the Value of Security, Not Just the Cost

Years ago, security was considered an isolated part of a company that did not have a direct role in company business. It was seen as purely physical protection of assets, so guards were hired for their size, not their knowledge. It was not seen as having inherent value to the company, except in the case of banks, perhaps, which saw security as a way to instill confidence in clients.

Changes over the past forty years, mainly through globalization and just-in-time supply practices, have placed greater demands on security, but without a change in understanding of the institutional value of security. Since businesses have failed to see security, business continuity, and emergency management as mainstream activity, they have failed to take advantage of the strategic planning opportunities inherent in the analysis conducted by these professionals.

Neither limiting thefts nor preparing for occasional catastrophic events was recognized as having a significant positive effect on the return on investment side of the balance sheet. As Ritter, Barrett, and Wilson note, "[d]ecisions to invest in day-to-day security and catastrophic preparedness often lose out to expenditures on advertising, research, or other activities that are presumed to create more immediate and assured economic rewards."[95] Deloitte Research notes that "an August 2004 Conference Board Survey found that 39 percent of executives at mid-level companies (with revenues between $20 million and $1 billion) saw security simply as a cost that should be strictly controlled."[96]

However, Deloitte Research has asserted that "measurable business benefits" are attached to security activities. "Businesses can look to security compliance as a strategic issue—an opportunity to create business value and realize a positive return on their security investment."[97] As noted earlier, IT tracking tools can not only prevent theft, but they can also enhance efficiency of supply chain management, ultimately lowering warehousing and shipping costs. Just-in-time management becomes most efficient when inventory tracking devices are included in the process, providing real-time information about supply chain elements' anticipated arrival and allowing for coordination of production elements and reduction of losses incurred through spoilage and outdating.

Risk management and security working together can not only lessen the incidences of business disruption, but they can also prevent some types of losses through mitigation steps and appropriate insurance coverage. Insurance premiums may be lowered based on good security practices.

Compliance with developing government security mandates may also result in savings across the supply chain. For example, Hasbro Toys spent $200,000 on its initial C-TPAT compliance, and spends $112,500 per year to maintain it. The benefit is that inspections dropped from 7.6 percent of its containers coming from foreign ports in 2001 to 0.66 percent of its containers in 2003. Hasbro estimates that it is saving $550,000 per year in inspection costs, a 5:1 ratio of savings to investment.[98]

CONTINUOUS ADAPTATION AS OUTCOME

Supply chain security requires continuous adaptation of routines and activities to match the evolving threat and operational environment. As has been noted above, external actors like government, criminal networks, and suppliers may change their regulations and routines, so continuous assessment will result in ever-evolving strategies and methods of security.

Continuous Adaption Defeats the Efficiency of Standardization

Because the supply chain involves a complex system of international stakeholders, it is impossible to communicate needed changes to all actors simultaneously. Adaptation to the changing environment requires changes to standard operating procedures in discrete portions of the supply chain, thereby defeating some of the efficiencies obtained through standardization.

For example, suppliers within the European Union now have to comply with the requirements of the Authorized Economic Operators regulations, but suppliers in China will not have that same set of requirements. Thus, security and quality inspections of raw materials coming from Europe will require a different level of testing than goods coming from China. Initially, this may be viewed as enhancing the value of products coming from Europe, but the need for changes in the product assembly line due to changes in testing and quality control will slow down the integration of raw materials from different sources. Since the just-in-time supply chain that is based on the daily cost of goods being ordered may see raw materials from China one day and from Europe the next, the constant change of testing protocols will be an added cost to the overall production.

NAFTA created common protocols at border checkpoints to enhance throughput of trade. Compliant shippers may use the FAST system's "green lane" to bypass many aspects of border inspections. However, because the NAFTA "green lane" regulations are publicized, smugglers and other criminals can get access to them and develop workarounds for their illicit cargo.

Changes in the border security picture, such as enhanced human trafficking, additional arms importation, and larger quantities of drugs, may require changes in inspection protocols that defeat the throughput efficiencies created in the standard inspection designs for "green lanes" and similar protocols. These border holdups may create unexpected delivery delays for supply chain components, defeating the efficiencies of just-in-time systems.

Continuous Assessment and Outside Stakeholders

Transition between one operational norm and another demands more manpower than traditional security operations. Continuous assessment demands that individuals be vigilant about their operations, with stakeholders all along the supply chain trained to detect irregularities and changes in the operating picture.

Involving stakeholders in supply chain vigilance inevitably opens the possibility of leaks and compromise of the new security apparatus. Manufacturers and transporters have access to information regarding the security of materials and parts as they move through the supply chain. Because the supply chain is multinational and cost-based, it is impossible to develop trusted agents in every company that serves as a supplier or transporter. Although historically security has been maintained by using only trusted agents, continuous assessment has to be open to stakeholders all along the supply chains—stakeholders whose loyalties and ethics may be unknown.

In order to obtain the most comprehensive view of the evolving status, security is forced to divulge information about intelligence collection and security practices. There is a cost–benefit tension between the sharing of information to improve security and compromising security.

Better Initial Data

Continuous assessment requires that security personnel remain proactive in seeking out information on evolving vulnerabilities. Reports from federal agencies and professional organizations will provide an environmental scan across sectors to understand the trends in criminal and terrorist activity. Security needs to receive open-source information and employee concerns to raise their situational awareness of issues that may impact the supply chain. For example, press reports of melamine in pet food traced to China would have raised quality control and product inspection levels at companies buying raw materials from China.

In 2009 peanut butter products were recalled in the United States due to a salmonella outbreak related to peanut paste processed in a single site in Blakeley, Georgia, on July 1, 2008. The products had gotten into the supply chain, requiring recalls of MREs, crackers, and a variety of consumer products.[99] This quality control breach in one plant constituted a breach in the food supply chain of the United States, raising questions about the effectiveness of U.S. food inspections overall. Ultimately, Peanut Corporation of America went bankrupt in February 2009.[100]

This points out the problem of stovepiping information from one part of the supply chain to another. The FDA is tasked with ensuring the safety of the U.S. food supply, and its inspectors had found some violations during visits in 2001 and in January 2009. Meanwhile the USDA, one of Peanut Corporation's largest customers, also had inspectors who visited the plant and found insecticide problems, but they were not trained in food safety issues and did not share their concerns with the FDA. The result is that although two federal agencies sent inspectors to the plant and noted deficiencies, they did not share their information and did not stop production until eight deaths had occurred. The tainted paste entered the nation's food supply chain through house brand products as well as through the USDA's surplus food programs, including the school lunch programs in California, Minnesota, and Idaho.[101]

Redundancy in the Supply Chain

Even with the best security plans, disruptions may occur. Natural hazards, strikes, and other breakdowns external to security control may stop access to products and delivery of goods. In addition, common vulnerabilities are currency fluctuations, exchange rate fluctuations, macroeconomic changes, transportation link failure, supply deviation, supplier bankruptcy, demand uncertainties, and factory shutdowns.[102] Thus, redundancy in the supply chain is crucial to maintaining the operations of a company.

Redundant sources of supply and transportation are crucial to the security of the supply chain. As Van Bodegraven and Ackerman note,

Redundancy is simply capacity that would be deemed excess, unless and until either a catastrophe or a demand spike occasions its use . . . . One great way to develop redundancy is to contract with third parties for capacity . . . . it is most often far less expensive than carrying redundancy year round. The redundancy can involve supply/manufacturing, transportation, and/or distribution space."[103]

As has been noted, single-source supply for parts in Kobe, Japan, closed down an automobile assembly line in Brazil after the 1994 earthquake. Other manufacturers in the United States, Malaysia, and Brazil could not get access to parts exclusively available in the Kobe region, such as LEDs.[104]

Due to the current business practice of shopping for just-in-time parts and materials based on global pricing, many companies already have multiple suppliers. However, competitors may also have the same suite of suppliers, meaning that if one supplier is unavailable the demand on the available suppliers may drive prices up to unacceptable levels. Predisaster agreements with suppliers should include exclusivity clauses in the event of supply chain failures.

Alternate shipping methods and costs should be investigated in advance of need. Alternate methods of delivery to customers, even at a temporary loss, is crucial to maintaining the good name of the product as well as the company's customer base. Porier and Zawada have noted that

> understanding the supply chain process, vendor criticality and vendor continuity maturity enables the organization to determine the best options (and associated costs) to mitigate likely risks. This will confirm suppliers, or alternate suppliers, will be able to deliver the specified component at the correct time, to the correct location and within specifications.[105]

In 2002 the West Coast longshoremen were locked out, causing cargo to pile up in ports, at sea, and in supply chains. The lockout of employees after days of labor slowdowns was estimated to cost $1.5 million per day. Noting the close ties of U.S. retailers to ports, one leader stated, "Christmas is sitting in the harbor out there."[106] So were parts for the NUMI auto plant in Fremont, California, and components for high-tech companies in the Silicon Valley.[107]

Technology as Vulnerability

While technology can greatly enhance supply chain security, as noted above, new technology may not be fully understood. Until it is exposed to a broader audience and practical pressures, it is impossible to know how well it will function and what its inherent vulnerabilities may be. Hacking, radio interference, and cross-band interference may not be discovered in the lab, but only in the application environment. RFID is a prime example of this. The ability to interrogate an RFID tag and then clone the tag, enabling a perpetrator to introduce a counterfeit item into the supply chain, or to use it to gain access to data, only surfaced to public view in 2006, although the RFID concept had been in use since the early 1970s. Likewise, the use of a GPS jammer that will disrupt the signals being sent from the satellite to the receiver—a technology that is both well known and readily available—disrupts a GPS unit's ability to locate itself, rendering it useless. Since it cannot tell where it is, it cannot provide the required tracking information or supply chain security to the products.

It should be realized that there is no single security mechanism. Changing and dynamic international, economic, and political factors require a constant environmental scan of all aspects of the supply chain to ensure that current risks are well understood. Security must then be applied in layers, using different policies and procedures based on a solid analysis of current, developing, and potential threats with the understanding that individual systems and techniques will fail from time to time. With appropriate redundancy in supply chain security, the failures will be caught by the other layers of the supply chain security matrix.

NOTES

1. Mark Mazzetti and Sharon Otterman, "U.S. captain is hostage of pirates; U.S. Navy ship arrives," *New York Times* online, April 9, 2009, http://www.nytimes.com/2009/04/09/world/africa/09pirates.html?_r=1&scp=1&sq=Mark%20Mazzetti%20and%20Sharon%20Otterman,%20%E2%80%9CU.S.%20captain%20is%20hostage%20of%20pirates&st=cse.

2. Edmund Sanders and Julian E. Barnes, "Somalia Pirates Hold U.S. Captain," *Los Angeles Times*, April 9, 2009, http://www.latimes.com/news/la-fg-somali-pirates9-2009apr09,0,3610259.story?track=ntothtml.

3. Edmund Sanders and Julian E. Barnes, "Somalia Pirates Hold U.S. Captain," *Los Angeles Times*, April 9, 2009, http://www.latimes.com/news/la-fg-somali-pirates9-2009apr09,0,3610259.story?track=ntothtml.

4. Katharine Houreld, "Owners Debate Arming Ships against Somali Pirates," *Associated Press*, April 10, 2009, ABC News online, http://abcnews.go.com/International/wireStory?id=7301262.

5. Katharine Houreld, "Owners Debate Arming Ships against Somali Pirates," *Associated Press*, April 10, 2009, ABC News online, http://abcnews.go.com/International/wireStory?id=7301262.

6. Katharine Houreld and Anne Gearan, "Escape from Pirates Thwarted," *Mercury News*, April 11, 2009, 9A.

7. Katharine Houreld and Anne Gearan, "Escape from Pirates Thwarted," *Mercury News*, April 11, 2009, 9A.

8. Mark Mezzitti, "Standoff with Pirates Shows U.S. Power Has Limits," *New York Times*, Metro Edition, April 10, 2009, 1A.

9. Arvinder Loomba, "Managing Supply Chain Risk," nd, concept paper, Lucas School of Business, San Jose State University, 1.

10. Siobhan Gorman, "Electricity Grid in U.S. Penetrated by Spies," *The Wall Street Journal*, April 8, 2009, A1.

11. Julia Prodis Sulek et al., "Phone Service Fully Restored; AT&T Offers $100,000 Reward," *Mercury News*, April 10, 2009, A1.

12. Julia Prodis Sulek et al., "Phone Service Fully Restored; AT&T Offers $100,000 Reward," *Mercury News*, April 10, 2009, A1.

13. Karen de Sa, "AT&T Boosts Reward," *Mercury News*, April 11, 2009, 1A.

14. Karen de Sa, "AT&T Boosts Reward," *Mercury News*, April 11, 2009, 1A.

15. Dave Foreman and Bill Haywood, *Ecodefense: A Field Guide to Monkeywrenching* (Chico, CA: Abbzug Press, 2002).

16. Arnold M. Howitt and Herman B. Leonard, *Managing Crises: Response to Large-Scale Emergencies* (Washington, D.C.: CQ Press, 2009), 6–8.

17. Jason Jackson, "Emergency Management: Evolution of the Private Sector—Walmart and Katrina," presentation at IAEM National Conference, Orlando, FL, 2007.

18. Mickey McCarter, "Commercial Transportation Lacks Vulnerability Assessments," *Homeland Security Today*, March 31, 2009, http://www.hstoday.us/content/view/7854/128/.

19. Government Accountability Office, "Commercial Vehicle Security: Risk-Based Approach Needed to Secure the Commercial Vehicle Sector," February 2009, http://www.gao.gov/new.items/d0985.pdf.

20. Steve Quinn, "Blow to Port Has Hindered Shipping," *San Diego Union Tribune*, September 10, 2005, http://www.signonsandiego.com/uniontrib/20050910/news_1b10port.html.

21. Marcia Clemmitt, "Global Food Crisis," in *Global Issues* (Washington, D.C.: CQ Press, 2008), 251–252.

22. Clifford Kraus, "Exports Fall, and It's Felt on the Farm," *New York Times* online, April 9, 2009, www.nytimes.com/2009/04/10/business/10agriculture.html?fta=y.

23. Peter Hulm, "Firms Gang Up against Bribes," January 2004, *International Trade Forum*, http://www.tradeforum.org/news/fullstory.php/aid/652/Firms_Gang_Up_Against_Bribes.html.

24. Peter Hulm, "Firms Gang Up against Bribes," January 2004, *International Trade Forum*, http://www.tradeforum.org/news/fullstory.php/aid/652/Firms_Gang_Up_Against_Bribes.html.

25. California Office of Homeland Security, "Fact Sheet: Mass Transit Security Grants in California from FY 2003 to FY 2006."

26. Department of Homeland Security, "DHS Announces $445 Million to Secure Critical Infrastructure," January 9, 2007, http://www.dhs.gov/xnews/releases/pr_1168366069190.shtm.

27. Department of Homeland Security, "Fiscal Year 2009 Port Security Grant Program Guidance and Application Kit," November 2008, 12.

28. Eric Napralla, Port of Redwood City, personal communication, March 18, 2009.

29. Anita Powell, "Ships Have Few Options against Somali Pirates," April 10, 2009, http://news.yahoo.com/s/ap/20090410/ap_on_re_af/af_piracy_scenarios.

30. Mark Mazzetti and Sharon Otterman, "U.S. captain is hostage of pirates; U.S. Navy ship arrives," *New York Times* online, April 9, 2009, http://www.nytimes.com/2009/04/09/world/africa/09pirates.html?_r=1&scp=1&sq=Mark%20Mazzetti%20and%20Sharon%20Otterman,%20%E2%80%9CU.S.%20captain%20is%20hostage%20of%20pirates&st=cse.

31. Anita Powell, "Ships Have Few Options against Somali Pirates," April 10, 2009, http://news.yahoo.com/s/ap/20090410/ap_on_re_af/af_piracy_scenarios.

32. Roger Turney, "Criminal Intent," November 2008, *Air Cargo World* online, http://www.aircargoworld.com/regions/euro_1108.htm.

33. Pierre Van Kleef, Note to Turney, "Criminal Intent," http://www.aircargoworld.com/regions/euro_1108.htm.

34. Gilad Solnik, "Changing Trends in Supply Chain Crime," presentation to TAPA Europe, Middle East and Africa Seminar, 2009, http://autoid.org/ISO_JWG/2009/11_ac11_seminar_pres06.pdf.

35. Gilad Solnik, "Changing Trends in Supply Chain Crime," presentation to TAPA Europe, Middle East and Africa Seminar, 2009, http://autoid.org/ISO_JWG/2009/11_ac11_seminar_pres06.pdf.

36. Peter Katel, "Rise in Counterinsurgency," *Global Issues* (Washington, D.C.: CQ Press, 2009), 19–20.

37. Sarah Glazer, "Radical Islam in Europe," *Global Issues* (Washington, D.C.: CQ Press, 2009), 106–107.

38. Peter Katel, "Oil Jitters," *Global Issues* (Washington, D.C.: CQ Press, 2009), 296–306.

39. Marcia Clemmitt, "Global Food Crisis," *Global Issues* (Washington, D.C.: CQ Press, 2009), 250–252.

40. Jia-rui Chong, Greg Krikorian, and Monte Morin, "Suspect in Firebombing a Hummer Dealership Released," *LA Times*, September 16, 2003, http://articles.latimes.com/2003/sep/16/local/me-hummer16.

41. Michael Wines, Keith Bradsher, and Mark Landler, "China's Leader Says He Is Worried over U.S. Treasuries, *New York Times*, March 14, 2009, 1A.

42. Shaila Dewan, "Extravagence Has Its Limits as Belt Tightening Trickles Up," *New York Times*, March 10, 2009, http://www.nytimes.com/2009/03/10/us/10reset.html?th=&emc=th&pagewanted=print.

43. Allison DeGaw, "Consumer Retailer Spending Down, but Walmart Sales Climb," November 6, 2008, http://www.abc15.com/content/news/phoenixmetro/story/Consumer-retailer-spending-down-but-Wal-Mart/wHRUilzrL0KlP9YOqq-hsA.cspx.

44. Ronald D. White, "Port Cargo Levels Are Sinking Fast," *LA Times*, March 2, 2009, http://www.latimes.com/business/la-fi-tradecrash2-2009mar02,0,807159.story.

45. Ronald D. White, "Port Cargo Levels Are Sinking Fast," *LA Times*, March 2, 2009, http://www.latimes.com/business/la-fi-tradecrash2-2009mar02,0,807159.story.

46. International Organization for Standardization, "New Suite of ISO Supply Chain Management Standards to Reduce Risks of Terrorism, Piracy and Fraud," October 25, 2007, http://www.iso.org/iso/pressrelease.htm?refid=Ref1086.

47. Mickey McCarter, "The Port Protection Challenge," *HSToday* 5, no. 7 (July 2008): 32–39.

48. Mickey McCarter, "The Port Protection Challenge," *HSToday* 5, no. 7 (July 2008): 32–39.

49. Public Law 109-347, October 13, 2006, "Security and Accountability for Every (SAFE) Port Act of 2006," http://www.hklaw.com/content/maritime/mardocs/SAFE_Port_Act.pdf.

50. Mickey McCarter, "Commercial Transportation Lacks Vulnerability Assessments."

51. Government Accountability Office, "Homeland Security: Preliminary Observations on Efforts to Target Security Inspections of Cargo Containers," GOA-04-325T, December 16, 2003, http://www.gao.gov/htext/d04325t.html.

52. Department of Homeland Security, Office of Inspector General, "Management of Department of Homeland Security International Activities and Interests," OIG 08-71, (June 2008), 3.

53. U.S. Customs and Border Protection, "Container Security Initiative, 2006–2011 Strategic Plan," ii.

54. U.S. Customs and Border Protection, "Container Security Initiative, 2006–2011 Strategic Plan," ii.

55. U.S. Customs and Border Protection, "Container Security Initiative, 2006–2011 Strategic Plan," 10.

56. U.S. Customs and Border Patrol, "Securing the Global Supply Chain: Customs Trade Partnership Against Terrorism (C-TPAT) Strategic Plan," November 2004, 12.

57. U.S. Customs and Border Patrol, "Securing the Global Supply Chain: Customs Trade Partnership Against Terrorism (C-TPAT) Strategic Plan," November 2004, ii.

58. U.S. Customs and Border Patrol, "Securing the Global Supply Chain: Customs Trade Partnership Against Terrorism (C-TPAT) Strategic Plan," November 2004, 29.

59. European Commission, Customs Security Programme, "AEO Pilot Report," August 24, 2006, http://ec.europa.eu/taxation_customs/resources/documents/customs/policy_issues/customs_security/AEO_pilot_report_en.pdf.

60. European Commission, Customs Security Programme, "AEO Pilot Report," August 24, 2006, http://ec.europa.eu/taxation_customs/resources/documents/customs/policy_issues/customs_security/AEO_pilot_report_en.pdf, 3.

61. Michael D. Laden, "The Genesis of the US C-TPAT Program: Lessons Learned and Earned by the Government and Trade," *World Customs Journal* 1, no. 2 (September 2007): 75.

62. European Commission, Customs Security Programme, "AEO Pilot Report," August 24, 2006, http://ec.europa.eu/taxation_customs/resources/documents/customs/policy_issues/customs_security/AEO_pilot_report_en.pdf, 6.

63. European Commission, Customs Security Programme, "AEO Pilot Report," August 24, 2006, http://ec.europa.eu/taxation_customs/resources/documents/customs/policy_issues/customs_security/AEO_pilot_report_en.pdf, 8.

64. Ron Eggers, "Protecting America's Busiest Port Complex," *9-1-1 Magazine*, August 2007, 14–16.

65. Guna Selvaduray, "Effect of the Kobe Earthquake on Manufacturing Facilities," paper delivered at the SEMI Workshop, March 19, 2003.

66. CNN, "Major Power Outage Hits New York, Other Large Cities," August 14, 2003, http://www.cnn.com/2003/US/08/14/power.outage/.

67. Port of Seattle, "New Container Cranes," http://www.portseattle.org/seaport/cargo/newcranes.shtml.

68. Poten & Partners, "LPG Vessels and Security," November 3, 2003, http://www.poten.com/Opinion.aspx?id=2482.

69. Poten & Partners, "LPG Vessels and Security," November 3, 2003, http://www.poten.com/Opinion.aspx?id=2482.

70. *New York Times*, "Indonesian Fires Blanket Central Malaysia with Smoke, Shutting Schools and a Port," *New York Times* online, August 12, 2005, http://spiderbites.nytimes.com/free_2005/articles_2005_08_00001.html.

71. *Foreign Policy*, "The List: Five Top Global Choke Points," May 2006, http://www.foreignpolicy.com/story/cms.php?story_id=3457.

72. *Foreign Policy*, "The List: Five Top Global Choke Points," May 2006, http://www.foreignpolicy.com/story/cms.php?story_id=3457.

73. UPI, "US and Mexico Cooperating to Restrict Radioactive Steel," *New York Times*, May 6, 1984, Susan Combs, http://spiderbites.nytimes.com/pay_1984/articles_1984_05_00001.html.

74. Brian Skoloff and Cain Burdeau, "AP Impact: Chinese Drywall Poses Potential Risks," April 11, 2009, http://news.yahoo.com/s/ap/20090411/ap_on_bi_ge/chinese_drywall.

75. U.S. Code Title 18, Part 1, Chapter 96, "Racketeer Influenced and Corrupt Organizations," 1970, http://www.law.cornell.edu/USCode/html/USCode18/USC_SUP_01_18_10_I_20_96.html.

76. Reuters, "U.S. Gasoline Theft on the Rise Along with Prices," April 24, 2008, http://www.reuters.com/article/idUSN2447526520080424.

77. Michael Harley, "Gasoline Theft in Hawaii on the Rise," May 27, 2008, http://www.autoblog.com/2008/05/27/gasoline-theft-in-hawaii-on-the-rise/.

78. *The Hindu*, "Gang Involved in Copper Wire Theft Held," December 8, 2007, http://www.hinduonnet.com/thehindu/thscrip/print.pl?file=2007120858240300.htm&date=2007/12/08/&prd=th&.

79. Federal Bureau of Investigation, "Precious Metal: Copper Theft Threatens U.S. Infrastructure," December 3, 2008, http://www.fbi.gov/page2/dec08/coppertheft_120308.html.

80. Julie Murphree, "Copper Theft at Epidemic Levels," *Arizona Agriculture*, March 13, 2007, http://www.videofied.com/nutech/pdfs/Copper%20Theft%20At%20Epidemic%20Levels%20March%2013.pdf

81. Julie Murphree, "Copper Theft at Epidemic Levels," *Arizona Agriculture*, March 13, 2007, http://www.videofied.com/nutech/pdfs/Copper%20Theft%20At%20Epidemic%20Levels%20March%2013.pdf

82. Pierce Adams, "Oconee Deputies Arrest Two for Live Wire Copper Theft," *Independent Mail*, June 29, 2007, http://www.independentmail.com/news/2007/jun/29/ocenee-deputies-arrest-two-live-wire-copper-theft/.

83. "Copper Theft Prevention Act of 2008," http://www.opencongress.org/bill/110-H6831/show.

84. Corey D. Ranslem, "Situational Awareness the Key: Deterring Pirate Attacks against Merchant Ships," *DomPrepJournal* (February 4, 2009): 20–22.

85. Corey D. Ranslem, "Situational Awareness the Key: Deterring Pirate Attacks against Merchant Ships," *DomPrepJournal* (February 4, 2009): 22.

86. Mark Mazzetti and Sharon Otterman, "U.S. captain is hostage of pirates; U.S. Navy ship arrives," *New York Times* online, April 9, 2009, http://www.nytimes.com/2009/04/09/world/africa/09pirates.html?_r=1&scp=1&sq=Mark%20Mazzetti%20and%20Sharon%20Otterman,%20%E2%80%9CU.S.%20captain%20is%20hostage%20of%20pirates&st=cse.

87. Edmund Sanders and Julian E. Barnes, "Somalia Pirates Hold U.S. Captain," *Los Angeles Times*, April 9, 2009, http://www.latimes.com/news/la-fg-somali-pirates9-2009apr09,0,3610259.story?track=ntothtml.

88. Edmund Sanders and Julian E. Barnes, "Somalia Pirates Hold U.S. Captain," *Los Angeles Times*, April 9, 2009, http://www.latimes.com/news/la-fg-somali-pirates9-2009apr09,0,3610259.story?track=ntothtml, 22.

89. Pauline Jelinek and Matt Apuzzo, "FBI Assisting the Efforts to Rescue US Ship Captain," *Associated Press*, April 9, 2009, Las Vegas Sun online, www.lasvegassun.com/. . . /fbi-assisting-in-efforts-to-rescue-us-ship-captain/.

90. Mark Mazzetti and Sharon Otterman, "U.S. captain is hostage of pirates; U.S. Navy ship arrives," *New York Times* online, April 9, 2009, http://www.nytimes.com/2009/04/09/world/africa/09pirates.html?_r=1&scp=1&sq=Mark%20Mazzetti%20and%20Sharon%20Otterman,%20%E2%80%9CU.S.%20captain%20is%20hostage%20of%20pirates&st=cse.

91. Mark Mazzetti and Sharon Otterman, "U.S. captain is hostage of pirates; U.S. Navy ship arrives," *New York Times* online, April 9, 2009, 22.

92. Anita Powell, "Ships Have Few Options against Somali Pirates," April 10, 2009, http://news.yahoo.com/s/ap/20090410/ap_on_re_af/af_piracy_scenarios.

93. Anita Powell, "Ships Have Few Options against Somali Pirates," April 10, 2009, http://news.yahoo.com/s/ap/20090410/ap_on_re_af/af_piracy_scenarios.

94. Beth Bacheldor, "Sam's Club Tells Suppliers to Tag or Pay," January 11, 2008, http://www.rfidjournal.com/article/articleview/3845/1/1/; Mark Roberti, "DOD Reaffirms Its RFID goals," April 5, 2007, http://www.rfidjournal.com/article/articleview/3211/1/1/.

95. Luke Ritter, J. Michael Barrett, and Rosalyn Wilson, *Securing Global Transportation Networks* (New York: McGraw Hill, 2007), 65.

96. Deloitte Research, "Prospering in the Secure Economy," 2005, 14, http://www.deloitte.com/dtt/cda/doc/content/Prospering%20Australia%20-%20high%20res.pdf.

97. Deloitte Research, "Prospering in the Secure Economy," 2005, 14, http://www.deloitte.com/dtt/cda/doc/content/Prospering%20Australia%20-%20high%20res.pdf.

98. Ben Worthen, "Customs Rattles the Supply Chain," *CIO Magazine*, April 12, 2006, http://www.cio.com/article/17906/Security_Compliance_Customs_Rattles_the_Supply_Chain.

99. FDA, "King Nut Issues Peanut Butter Recall," January 10, 2009, http://www.fda.gov/oc/po/firmrecalls/kingnut01_09.html.

100. Peanut Corporation of America, http://www.peanutcorp.com/.

101. Associated Press, "FDA: Georgia Plant Knowingly Sold Peanut Butter Tainted with Salmonella," *New York Daily News*, February 6, 2009, http://www.nydailynews.com/news/us_world/2009/02/06/2009-02-06_fda_georgia_plant_knowingly_sold_peanut_.html.

102. Indian School of Business, "Global Supply Chains," nd, http://www.isb.edu/glams/GlobalSupplyChains.shtml.

103. Art Van Bodegraven and Kenneth B. Ackerman, "Basic Training: The Hard Work of Getting Flexible," *DC Velocity*, March 2008, http://www.dcvelocity.com/viewpoints/?article_id=1734.

104. Guna Selvaduray, "Effect of the Kobe Earthquake on Manufacturing Facilities," paper delivered at the SEMI Workshop, March 19, 2003.

105. Michael Porier and Brian Zawada, "Risky Business: Failure to Assess Supply Chain Continuity," nd, http://www.disaster-resource.com/articles/03p_032.shtml.

106. Rick Del Vecchio, "Determined Men Battle over Future of Waterfront," October 3, 2002, http://www.sfgate.com/cgi-bin/article.cgi?file=/chronicle/archive/2002/10/03/MN98447.DTL&type=printable.

107. David R. Baker, "Economy May Sink If Strike Shuts Ports," August 28, 2002, http://www.sfgate.com/cgi-bin/article.cgi?file=/chronicle/archive/2002/08/28/BU88270.DTL&type=printable.

CHAPTER 2

Innovative Global Risk Management to Reinforce Supply Chain Security

R. Ray Gehani and G. Tom Gehani

> Every morning in Africa, a gazelle wakes up.
> It must outrun the fastest lion, or it will be killed.
> Every morning, a lion wakes up.
> It must run faster than the slowest gazelle, or it will starve.
> It doesn't matter if you are gazelle or lion,
> When the sun comes up, you must start running.
> —Anonymous African Proverb
> Cited by Friedman (2005, 2006: 137)

INTRODUCTION

As supply chains and operations are globalized, they become increasingly complex, dynamic, and interdependent across multiple suppliers located in multinational geographic locations. Typically, risks of global suppliers are less well known compared to the risks of domestic suppliers. And, therefore, security of more widespread global supply chains is exposed to higher risks.

Global supply chain managers (GSMs) must pay attention not only to risks related to their direct tier 1 suppliers, but also to the risks related to their entire extended supply chains. By planning for business continuity, they need to identify all vulnerable partners likely to fail in their supply chains and estimate their risk implications. The GSMs should be able to comprehend, anticipate, and monitor the more likely risk-laden episodes. They must anticipate their interdependencies with other collaborators, which may hamper the overall performance of their own supply chains or the reputation of their enterprises. GSMs must be capable of institutionalizing a secure and safe strategic plan that helps them appropriately intercept the individual risk elements as they are likely to occur.

A resilient and robust global supply chain has the dynamic capability to withstand and recover quickly from a disruptive episode. Resilient supply chain managers proactively anticipate and plan steps to prevent or respond quickly to disruptive security events by building alternatives operations.

GLOBAL EVOLUTION OF SUPPLY CHAINS

Innovations in telecommunication, transportation, and information technologies since the mid-1990s have accelerated the globalization of economies in general, and offshore outsourcing of supply chains in particular.[1] Thomas Friedman[2] noted three convergences (new platform technology, new business model, and new human talent) and ten forces that flattened the world. As a result of these convergences, by the dawn of the twenty-first century, close to 20 percent of production of U.S. enterprises was done abroad, and close to 25 percent of U.S. imports were between the U.S. enterprises and their foreign affiliates.[3]

The fall of the Berlin Wall on November 9, 1989, opened the global market economy to hundreds of millions of people living in former communist economies. Earlier these people did not have much access to global free markets.[4] In the mid-1990s, Netscape launched their public Internet browser that instantly linked distant corners of the World Wide Web.

The crisis of Y2K upgrading was averted when the world's computers and computerized equipments were updated before January 1, 2000, with the help of extensive outsourcing to a rising software service industry in India. After the Y2K crisis was averted, there was a boom in e-commerce. Once again, many Western companies outsourced their key projects and applications to time-tested Indian software service providers such as Infosys, Wipro, Tata Consultancy Services, and others. Using the undersea fiber-optic cable technology, the marginal costs for outsourcing their IT projects was low, and the savings gained were enormous, resulting in large bonuses for executives.

On December 11, 2001, China formally joined the World Trade Organization. Thereby, China agreed to abide by the global rules regulating international trade and foreign direct investments that most other countries of the world were already following. This boosted offshore outsourcing and globalization of supply chains to China.

What kinds of goods and services are likely to be sourced globally? Labor-intensive goods and services tend to help leverage the comparative advantages of low-cost sourcing countries such as China (for manufacturing goods) and India (for information technology services). Gradually, however, the momentum is shifting to global sourcing of more technology-intensive goods and services for which the global suppliers also contribute collaborative innovation based on their specialization and deeper knowledge of their industry. China's supernatural economic growth has lately put pressure on its own natural, environmental, and manufacturing resources.

RISK AND GLOBAL SUPPLY CHAIN SECURITY

The terrorist attack on September 11, 2001, in which hijacked aircraft flew into the ninety-fourth and ninety-eighth floors of the twin towers of the World Trade Center in New York City, shut down many newly opened U.S. windows to the world. Unfortunately, these supply chain disruptors learned and adopted the same technological innovations as the leading business enterprises. Globalization of businesses and supply chains also proliferated and integrated the sources of disruption distributed around the world.

The deeper, extended, and more globalized supply chains incur higher risks. This urgently demands adoption of innovative risk management. Many supply chain management researchers[5] have pointed out to the gap and the need for more systemic research in this area.

The Royal Society[6] defines risk as the quantitative chance of the occurrence of a defined hazard. This combines the probabilistic occurrence of certain disruptive events in conjunction with the consequences of those disruptive occurrences. In a similar manner, Deloach[7] defines business risk as the level of exposure to certain uncertainties that the business enterprise must effectively understand and manage as it implements its strategies to accomplish its business objectives and value-adding activities.

It is interesting to note that whereas many uncertainties, coming from the national-level macroenvironment and industry-level microenvironment, cannot be "controlled," their associated risks can nevertheless be estimated and assessed.

A number of researchers, including Andreas Norman and Ulf Jansson,[8] have stressed that business enterprises (such as those involved in a global supply chain) should focus not only on their own risks, but also on the risks in other linked enterprises in their global supply chains. They believe that a key component of supply chain management is the sharing of joint risks and rewards among different members of a supply chain.

Strategic collaboration between buyers and suppliers help mitigate risks and share rewards. Giant diversified manufacturers such as Procter & Gamble and Kimberly Clark, as well as retailers like Wal-Mart and Target, increasingly collaborate with other enterprises in their global supply chain. The textile and chemical company Milliken and Company collaborates with several major department store buyers and many key textile suppliers by sharing store-level point-of-sales (POS) information. This information helps all parties synchronize their production and ordering plans. This has helped speed order-to-fill cycle time from eighteen weeks to just three.[9]

A Supply Chain Performance Scorecard

Ray Gehani and Tom Gehani[10] developed a multivariable composite supply chain performance scorecard to compare and contrast the impact and efficiencies of alternate modes of transportation. This was also used to compare the performances of alternate transport service providers. In the context of the present study on supply chain risk management, the supply chain performance scorecard can be used to measure balanced performance of a supply chain before and after mitigating its risk. Figure 2.1 shows the supply chain performance scorecard, and the performance of a supply chain under (A) optimistic risk-free circumstances, and (B) pessimistic risky circumstances.

In strategic global sourcing of auto parts, faster delivery times are sought without compromising or increasing the cost of procurement (for specific supply chain performance). Use of the third-party logistics (3PL) providers, who offer differentiated value-adding services such as warehousing, repair and assembling, and inventory management, is preferred. High reliability and flexibility are sought, coupled with suppliers' attentiveness and responsiveness to the needs of their key customers. To a great extent, this relies on visibility and transparency of a robust and resilient global supplier with high tolerance for failures and disruptions. Thus, strategic suppliers should be able to easily handle the variability in large-scale transportation over long distances.

Under the growing threats of terrorism in the twenty-first century, the national macroenvironment and industrial microenvironment under which global supply chains must operate have changed drastically. As a result, more innovative global risk management methods are required to replace the

Figure 2.1
Measuring Variations in Performance Scorecard for Global Supply Chain Management

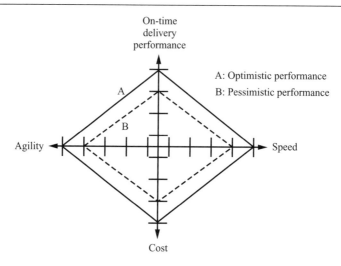

traditional risk management methods developed under much more secure national and industrial environments.

Traditional Supply Chain Risk Management

Traditionally, purchasing and procurement functions were treated as operational activities in conjunction with vendor/supplier management. Even though these activities had significant impact on the overall performance of an enterprise, these activities were not perceived as strategic resources for the enterprise.

Traditional supply chain security often implied a firm-level focus on the theft and damages in a firm's supply chain. Some attention was paid to transportation of counterfeit goods or illegal contraband. Traditional supply chain security implied securing only the facilities directly under the control of the firm. The focus for security of a global supply chain system was primarily limited to controlling shrinkage along its various handover points and transportation routes. This usually involved tracking misrouting or losses of cargo shipments through theft or damages. Another common traditional concern with supply chain security was the transportation of contraband such as illegal drugs, stolen goods, or illegal immigrants. With the recent terrorist attacks, transportation of terrorists and weapons of mass destruction were included in this list.

INNOVATIVE RISK MANAGEMENT FOR THE TWENTY-FIRST-CENTURY SUPPLY CHAIN: AN OVERVIEW

Globalization of a supply chain, involving multiple cross-national handovers and changes in ownership, demands higher security to protect the firm's goods, distributed facilities, and reputation.

After the 9/11 terrorist attacks in 2001, the London transportation bombing, Madrid commuter train attack in 2004, and the most recent Mumbai terrorist attacks in November 2008, a heightened worldwide awareness of terrorism has emerged, and it is escalating steadily. In 2003, it was estimated that new security measures put in place to reduce terrorist threats to security in the United States incurred additional $151 billion in annual costs.[11] Of this total amount, $65 billion, or over 40 percent, was to upgrade the supply chain logistics. As a result, the focus of supply chain security has been radically transformed.

The disruptive consequences of a terrorist attack at or through a critical supply chain node carries with it the enormous risk of losing precious lives, destruction of vital infrastructure, and loss of faith in a nation's ability to maintain its law and order. These effects can be a crippling blow to a nation's economy. More than 90 percent of the world's trade is carried every year in 20 million container shipping trips. In the United States, this comes to close to 20,000 containers arriving at U.S. ports every day.[12] The general public is extremely concerned with the undetected importation of weapons of mass destruction (WMD) embedded into the shipments of regular commercial cargo.

Figure 2.2
Innovative Supply Chain Risk Management: Three-Step Process Model

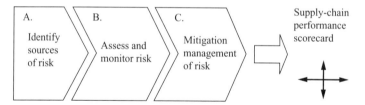

Innovative supply chain security in the twenty-first century, as suggested earlier in this study, demands paying increasing attention to protecting not only (1) products, but also (2) facilities, (3) assets and equipment, (4) personnel, and (5) information having to do with any acts of terrorism and sabotage. This includes illegal transportation of terrorists or weapons of mass destruction. This extended definition of supply chain security in the twenty-first century has substantially increased the potential risks associated with any breach of security of a global supply chain.

As noted earlier, securing such a global supply chain in the twenty-first century requires the firm to collaborate with multiple partners in its supply network. These include first-tier and second-tier suppliers, buyers and consumers, and global trading partners, including carriers, terminals, and government officials.

A critical element of global supply chain management is managing the sources and effects of risks affiliated with its disruption. Three key strategic processes (see Figure 2.2) involved in innovative supply chain risk management (ISRM) are given below:

Step I: Identify Environmental and Enterprise Sources of Disruption

The first strategic step in innovative supply chain risk management is identifying the sources of potential risks per the extended scope of the twenty-first-century global supply chain management. In this study, a multilevel identification of external and internal sources of risk is proposed. These include the external sources of the country-level and industry-level risks, and the internal sources of the firm-level risks.

Step II: Assess and Monitor the Devastating Dynamic Effects of the Abovementioned Sources of Supply Chain Risk

Assessment of risks in global supply chain management can be done qualitatively and quantitatively. A qualitative risk assessment helps prioritize the risks identified in the previous step based on the likelihood of a disruptive risky episode and its most likely disruptive impact. If a global supply chain project seems qualitatively too risky, it may be terminated early without much quantitative analysis. The quantitative risk assessment involves quantifying the additional margins in costs, delivery times, and performance deliverables needed to compensate for the variances in risky supply chain activities. Usually, the quantitative risk assessment focuses on the risks with the largest disruptive impact.

Step III: Mitigate the Rippling Bullwhip Effects of Risky Disruptions

Different enterprises manage their global supply chains with different levels of maturity. In general, the managerial responses to a security risk are as follows:

1. Avoid the potential cause of risk.
2. Transfer the risk to another party.
3. Accept the risk and cope with it.
4. Mitigate the risk by reducing the probability of its likelihood or the severity of its disruptive impact.

For example, a distribution center of the fictive Acme Global Corporation on the Florida coast (or in Louisiana, on the Gulf of Mexico), can be affected by a natural source of risk, such as a hurricane. Acme Global can avoid the risk by transferring the distribution center away from the coastal regions. Acme can also transfer the risk to an insurer by buying natural disaster insurance. Acme can build agility into its process operations to cope in the event that such a disaster occurs. And, finally, Acme Global can hire weather forecasters and subscribe to satellite services to become able to divert shipments in case of an approaching hurricane. It is quite likely that Acme Global may choose to use a hybrid portfolio, using all these alternative ways to mitigate its global supply chain risks.

IMPLEMENTING THE THREE-STEP PROCESS

Specific, innovative practices are discussed here for each of the three steps of the innovative supply chain risk management models.

Step I: Identify Environmental and Enterprise Sources of Disruption

George Souter[13] highlighted the significance of including risks in internal as well as external links in a supply chain. This significance enhances many-fold when parts of a supply chain get outsourced or offshored. Given below are some recent examples.

A Greenville (North Carolina)–based Daimler–Chrysler plant making suspension parts was flooded by Hurricane Floyd. This shut down seven of the company's other plants in North America for seven days.

A fire at Aisin Seiki's brake fluid proportioning valve plant in February 1997 shut down Toyota's eighteen plants for two weeks.[14] The disruption cost 70,000 vehicles and an estimated $325 million.

Cisco took a $2.5 billion inventory writeoff in Q2 2001 because of falling demand and locked-in supply agreements.[15]

Based on these empirical illustrations, in this study, we propose that innovative supply chain risk managers carefully identify all potential sources of risk in the following three layers (see Figure 2.3):

1. Country-level sources of risk
2. Industry-level sources of risk
3. Firm-level sources of risk

Figure 2.3
Identify Multi-Level Sources of Risk in Innovative Global Supply Chain Management

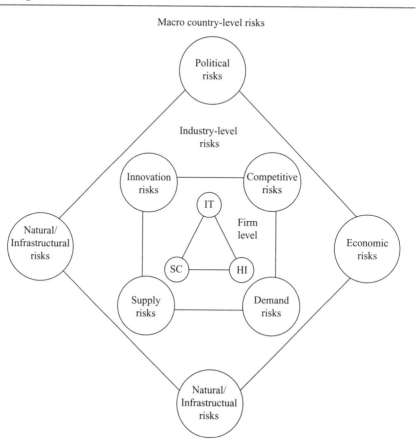

These layered sources of risk are described in detail next.

Country-Level Sources of Risk

Uninterrupted management and risks of global supply chains depend quite heavily on the contextual country-level macroenvironments of the different relevant trading partners. For example, economic and regulatory environments vary from one country to another. Some countries enforce antitrust policies more stringently than other countries. Regulation of corporate tax rates and employees' individual tax rates vary from one geographic region to another.

The variety of country-level sources of risk can be clustered as follows:

1. Political and regulatory risk
2. Economic fluctuation risk
3. Natural disaster and infrastructural risk
4. Sociocultural risk

Political and Regulatory Sources of Risk   Political environment drives the credibility and effectiveness of a country's ruling governing body. A country at war promises less credibility and effectiveness to global supply chain managers than a country that enjoys harmonious political relations with its geographic neighbors and distant allies. Similarly, a country with large number of fragmenting parties may pose more supply chain risks when a new election swings the political mood of the country from ultra-right capitalism to ultra-left socialism.

The regulatory and legal policies of a country frame the rules guiding the various business transactions across a global supply chain. The efficiency and effectiveness of regulatory policies are heavily dependent on the enforcement capability of legal and judicial institutions. Rules without teeth are often overlooked, thereby enhancing the risks for disruption of a global supply chain. An ill-defined and opaque judicial system riddled with corruption and bribery increases the risks for global firms to engage in long-term transactions with anonymous parties within a country. This denies production specialization and competitive advantages along the different segments of a global supply chain.

Traditionally, each state in the United States enacted its own bodies of regulating laws and statutes to govern different spheres of business activities within its jurisdiction. This resulted in development of divergent commercial laws, causing serious obstacles to interstate and international flows of commercial goods. The American Bar Association constituted the National Conference of Commissioners on Uniform State Laws (NCCUSL) to codify the laws governing different business transactions.

During the early 1980s, the United Nations helped enact a uniform body of laws governing commercial contracts for the international sale of goods. This is known as the United Nations Convention on Contracts for the International Sale of Goods, or CIGS.

Since the 9/11 terrorist attacks, a number of new measures have been adopted to prevent similar mishaps in future. Traditionally, regulatory government agencies involved in a global supply chain were mainly concerned with controlling import and export trade, collecting duties, fees, and taxes, and restricting any inflow and outflow of legally banned items. Because of the newly defined terrorist threats to a country and its commerce, government regulatory agencies are increasingly securing operations of supply chain to promote trade with trusted partners. This has inevitably increased higher inspection of goods, cash transfers, and information flows.

The U.S. Congress authorized the Department of Homeland Security (DHS)[16] Directorate of Border and Transportation Security to ensure efficient and speedy flow of lawful goods and services. The U.S. Customs and Border Protection agency, under DHS, has instituted a number of specific initiatives to meet its demanding mandate in an increasingly less secure world.[17]

1. The **Customs-Trade Partnership Against Terrorism (C-TPAT)** is a voluntary precertification program instituted by the Congress-mandated Directorate of Border and Transportation Security of the U.S. Department of Homeland Security (DHS). Selected shippers do self-appraisals of their security procedures. These are coupled with custom audits and verifications. Precertified firms are required to do business and collaborate with other precertified suppliers, customers, and intermediaries.

2. The **Container Security Initiative (CSI)** prescreens cargo containers and provides fast tracking as they reach the shores of the United States.

3. The original **Advanced Manifest Rule (AMR)** and the updated **Advance Cargo Information (ACI)** mandate providing detailed data about cargo long before the cargo is either shipped from or shipped into the United States by air, road, or rail.

4. The **Free And Secure Trade (FAST) program** permits faster transportation and passage through borders for low-risk goods of trusted firms using trusted carriers, reserving detailed inspection for high-risk and unknown shipments.

5. The **Bioterrorism Act of 2002** implemented by the U.S. government mandates that firms involved in food processing be able to trace their raw materials one step back, and their finished goods one step forward, along their supply chain.

6. **New country of origin labels (COOL)** for some food and agricultural products provide consumers with more information about product origins, and how certain products meet and exceed voluntary and regulatory guidelines.

7. Just like the United States, the governments of other countries, as well as international organizations such as the World Trade Organization (WTO) and the World Customs Organization (WCO), are also actively seeking to streamline global trade and safe transportation of goods and services internationally. More than 160 members of the WCO have agreed to share information in their **Global Standards for**

Supply Chain Security initiative to facilitate safer and faster clearances of low-risk shipments through their borders. The International Standards Organization (ISO), in collaboration with Strategic Council on Security Technology is developing **Smart and Secure Tradelanes (SST)** technology platform to track chain-of-custody audits as containers move globally.

Economic Sources of Risk   The 2008–2009 meltdown of the U.S. banking sector, including the nation's leading enterprises such as Citibank and AIG, has resulted in a serious decrease in global supply chain managers' trust in the American financial and capital goods markets. It is suspected that as of March 2009, a large number of investors with millions to invest in production industries and supply chain services were sitting on the sidelines waiting for the nation's capital goods and financial goods markets to calm down.

Economic Reforms and Supply Chain Risks   Since the dawn of the twenty-first century, China's sprawling banking system, playing a critical role in the risk management of global supply chains, was riddled with bad loans, bureaucracy, and corruption. In its 2005 report, Moody's Investors Service estimated that from 1998 to mid-2005, the Chinese government injected estimated $443 billion in capital to dispose of bad debts and strengthen the Chinese banking system.[18] Chinese banks listing on foreign stock exchanges were subjected to higher transparency requirements and were required to collaborate with foreign investors with innovative risk-management techniques and banking industry knowhow. According to the accounting and consulting firm KPMG, this boosted the net profits of China's banking sector 50 percent in 2007. The KPMG report also noted that seventy-five of eighty-three Chinese banks surveyed dropped their nonperforming loans (NPLs) to below 5 percent—below 2 percent for thirty-four banks.

The global economic slowdown has hit China's export-led growth hard. Chinese manufacturing declined month after month, and China's exports, in yuan, dropped in double digits. According to deputy governor Huang Longyun, Guangdong province saw[18] its export growth drop from 22.3 percent in 2007 to only 5.6 percent.

China's banks and state-owned construction and building companies in cement, glass, steel, copper, and aluminum are heavily invested in China's big real estate development projects. According to China's National Development and Reform Commission (NDRC), all these entities are facing high risks because of a drop in real estate prices in China's seventy large and medium cities. To bolster the construction sector, China announced a highly ambitious 4 trillion yuan ($585 billion) stimulus plan, with heavy investments in infrastructure construction. Additional efforts are being made to increase bank lending to small and medium-sized enterprises (SMEs).

Natural and Infrastructural Sources of Risk   Each country may have unique natural sources of risk for a global supply chain. U.S. supply chains were severely disrupted when suppliers in southeast Asia were devastated by a tsunami, and when petroleum refineries were damaged by Hurricane Katrina. Global supply chain managers must carefully and continually monitor the changing dynamic risks due to natural factors in different countries.

To estimate natural weather-related risks to sugar and other crops of key ingredients, the global candymaker Mars has hired the services of full-time meteorologists on its staff.[19]

The state of the manmade physical and informational infrastructure of a country can also play a determining role in the economic productivity and the efficiency of managing a global supply chain in that country. The recent collapse of an important bridge in Minneapolis, Minnesota, has many global supply chain managers concerned about the vulnerability of the aging U.S. physical infrastructure.

The strike at Long Beach port in California, for example, caused a backlog of shipping for some companies for more than six months—with devastating financial risks.

Sociocultural Sources of Risk   A country's sociocultural environment is its norms, and the level of trust, for cooperative and associational activities within its boundaries. Distinctive local norms for hiring and firing can become a minefield for a global enterprise. For example, the U.S. letter of offers, with its uniquely Americacentric terminology, may not be quite convincing to potential sales employees in Europe.

National societies or smaller communities with higher levels of mutual trust tend to conduct more personal business transactions. High levels of trust discourage individual actors from acting primarily out of opportunistic self-interest. They are likely to forego some of their self-interest for collective societal benefits. Close-knit civic activities between cultural groups build trust and collaboration in a country.

Industry-Level Sources of Risk

Each industry has certain unique traditions and ways of conducting business. Use preventive proactive initiatives rather than relying on reactive corrective actions to address key negative trends in your industry. Rather than waiting for your key suppliers to declare bankruptcy and disrupt your supply chains significantly, proactively investigate why your key suppliers are having financial difficulties or incurring delays in procuring raw materials. If your major customers frequently make late payments, offer them incentives by giving discounts for prepayments.

Industry-level sources of risk can be clustered as follows:

1. Demand-related risk
2. Competitive-risk
3. Supply-related Risk
4. Disruptive innovation-related risk

Demand-Related Risk The economic slowdown of 2008–2009 has demonstrated that demand of goods and services can fluctuate drastically. Global automotive giants such as General Motors and Chrysler have seen demand for certain models slashed by more than half. In many other sectors, buyers may choose to sit on the sidelines, throwing off forecasts about orders of products subject to discretionary demand. If a buyer accounts for a significant percentage of a producer/supplier's overall supply capacity, this can drastically affect the financial survivability of the concerned producer/supplier.

Innovative buyers are increasingly seeking financially stable global suppliers who are likely to be more reliable in making their promised deliveries even during the difficult economic times. According to the senior managers of global transactions banking units at Deutsche Bank, the Swedish banking giant SEB, and J. P. Morgan, their big anchor clients and distributors were using supply chain finance to extend payment terms and provide liquidity at reasonable prices to their key suppliers.[20] Top 40 global banks such as CitiBank and J. P. Morgan were seeking integrated end-to-end supply chain finance for upstream as well as downstream. U.S. Bank recently acquired logistics provider PowerTrack to integrate freight payments with payables and receivables management.

Competitive Risks Global competitors can pose serious sources of risk for global supply chain management. In the case of suppliers of commodity goods with low switching costs, competitors are likely to engage in price wars and entice some the key customers away. Product differentiation and brand reputation (such as of Intel microprocessors), helps hedge the intensity of such competitive pressures.

Very often, when a major rival (such as Coca-Cola for Pepsi) is launching or test-marketing an innovative product, the competitors may sabotage their test-marketing by subsidized offerings of their own. Such actions may have a significant erroneous impact. In 1993, IBM was significantly short of its projected $100 billion in annual sales because its rivals in the personal computer (PC) industry, including Compaq, Dell, and others, were offering their comparable clone PCs at much lower prices and through mass merchandisers.

If an industry has low barriers to market entry due to low fixed capital requirements, new competitive entrants can enter that industry relatively easily and fragment that industry's markets significantly. This led to the Dot-Com bust in 2000.

Poor Supplier Integration-Related Risks   Growing global enterprises must offer and deliver high-quality goods and services at competitive prices. These enterprises must carefully choose the goods and parts they will continue to produce internally, and the goods or parts that they will outsource globally. Global outsourcing has emerged as a strategic weapon for an increasing number of global enterprises to gain additional competitive advantage. Such make-versus-outsource decisions are strategic decisions with both short-term and long-term implications. For example, in general, global outsourcing of a product or its parts will tend to make it generic over the long term. The need to share technology with suppliers makes the product or its parts somewhat commoditized.

The global outsourcing decision requires building collaborative strategic alliances. Some of the key supplier-related risks associated with global outsourcing are

1. Risks caused by inadequate or unrealistic understanding of a global supplier's actual or potential technical capabilities

2. Risks caused by inability of a global supplier to scale-up its capacity economically at the desired growth rate.

3. Risks caused by significant cultural differences between a buyer and its global suppliers (for example, different national cultures have different attitudes toward timely completion of a task)

4. Risks caused by leakage of intellectual property shared or co-developed with the global suppliers (a global supplier supplying to competing companies may share with each company capabilities acquired or developed by the other)

5. Risks caused by breakdown in communication with global suppliers

For example, NASA's Mars Climate Orbiter, which cost $250 million, disappeared in 1999.[21] The construction of the Orbiter was outsourced by NASA to its tier 1 supplier Lockheed Martin. An independent review board assigned the cause of the loss of the Orbiter to poor supervision and communication, poor project management procedures, and short-sighted engineering. The Orbiter's navigation team was not trained appropriately and lacked familiarity with the spacecraft. The outsourced supplier did not provide the navigation information in metric units, and the NASA project team failed to detect this risk in advance. Proper contingency plans were not developed under a variety of simulated climate conditions.[22]

Disruptive Innovation-Related Risks   Innovative substitutes are goods and services that meet a given set of customer needs in alternate ways. The transportation needs met by horse-and-buggy suppliers were disrupted by the innovation of the horseless carriage.[23] This made leather harness suppliers obsolete. Personal computer makers such as Dell, Apple, and Sony relied heavily on suppliers of first $5^1/4$" and then $3^1/2$" diskette drives. But these were made obsolete by first the CD-ROM and then the more compact flash storage drives. In the same manner, the suppliers of audiocassette tapes came under competitive pressure from the suppliers of compact discs, and video cassette suppliers by DVD suppliers.

Firm-Level Sources of Risk

Inadequate firm level value-adding activities and business processes can also contribute some sources of risk. After polling 273 global executives in early 2008, a McKinsey Quarterly Survey by Pentilla reported[24] that a majority of global executives felt that their enterprises were not fully addressing most of the risks to their supply chains from a variety of global factors. To highlight the high exposure to business and supply chain risks, large multinational enterprises such as Navistar and Walgreens have redesignated their chief financial officers (CFOs) as chief risk officers (CROs).

Traditionally, some of the largest buyers (such as the Big Three American automobile makers) having the greatest bargaining power have sometimes treated their suppliers as hands-off adversaries. Supplies were procured from these key suppliers on a transaction-by-transaction basis and were primarily based on minimum costs. Their global rivals, such as Toyota, Honda, and Nissan, on the other hand, often treated their key tier 1 suppliers, such as Nippon-Denso, as family members of their groups. Their business was conducted on a collaborative basis while cultivating long-term win–win relationships.

Strategic sourcing, pioneered by General Motors[25] in the 1980s, uses procurement process as an integral process of supply chain management that continually evaluates and improves the sourcing and purchasing of an enterprise. Strategic sourcing enlarges the focus to a broader set of processes to help the enterprise minimize its costs and maximize its value under dynamic competitive conditions.

Some of these processes include supplier precertification and relationship management, enterprise-wide sourcing, supplier–vendor inventory management (also known as just-in-time II), and blanket contract agreements. Strategic sourcing can have a significant impact on the overall enterprise performance as well as on its new product development, differentiation, and quality. These accelerate the ability of an enterprise's speed to market. In strategic sourcing, better collaboration is innovated with cross-functional, cross-divisional, cross-geographic teams for sourcing, new product innovation, and other functional value-adding activities.[26]

In the face of the 2008–2009 global economic slowdown and credit crunch, many innovative global enterprises revamped financing of their enterprise-wide supply chains. Supply chain financing, a relatively innovative business practice, reduces risks by ensuring smooth flow of goods and information across from the enterprise supply chain, from suppliers to producers to distributors, by providing adequate liquidity to all partners involved.[27]

Appropriate investments in information technology platform of a firm play a strategic role in maintaining reliable critical communication needed for global outsourcing.[28] In a worldwide economic slowdown, such as in January 2009, an interdependent global supply chain is likely to be driven by its information technology platform and processes.

For example, a global enterprise[29] had 40 percent of its workforce in London and southeast England, areas that were adversely affected by an unprecedented storm in January 2009. A large number of sales associates could not take customer calls coming into their offices. This could have resulted in high levels of customer dissatisfaction and significant loss of business revenues, but the company called outsourcing IT provider TeleTech, headquartered in Englewood, Colorado. By deploying an innovative Internet-based IT platform, with a push of a button, TeleTech migrated its client's farflung virtual workforce working out of their homes in the United States, Britain, and Australia. Within minutes, 175 home-workers went online to provide much-needed customer support. By the end of the week, 700 extra customer orders were processed, resulting in 33 percent more sales than the client's weekly average.

Resilient global supply chains require well-coordinated teamwork between many professionals connected with a global supply chain. Often a number of professionals so affected deny the need to identify, assess, and mitigate their risks. They may either refuse or be reluctant to participate in team-based risk management. Some individuals argue that there is no risk in their areas—so they do not need to participate in risk management teams. Others claim that they have already responded to risks due to disruptive events and thus know what to do in the case of a disruptive event. A third group may not enjoy conjuring up all the disruptive events that may occur, dealing beforehand with potential negative problematic events. All these professionals illustrate a lack of comprehension of the innovative risk management process outlined in this study.

In progressive enterprises, innovative GSMs inspire and engage their employees who span the boundaries of their enterprises as they interface with their industry-level market environment and the national-level macroenvironment. These innovative GSMs share with these boundary-spanning employees all the needed information and resources needed to achieve superior supply chain performance and enterprise-wide results.

Step II: Assess and Monitor the Devastating Dynamic Effects of the Abovementioned Sources of Supply Chain Risk

Global supply chain managers (GSMs) need to develop their abilities to predict and anticipate, rather than be forced to react to and cope with, disruptive events in their worldwide supply chains. Instead of relying on intuition and gut reaction, GSMs must develop and promote the use of a structured process for assessing risks and vulnerability due to likely disruptions in their global supply chains.

After the likely causes—based on the sources of risk outlined earlier—have been clearly identified, GSMs can help brainstorm what-if questions to develop alternate states-of-nature scenarios. This will produce the severity of likely disruptive impacts of the various relevant national- and industry-level macro and micro sources of risk. All variances are monitored over a predetermined threshold of disruption (such as an increase in cost of more than $100,000, or a delay of more than two days). These disruptive impacts may be weighted disproportionately, if so desired. Severities of disruption are estimated for the best-case risk, the worst-case risk, and the most likely risk for each of the disruptive causes and sources of risk. The most likely risk impact is weighted at four times the weight of the best-case risk impact and the worst-case risk impact.

A careful monitoring of historical data, coupled with new what-if causal questions, can provide a reliable justification for the cost or time overrun needed for contingency planning under risky conditions.

This assessment can also provide guidelines for the probabilities of each of the disruptive events.

For each disruptive cause, the severity of adverse impact and its probability are plotted on a matrix such as that shown in Figure 2.4. Thus a portfolio

Figure 2.4
Monitor Risks and Assess Vulnerability due to Supply-Chain Disruptions

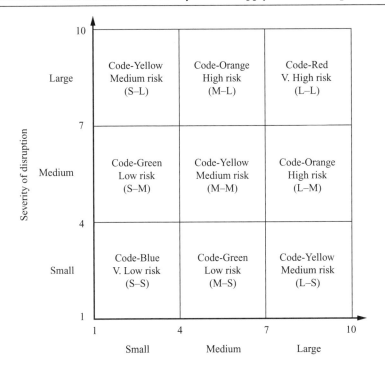

Likelihood of supply-chain disruption

of severities and probabilities of likelihood of all possible disruptive events is developed. This portfolio monitors nine color-coded zones of riskiness. For example, very risky events, coded red, have been assessed a high severity of disruption impact and a high likelihood of supply chain disruption. Code orange events, which are highly risky, have been assessed as having either high severity of disruption impact with medium likelihood of occurrence, or medium severity of disruption impact with high likelihood of occurrence. Similarly, code yellow events, code green events, and code blue events have been assessed as having successively lower risk.

Terrorist acts, however, are exceptional "Black Swan" episodes, unlike all other routine disruptive episodes contributing to supply chain risk. Contingency plans for these terrorism-related disruptions must be prepared and rehearsed separately. Given below is a brief description of the likely bullwhip impact of terrorist disruption of a global supply chain.

The goal of securing a global supply chain is to improve its resiliency and reduce the risk associated with any disruption. A resilient supply chain can withstand a disruptive incident and rapidly recover to a stable and reliable level of performance. With the acceleration of global supply chains, the potential threat of a disruptive incident increases geometrically into an unpredictable and cascading bullwhip effect.

In phase 1, a terrorist disruption of supply chain security can seriously hamper delivery and service capabilities of a supplier's key customers in terms of meeting the demands of their ultimate consumers. This can result in a serious shortfall of their short-term revenues. These customers can permanently lose some of their underdelivered or underserviced consumers.

In phase 2, these key customers can lose some or a substantial part of their intangible brand equity in the long run due to their lack of reliability. This damage can be severe if consumers believe that the disruption in delivery or service was due to negligence and inadequate protection from terrorist acts.

In phase 3, any sustained loss in key customers' revenue or brand equity reduces the supplying firm's own performance. This could erode the confidence of equity investors and lenders of debt or credit.

In phase 4, such shortfall in promised deliveries, service, or financial performance is likely to incur some legal liability.

In phase 5, a terrorist disruption of a supply chain is likely to cause a loss of faith and trust among many employees of the disrupted supplier toward their leaders' abilities to manage their global operations. In the case of severe disruptive situations, employee turnover or absenteeism may increase to unmanageable levels.

Finally, in phase 6, terrorist breach of security and any collateral damage are likely to increase regulatory scrutiny. This may add unnecessary costs to doing business in a particular industry or service sector. The tire failures in the early 2000s of Ford Explorers equipped with Firestone/Bridgestone tires resulted in increased regulation of tire pressure by the National Highway Traffic Safety Administration.

Step III: Mitigate the Rippling Bullwhip Effects of Risky Disruptions

Innovative management of risk in global supply chains evolves supplier sourcing over four maturity stages.

Stage 1, the elementary level, uses traditional sourcing; one-time cost reduction may be gained by consolidation of suppliers and aggregation of demand. The primary weapon is via price negotiation. This may, however, add some new sources of disruption and risks.

Stage 2, the junior level, uses analytical sourcing; deeper understanding is pursued in grasping the microeconomics of supply and demand. At this stage, all aspects of relationships with suppliers are developed and negotiated. This integrates macrolevel environmental risks.

Stage 3, the senior level, uses integrated sourcing; enterprise-wide integration of supply chain management with information technology, financial and taxation optimization, and change management are examined and streamlined. At this stage, enterprise-wide partnering with suppliers is pursued. In this case, microlevel industry level sources of risk are well grasped.

Stage 4, the master level, uses strategic global sourcing; continuous cost reduction is achieved by developing institutional dynamic sourcing capabilities. Customized global sourcing strategies are developed for the different commodities and critical supplies of the firm. Stage 4 risk management maturity translates the strategic goals and business objectives of an enterprise into an enterprise value innovation network that enhances the overall performance

Figure 2.5
Risk Mitigation Maturity Model for Innovative Global Supply Chain Management

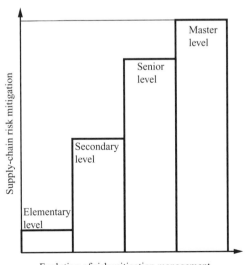

Evolution of risk mitigation management

of the global supply chain. This seamlessly integrates the value-adding chain of an enterprise with the value-adding chain of its key suppliers into an integrated value-adding network producing and sustaining superior performance over extended periods of time.

CASE STUDY: A GLOBAL SUPPLY CHAIN DISRUPTION AT ERICSSON

Ericsson, established in 1876 (employing 61,000 people in over 140 countries in 2004), is one of the world's largest suppliers of telecommunication systems.[30] In 2004, estimated 40 percent of all mobile phone calls were made using Ericsson's systems. The world's ten largest mobile-phone service providers were among Ericsson's customers.

In the past ten years, Ericsson had globally outsourced a large percentage of production and assembly of its products to contract manufacturers and suppliers. This exposed Ericsson to a variety of risks associated with its global supply chain.

On March 18, 2000, a minor fire accident took place in Ericsson's supplier's plant based in Albuquerque, New Mexico, the sole supplier of radio frequency chips for its equipment. The ten-minute fire involved a small area of a production cell, the size of a conference room for ten people. The fire hit an electric line that caused power fluctuations and outage throughout the state of New Mexico. Without any spare diesel power, the fans in the "clean room" stopped. The smoke and sprinkler water in the "clean room" took three weeks to clean before production could be restarted.

The production yield recovered to less than 50 percent after six months. Purchasing and installing new equipment took a few years. Ericsson could not sell and deliver its key consumer products because of its heavy reliance on this supplier. In spring 2001, Ericsson's annual report accounted a major loss of $400 million, primarily due to this disruption. This was later adjusted to $200 million and paid by insurance companies.

This supply chain disruption forced Ericsson not only to measure, monitor, and mitigate risks within Ericsson, but also to improve supply chain risk management to better measure, monitor, and mitigate risks along Ericsson's entire extended supply chain. After revamping its risk management procedures, Ericsson has adopted the philosophy[31] that "everyone is a risk manager."

Prior to the Albuquerque supply disruption incident on March 18, 2000, risk management at Ericsson was a corporate function primarily dealing with insurance and security service providers. After this disruption, the supply chain risk management was handled by a matrix organization under a risk management council with representatives from diverse parts of Ericsson's supply-related organizations.

After the Albuquerque supplier disruption incident, Ericsson's innovative risk management includes risk assessment and identification of sources of risk, risk monitoring, and risk management including contingency planning and incident handling procedures.[32]

Ericsson must map upstream and downstream operations to assess its supply chain risks. More attention must be paid to critical parts. Ericsson classifies different parts into four categories based on their sourcing. Some products are sourced from two or more approved sources (one manufacturer with two or more sites, or two or more manufacturers). Other products are sourced from one approved source, with other sources either approved and ready to be used, or other sources approved but not ready to be used. Finally, there are products with only one approved supplier.

For each of these four types of products, the impact of a disruptive accident is measured in terms of "business recovery time," ranging from less than 3 months to 3–8 months, 9–12 months, and more than 12 months (demanding redesign of a highly complex unit or product).

Ericsson's risk assessment process must involve evaluating external and internal disruption threats for the business enterprise as well as for its outside suppliers. These should be regularly assessed and revised.

The risk assessment must consider not only sources and risks from its current operations, but also assess the catastrophic effects of industry-level risks such as a shift in a rival's business strategy, entry of a new rival in the relevant market space, and the disruptive effect of an innovative substitute product.

When specific sources of risk and business interruptions are identified, squat teams should be formed of members from different parts likely to be affected to discuss potential vulnerability and develop proactive preventive actions.

Assessment and Monitoring of Supply Chain Risks for Ericsson

As suggested before, value of risk at Ericsson can be monitored using a risk map, based on the likelihood/probability and severity of disruption. Ericsson uses business interruption value, calculated by multiplying business recovery time by the gross margin of a product. Other costs for idle capacity of equipment and labor, as well as lost goodwill, can be added to this. The business interruption values are clustered in terms of negligible ($10 million), minor ($10–50 million), major ($50–100 million), and severe ($100 million). Using the proposed likelihood–severity matrix, Ericsson risk management spends less time, attention, and effort on sources of disruption that incur high severity with high likelihood than disruptive sources with low severity and low likelihood.

In case of disruptions with high business interruption value, risk monitoring is continued even after taking some risk mitigation actions.

Mitigation of Supply Chain Risks for Ericsson

At Ericsson, supply chain risk mitigation is a line responsibility. For each source of potential disruption, likelihood/probability and severity can be compiled by the persons responsible for alternate risk mitigation strategies.

The business interruption value may be used to determine the cost of alternate preventive actions.

In case there is a high residual risk even after taking some risk mitigation actions, that risk must be closely monitored for longer period.

Ericsson is also concerned about planning for business continuity. Specific responsibilities must be assigned for reporting disruptive events and taking emergency corrective actions. These disruptive incidents must be reported promptly to appropriate task forces and all the people most likely to be affected by the disruption.

Ericsson has a mitigating toolbox available on its intranet for access to all its subsidiaries linked to its global supply chain around the world.

In the advanced stages of a risk management maturity model, Ericsson must manage not only its own risk, but also the risk of its suppliers and these suppliers' suppliers. Thus, Ericsson's suppliers and the suppliers' suppliers must also promptly report their disruptive incidents. Critical suppliers and their key sites must be identified to be prioritized for appropriate risk management, including risk assessment, risk monitoring, and risk mitigation.

Expected Benefits of the Innovative Risk Management Model

After the Albuquerque fire disruption, telecommunication world-leader Ericsson had a hard time getting new business-disruption insurance.[33] Most insurance companies were skeptical, and they wished to hedge their risks by charging Ericsson high insurance premiums. They also demanded disclosure of more information about Ericsson's global supply chain operations and risks.

After Ericsson implemented some of the steps in the proposed innovate risk management, Ericsson's insurance companies praised their client's approach, and recommended the same practices to their other clients. The insurance companies reduced Ericsson's premium to 50 percent lower than what Ericsson was expecting to pay.[34]

Later, Ericsson had another disruptive incident of a fire in a plating plant. The innovative risk management model correctly estimated a disruption of three months. Ericsson promptly allocated adequate resources per the innovative risk management process, and there was no disruption in inbound supply.

CONCLUSIONS

Often in supply chain risk management there is an operational tug of war between the likely cost of disruption and the anticipated cost of mitigating that disruption. Investing resources in mitigating risks for disruption that are yet to occur seems futile to many bottom-line-driven accountants and global supply chain managers. On the other hand, strategically, any minor or major disruption in a global supply chain caused by a breach in security may cause an irreparable and irreversible damage to brand reputation and customer trust and goodwill.

Accidental importation of food products infected with mad cow disease from North America had a significant impact on the brand reputation of a number of enterprises involved. Small quantities of lead found in children's toys produced in China adversely affected the reputation of a number of Chinese toymaking producers and suppliers.

In this research study, we have proposed a multilayered innovative risk management framework to secure and reinforce global supply chains. To develop this innovative risk management model, we have synthesized principles and practices related to risk management in many interrelated disciplines such as strategic management, production planning, cross-cultural international management, finance management, microeconomics, and more. This synthesis demanded that we harmonize the different terminologies used in these diverse disciplines.

First we defined the scopes of our terms: supply chain management, risk, and supply chain risk management. A number of actual disruptive incidents in global supply chains were shared, along with their adverse direct and indirect consequences.

We outlined the objectives of the innovative risk management as to streamline global supply chains and to attain sustainable superior strategic performance for the business enterprise. We then identified the building blocks of the innovative risk management as (1) identification of multiple layers of sources of risk, (2) risk assessment and monitoring based on the likelihood/probability of disruption, and the severity of disruption, and (3) a risk mitigation model describing the elementary, junior, senior, and master levels of risk mitigation.

In a future study, we will review risk-related research studies in depth in the spirit of the "management science" discipline. These include modeling inventory management under uncertain supply and under uncertain demand, as well as alternate modes of transportation and logistics. In this study, however, we confine ourselves to the role of global supply chain managers (GSMs), managing the interactions and interrelationships with a variety of stakeholders.

With a growing focus on security and risks in global supply chains,[35] risk and security in global supply chains will continue to hold the attention of many more global supply chain managers and leaders in upper echelons. The innovative risk management framework proposed here has a wide variety of applications in risk management and other related areas of production planning. We propose to build on this framework in a variety of ways, including (but not limited to) empirical validation through in-depth case studies, surveys of practicing supply chain managers, and more.

This research study has provided us a renewed conceptual clarity for further research in global supply chain management, and it has helped us as practitioner supply chain managers. Unlike some successful supply chain managers who are able to guess and mitigate their risks intuitively, we can use this study to anticipate and assess how various sources of risk are most likely to affect the performance scorecards of our global supply chains and our business enterprises.

NOTES

1. Toshihiro Nishiguchi, *Strategic Industrial Sourcing* (New York: Oxford University Press, 1994).

2. Thomas Friedman, *The World Is Flat: A Brief History of The Twenty-First Century* (New York: Farrar, Strauss and Giroux, 2005, 2006).

3. P. Dornier, R. Fender, and P. Kouvalis, *Global Operations and Logistics* (New York: John Wiley, 1998).

4. Friedman, 2005, 2006.

5. F. Niederman, S. Kundu, and S. Salas, "IT Software Development offshoring: A Multi-Level Theoretical Framework and Research Agenda," *Journal of Global Information Management* 14, no. 2 (2006): 52–74.

6. The Royal Society, *Analysis, Perception and Management* (London: The Royal Society, 1992).

7. J. W. Deloach, *Enterprise-wide Risk Management: Strategies for Linking Risk and Opportunities* (London: Financial Times/Prentice-Hall, 2000).

8. Andreas Norrman and Ulf Jansson, "Ericsson's Proactive Supply Chain Risk Management Approach after a Serious Sub-Supplier Accident," *International Journal of Physical Distribution & Logistics Management* 34, no. 5 (2004): 435–456.

9. R. J. Schoneberger, "Strategic Collaboration: Breaching the Castle Walls," *Business Horizons* 39 (1996): 20.

10. R. Ray Gehani and G. Tom Gehani, "Air Transportation in Evolving Supply Chain Strategies," in *Aviation Security Management, Volume 1: The Context of Aviation Security Management*, ed. R. Andrew Thomas (Westport, CT: Praeger Security International, 2008), 25–40.

11. Dawn M. Russell and John P. Saldhana, "Five Tenets of Security-Aware Logistics and Supply Chain Operation," *Transportation Journal* 42, no. 4 (2003): 44–54.

12. E. C. Cuneo, "Safe at Sea," *Information Week* (April 7, 2003): 15.

13. G. Souter, "Risks from Supply Chain also Demand Attention," *Business Insurance* 34, no. 20 (2000): 26–28.

14. Converium, "Suppliers' Extension or Contingent Business Interruption Insurance," 2001, http://www.converium.com/web/.

15. Norrman and Jansson, 2004.

16. U.S. Department of Homeland Security, http://www.dhs.gov.

17. Donald J. Bowersox, David J. Closs, and M. Bixby Cooper, *Supply Chain Logistics Management* (New York: McGraw-Hill, 2007).

18. Thomas Clouse, "Fuel for the Growth Engine," *Global Finance* (February 2009): 34–35.

19. Chris Pentilla, "Risky Business," *Entrepreneur* (November 2008): 17–18.

20. Denise Bedell, "Tightening the Supply Chain," *Global Finance* (February 2009): 27–30.

21. CNN.com, "NASA Human Error Caused Loss of Mars Orbiter," 1999, http://mate.dm.uba.ar/~jetchev/Horror/CNN%20-%20NASA%20Human%20error%20caused%20loss%20of%20Mars%20orbiter%20-%20November%2010,%201999.htm.

22. Peter Finch, "Supply Chain Risk Management," *Supply Chain Management* 9, no. 2 (2004): 183–196.

23. R. Ray Gehani, *Management of Technology and Operations* (New York: John Wiley & Sons, 1998).

24. Pentilla, 2008.

25. Nishiguchi, 1994.

26. Gehani, 1998.

27. Bedell, 2009.

28. Gehani, 1998.

29. "2009 Global Outsourcing," International Association of Outsourcing Professional (IAOP) report, *Fortune*, May 4, ad section.

30. Norrman and Jansson, 2004.

31. Norrman and Jansson, 2004.

32. Norrman and Jansson, 2004.

33. Norrman and Jansson, 2004.

34. Norrman and Jansson, 2004.

35. Andrew R. Thomas, *Aviation Insecurity: The New Challenge of Air Travel* (Amherst, NY: Prometheus, 2008).

CHAPTER 3

Supply Chain Security Management and Its Effect on Shareholder Value

Mary F. Schiavo

TYLENOL, 1982

In September 1982, the parents of a twelve-year Chicago girl with a cold gave her a capsule of Extra-Strength Tylenol. Hours later, the child was dead. Within days, six more lives were claimed in the Chicago area. The ensuing investigation revealed that the victims were poisoned. Though initially baffled, the Chicago police and the Federal Bureau of Investigation soon found the link. All of those who died had ingested capsules of Extra-Strength Tylenol.[1] All levels of the supply chain were suspect—the production plants, the distributors, and the retailers. Law enforcement officials concluded most likely someone had taken Tylenol bottles off the store's shelves and stuffed the capsules with deadly levels of cyanide.[2] Obviously, the supply chain was intentionally breached. Every media outlet in the world, as well as loudspeakers mounted on vehicles traversing Chicago streets, broadcast warnings against taking Tylenol.[3] Johnson & Johnson, the manufacturer of Tylenol pulled the product and offered free replacements. In November 1982, the company resumed production and continued to manufacture and sell Tylenol capsules, reassuring its customers that they had taken control of their supply chain security through tamper-*resistant*—probably more realistically called tamper-*evident*—packaging. Many market analysts believed that Tylenol would never be able to regain its market share. The recall and relaunch was reported to have cost Johnson & Johnson over $100 million. Many pundits praised the company for its handling of the crisis. Tylenol's market share rebounded within a year and its tarnished image—although not its supply chain security—was significantly repaired.[4] The company's reaction to this negative situation was praised in a Harvard Business School case study that credited the company for its robust response and for tamper-resistant packaging.[5] The pundits and Harvard Business School were wrong. The company's actions to secure its supply chain were neither sufficient nor effective—it was a bandage on a vein of vulnerability.

TYLENOL, 1986

Four years later, in 1986, a 23-year-old Yonkers, New York, woman took two Tylenol capsules from a sealed Tylenol bottle equipped with tamper-resistant—or, rather, tamper-evident—packaging. No tampering was evident. She was found dead a few hours later. Once again, Tylenol capsules had been filled with cyanide. There was no evidence of tampering with the three protective seals on the packaging. Investigators initially concluded that the tampering must have been done during the manufacturing process. Tylenol was again removed from store shelves. The investigation revealed another cyanide-laced bottle of Tylenol with all tamper-resistant seals intact. The second bottle of Tylenol was from a different manufacturing plant than the first bottle of Tylenol.[6] To this day, both the 1982 and 1986 Tylenol cyanide supply chain cases remain unsolved murders.[7] In both the 1982 and 1986 episodes, extortionists unsuccessfully attempted to profit from the situation, demanding $1 million in 1982, and $2 million in 1986, to stop any future poisonings, demonstrating even further supply chain vulnerabilities—extortionate demands threatening supply chains much like modern-day pirates attacking ships and holding them for ransom.

The Food and Drug Administration counted 270 incidents of copycat supply chain tampering in the month following the 1982 attacks. Many different lines of products and supply chains were attacked. Halloween was canceled in several cities that feared the opportunity presented for new threats in Halloween trick or treat candy. These attacks on the supply chain affected not only the company that was the direct target, but also hundreds of other supply chains, companies, markets, and sales—and, ultimately, the shareholders who invested their equity in companies with vulnerable supply chains.[8]

Despite the Harvard Business School's touting Tylenol as a model for corporate case study reaction during an emergency, Tylenol's repairs should not be praised as a success story. The supply chain was breached not once, but twice, and by the same threat and method of supply chain interruption—cyanide poison in capsules. A company falling victim to the same supply chain attack within a span of four years is not a success. Evidently "tamper-resistant" packaging wasn't tamper-evident. It was only after the second attack that the cheaply produced Tylenol capsules were replaced with new coated caplets. In 1989, federals laws required that all over-the-counter products be secured by protective packaging protecting consumers from compromises in supply chain security.[9]

BHOPAL, 1984

Between the 1982 and 1986 Tylenol supply chain disasters came a 1984 supply chain attack that resulted not only in shareholder losses, but in massive loss of life as well. Originally thought to be a failure in a manufacturing plant pipe, the Union Carbide disaster in Bhopal, India, was believed to be a deliberate sabotage attack. A large amount of water was intentionally released into a methyl isocyanate gas tank, causing a chemical reaction that forced open the chemical release valve. As in the Tylenol sabotages two years before and two years after, the perpetrators were never caught. Union Carbide made approximately $600 million in payments to or on behalf of victims. That sum does not include cleanup, investigation, and legal costs, or, ultimately, the sale of Union Carbide's interest in the Bhopal plant.[10]

Investors in the above companies and products have not been alone in suffering losses due to chain security holes. Threats in the twenty-first century are even more alarming. Supply chain security threats are not, and cannot be, contained within the boundaries of the United States, or any other country. Companies have globalized their product supply lines in an effort to reduce costs; because of this, supply chains span the global market. The global market is now so integrated that security breaches in one part of the process in one location have domino effects that reach around the world. The secretary general of the International Standards Organization (ISO) concluded that "[t]hreats in the international market-place know no borders."[11] These acts of supply chain attacks can weaken a company to the point of collapse. Anyone alive in the three decades since the Tylenol and Bhopal disasters has heard news reports of hundreds of supply chain disasters, intentional or unintentional, resulting in market interruptions of peanut butter, milk, orange juice, dog food, produce, hamburger and many other meat products, plastic toys, toothpaste, baby food, baby formula, drywall, insulation, potting soil, bottled water, and countless other goods.[12, 13]

WHO OWNS THE SUPPLY CHAIN, AND IS THE SAME ENTITY RESPONSIBLE FOR IT?

Before there can be a supply chain process, there must be goods that generate a supply chain, a business entity to produce the goods and be responsible for them and investors to finance the goods production and supply chain process. The business will choose how it wishes to be structured (as a partnership, limited liability company (LLC), corporation, etc.). Because of liability limitations, most business entities choose incorporation and financing by the investment of shareholders who entrust the management and the board of directors with their investments.[14]

Even without supply chain security, owning stock in a company can be a crap shoot—it may be a lucrative short-term or long-term investment and provide a steady stream of income through dividend payments, or it may be a disastrous loss or a flat line on stock price charts. But when a company suffers a supply chain disaster, shareholders shoulder and suffer the loss. When companies experience incidents such as the Tylenol or Bhopal incidents, stock prices drop precipitously, and shareholders can lose part and or all of their investments. The shareholders' risk is greater than that of the management or the company's security holders; management and bond holders enjoy priority over shareholders. While brokerage firms and Wall Street pundits can frequently be heard touting some stock as "recovered," a stock recovery does not make the shareholders whole—they still suffered a loss in value that does not simply evaporate with the advent of future earnings.

At every step in the lifecycle of a product, a breach in supply chain security compromises shareholder investment. Through research and development, production, outsourcing, parts, supply, packaging, shipping, distribution, placement, sales, and aftermarket uses, this division of labor ideally allows greater economic efficiency, but it also provides increased opportunity for supply chain compromises, and loss of control and security that can decrease shareholder value.

Even if a company rebounds from a supply chain disaster, the Wall Street myth that a recovery in stock value somehow erases the earlier losses suffered by shareholders is belied by simple arithmetic: Investor A buys $1.00 in stock before a supply chain disaster. After a breach in the chain, the stock falls to 50¢. Investor A loses 50¢. Investor B buys his share while the stock is at 50¢. Even if the stock subsequently rises to $2.00, Investor A still lost 50¢. Investor B realizes a $1.50 gain in value while investor A realized only $1.00. Praising the Tylenol manufacturer and seller Johnson & Johnson for its eventual recovery obscures the fact that supply chain disasters twice cost investors and shareholders hundreds of millions of dollars. Johnson & Johnson has been listed on the New York Stock Exchange (NYSE) since 1944.[15]

WHY SHAREHOLDERS PAY ATTENTION TO THE SUPPLY CHAIN

Supply chain security has come to the forefront of corporate concerns because the exposure to risk and the potential for a devastating impact is so enormous. Johnson & Johnson paid over $100 million dollars for the 1982 recall and relaunch of Tylenol.[16] Union Carbide's costs were well over $600 million.[17] Furthermore, securing the supply chain since September 11, 2001, has required even closer scrutiny. Supply chain attacks have more sophisticated plots. Unhampered by national boundaries, the implements of terror are far more diverse than cyanide or melamine and range from cyberattacks to missiles and include everything in between. The recognition of supply chain security has become so much a part of modern life that preschoolers know that they are not supposed to eat trick-or-treat candy that is not commercially packaged or whose packaging is damaged. U.S. schools require that food shared in the classroom be commercially prepackaged. Homemade treats are from an unsecured or unknown supply chain and are not allowed. Kindergarteners now know the importance of supply chain security, even if they cannot name it or spell it.

WHY VIGILANCE AND ALERTS ALONE FAIL

Attempted security breaks can and have been foiled by an educated populace on vigilant alert. The United States Postal Service relies on these four steps: educate, investigate, intervene, and prevent.[18] But being on continuous or near continuous high alert levels quickly reduces the focus attention and sense of urgency of the vigilant. The best example may be the color-coded airport threat level introduced by the TSA after September 11, 2001. The threat level has stayed at orange for so long that no one pays attention, despite the fact it is the second highest of five levels of alert.[19] Clearly, then, supply chain security must include the minimization of risk, not just elevation of alert.

THE TROJAN HORSE

Throughout history it has been transportation that has been used as the point in the supply chain to disrupt and terrorize. So ubiquitous is this form of threat that Virgil's *The Aeneid* and Greek mythology provide us a name— trojan horse. Countless attackers have used the same modus operandi. The man that the world would eventually know as the Unabomber exploded his first homemade bomb at a Chicago university. For the next seventeen years, Ted Kaczynski mailed or hand-delivered a series of increasingly sophisticated bombs that killed three Americans and injured twenty-four more. He also threatened to blow up airliners.[20] Years before September 11, 2001, in 1972 and 1977, in just two of many attacks, letter bombs from the Mideast traveled overseas on commercial planes and were delivered within the United States by the U.S. Postal Service.[21,22]

The airline industry has long been a direct target of terrorism. Just-in-time manufacturing and warehousing pose additional risk to transportation because the time constraints leave little to inspect and double check, especially in a global market. The major players in the rapid transport of packages all use airplanes in their supply chains. Unfortunately, aviation history demonstrates that the airline industry has been more reactive than proactive in assessing, managing, and forecasting risk. Passengers, passenger baggage and carry-ons, and cargo unassociated with passengers are all causes for concern, especially in light of the number of attacks after security was introduced over fifty years ago. There have been well over 1,000 documented attacks on aviation.

For a laundry list of hijackings and other aviation security too lengthy to list here, see *Aviation Security Management, Volume 1*, Chapter 10.[23] The U.S.

Centennial of Flight Commission also outlined a history of aviation security. The first hijacking of an aircraft was reported in May 1930 when Peruvian rebels hijacked a Pan American mail plane to drop propaganda leaflets. And that was just the beginning. Demands for baggage inspection in the United States came in November 1955 after a man wanting to cash in on his mother's life insurance policy packed a bomb to detonate midflight on a plane bound for Denver, Colorado. By December 1972, an emergency rule was issued by the Federal Aviation Administration (FAA) that all passengers and carry-on baggage had to be inspected by the start of 1973 because three bombs were discovered on three different airliners. In December 1988, security measures were put in place at European and Middle Eastern airports inbound to the United States to examine all checked bags and match luggage to passengers after the Lockerbie, Scotland, terrorist attack, in which Pan American Airways Flight 103 was blown up on a flight between London and New York by a bomb hidden in a cassette tape player.[24] This tragedy followed an FAA bulletin issued in mid-November 1988 that warned of such a device, and another warning on December 7 of a possible bomb to be placed on a Pan Am plane in Frankfort.[25] In 1996, attention was again focused on the danger of explosive devices on board aircraft, including hazardous cargo, after the crash of TWA Flight 800, at first thought to be caused by a terrorist bomb. For over a decade after the Pan Am 103 bombing, the United States continued to focus on the threat vector of explosives in baggage by devoting nearly tunnel vision to looking for bombs in bags, giving a false sense of security and complacency. The United States overlooked other vulnerabilities and concentrated on one preventative technology, much like the 1982 Tylenol attacks. There was a false sense of tranquility accompanied by unjustified reliance in the illusory bag checks, just as was placed in the safety seals on the tamper-resistant packaging.

The false sense of security was shattered on September 11, 2001, when terrorists hijacked four airliners and crashed them into the World Trade Center, the Pentagon, and a field near Shanksfield, Pennsylvania (after passengers prevented the terrorists from reaching the U.S. Capitol). After the 9/11 attacks, security changed hands from the airlines and their contractors to the federal government with the passage of the Aviation Transportation and Security Act. The act also created the Transportation Security Agency (TSA) and, later, the Department of Homeland Security, which oversees security for all modes of transportation.[26]

As tragic as the 9/11 attacks were, they, too, were copycat attacks. Multiple simultaneous hijackings had already occurred thirty years before. In September 1970, a hijacking occurred involving four airplanes and five governments (the United States, Germany, Switzerland, Israel, and Britain).[27] Moreover, al-Qaeda's 1995 "Bojinka" plot was foiled only a few days before its execution. It included plans to bomb multiple U.S. airlines over the Pacific Ocean on the same day and fly one hijacked aircraft into CIA headquarters.

Hijackings and bombs and missiles aimed at transportation pose grave concerns for the supply chain. The 9/11 attacks pushed many airlines over the edge and many other industries to the verge of bankruptcy. Bailout money was provided from the government to many supply chain–related companies, but not to shareholders. The owner–investors' or shareholders' equity in those businesses plummeted. Despite the fact that to date not one airline, airport, or security company has paid so much as one dime to its victims,[28] many airline stocks after 9/11 became junk.

To make matters worse for supply chain stakeholders, the state of cargo aircraft security is worse than that of passenger aircraft. In October 2006, the International Air Transport Association (IATA) concluded that "[c]argo security is in a state of relative infancy when compared with aircraft, passenger and baggage security . . . . Supply chain security is much talked about but insufficiently understood. Acceptance of the key principle—that each supply chain member must accept and deliver their proper component of cargo security responsibility—is inadequately embraced."[29] The old saying that a chain is only as strong as its weakest link certainly holds true in the world of supply chain security.

With the advent of just-in-time manufacturing and global supply chains, much as in the Industrial Revolution, "economic changes caused far-reaching social changes, including the movement of people to cities, the availability of a greater variety of material goods, and new ways of doing business."[30] Seventy years ago, much of the manufacturing process was done in-house, and shipping contained within certain geographical boundaries. Today, this is no longer the case as companies search for the most cost-efficient methods to manufacture goods or services. For example, at least sixty international suppliers were contracted to make parts for the Boeing 777.[31]

The linked chain analogy is also useful in consideration of the fact that each link of a multilink chain may be contracted out to the lowest bidder and transported between each link in some manner, such as by truck, ship, rail, plane, or Internet, also by the lowest bidder. The charts below give examples of points in an international supply chain. Each transfer represents a link, a point of vulnerability, and an opportunity for a breach.

According to an April 2008 U.S. Government Accountability Office (GAO) report on supply chain security,

[c]ontainer ships carry cargo for thousands of companies and the containers are loaded individually away from the port. Each transfer of a container from one party to the next point is a point of vulnerability in the supply chain. The security of each transfer facility and the trustworthiness of each company are, therefore, critical to the overall security of the shipment. Cargo must be loaded in containers at secure facilities and the integrity of the container must be maintained to its final destination.[32]

Every point in the supply chain has an exposure to risk.

As companies look to increase efficiency in every area in the service sector, there has been a mass offshore migration. Offshoring generally refers to a company's "purchases from abroad (imports) of goods or services that were previously produced domestically. A company may offshore either by purchasing services from another company based overseas or by obtaining services in-house through an affiliate located overseas."[33] According to a 2005 GAO report on off-shoring, there are three main reasons for this increase. First, technological advances, such as the Internet and other telecommunication devices, facilitate communication amongst people around the globe. Second, many countries have opened their borders for trade and business, be it goals or service—China and India being two such examples. Third, technically skilled populations now exist around the globe to perform services and technological work. Offshoring presents increased vulnerabilities in not only consumer privacy and national security, but in corporate supply chain security.

The GAO report also posits that many benefits are derived from offshoring: reduction in labor costs (from hourly wages to employee benefits, taxes, or tax credits, depending on country-specific requirements), expanded access to markets, and better currency exchange rates. Additionally, having locations in different time zones allows the business to operate twenty-four hours a day, thus meeting the demands of worldwide customers. However, most benefits do not come without their counterpart risks. The GAO identified risks such as "possible political instability in overseas locations, less reliable civil infrastructure, exchange rate volatility, less developed legal and regulatory systems, and risks to intellectual property."[34] Any one of those vulnerabilities, if exploited by terrorists, other criminals, corporate espionage, or hostile governments could quickly destroy shareholder or owner–investor value.

Supply chain security vulnerabilities are not only risks for private industry, but also a huge concern for the U.S. government. For example, the decision of the U.S. government to offshore the manufacturing of passports was made without a full appreciation of the vulnerabilities and risks in the passport supply chain. According to the United States Department of State Web site,

The U.S. passport, also called the Electronic Passport or e-passport, looks almost the same as a regular passport but it contains a small contactless integrated circuit (computer chip) embedded in the back cover. The chip contains the data visually displayed on the photo page of the passport, including a digital photograph. The inclusion of the digital photograph is to enable biometric comparison, through the use of facial recognition technology, at international borders. The U.S. e-passport also has a new look, incorporating additional anti-fraud and security features.[35]

In March 2008, the *Washington Times* published its first piece in a three-part series regarding this very topic. According to the *Times*, some of the companies installing the computer chips are located in Europe, but after the chips are installed, the products are shipped again—to companies in Thailand. And one of these was infiltrated by Chinese espionage, and passports were outfitted with radio frequency identification antennae. Furthermore, in addition to Chinese espionage, Thailand has been affected by social unrest and the target of terror threats from Islamic antigovernment groups, including al-Qaeda, the same terrorist organization responsible for breaching both the United Airlines and American Airlines supply chains and getting into the cockpit on September 11, 2001. The "United States Passport supply chain puts cost savings ahead of national security."[36] Lowest-cost bidder selection for each link of the chain is not always prudent or responsible.

INSPIRATION VERSUS IMPLEMENTATION

Even if there are written safeguards in place, the benefits they offer can only be fully recognized if they are implemented, enforced, and continuously reviewed and revised to keep current with potential threats. Risk assessment must be ongoing and proactive, not just reactive and per occurrence. This continuous risk assessment is necessary for the supply chains of both the manufacturing and service sectors. Some of today's most prominent threats were not on most companies' lists of concerns thirty years ago.

MY BROTHER'S KEEPER

Companies have a number of different influences directing their supply chain security best practices: federal regulation, industry standards, and their own prior experience—and the industry's prior experience—with intentional breaches in the supply chain. Companies should strive to make supply chain security a lesson they learn from others' mistakes, not from their own. One person's mistake can cause shareholders industrywide to suffer, so companies and shareholders should take a keen interest in industry practices and the effects on their own company.

Federal regulations and programs can be a driving force behind a company's supply chain security program—if it is not followed, enforceable provisions may bring legal repercussions. A cost–benefit analysis of implementing security measures always shows a price increase to the consumer, and consequently a loss of some price-competitive points. Companies strike a balance between cost and security in an effort to make their prices competitive while simultaneously reducing the risk of security breaches in the supply chain. The government does the same cost–benefit analysis. As a result, government-imposed security regulations are minimums, not maximums, and companies are always able to improve their supply chains' security above government-mandated minimums. According to a 2008 GAO report on supply chain security,

[i]n an effort to strike a balance between the need for security and free-flowing maritime commerce, U.S. Customs and Border Protection (CBP) (a component of DHS responsible for protecting the nation's borders at and between official ports of entry) oversees the Customs-Trade Partnership Against Terrorism program, known as C-TPAT. CBP's port of entry responsibilities encompass 326 airports, seaports, and

Table 3.1

Table 2: Examples of Minimum Security Criteria That Trade Sectors Must Meet for C-TPAT Participation

Trade sector	Examples of minimum security criteria	Month/year revised minimum criteria effective
Importers	Written procedures must stipulate how seals are to be controlled and affixed to loaded containers.	March 2005
Sea carriers	A vessel visitor log must be maintained and a temporary visitor pass must be issued.	March 2006
Highway carriers	Trailers must be stored in a secure area to prevent unauthorized access and/or manipulation.	March 2006
Foreign manufacturers	To help ensure the integrity of cargo, procedures must be in place to ensure that information received from business partners is reported accurately and timely.	August 2006
Rail carriers	Rail carriers must have procedures in place for reporting unauthorized entry into rail cars and locomotives.	August 2006
U.S. customs brokers	For all brokers, procedures for the issuance, removal, and changing of access devices (e.g., keys, key cards, etc.) must be documented.	January 2007
U.S. and foreign marine port authorities and terminal operators	An employee identification system must be in place for positive identification and access control purposes.	August 2007
Long haul highway carriers in Mexico	Written procedures must exist which identify specific factors or practices, that may deem a shipment from a certain shipper of greater risk.	August 2007
Air carriers	Procedures must be in place to prevent, detect, or deter unmanifested material and unauthorized personnel from gaining access to aircraft, including concealment in cargo.	November 2007

Source: CBP.

Note: CBP has not issued minimum security criteria for one trade sector—freight consolidators/ocean transportation intermediaries and nonvessel operating common carriers. CBP projects that criteria will be issued and effective for the trade group by mid-2008.

U.S. Government Accountability Office, *Supply Chain Security: U.S. Customs and Border Protection Has Enhanced Its Partnership with Import Trade Sectors, but Challenges Remain in Verifying Security Practices* (GAO-08-240, 2008), 18.

Table 3.2

Table 3: Summary of C-TPAT Tiered Benefits Structure from the SAFE Port Act

C-TPAT benefit level	When benefits are awarded	Time frame for benefits determination	Benefit examples
Tier 1	Upon CBP's certification of applicant as a C-TPAT member	Within 90 days of CBP's receipt of an application for C-TPAT membership, to the extent practicable	May include: • a maximum 20 percent reduction in Automated Targeting System score for an importer
Tier 2	Upon validation of member's security measures and supply chain security practices	Within 1 year of a member's certification into C-TPAT, to the extent practicable	May include: • reduced scores in Automated Targeting System for importers • reduced cargo examinations[a] • priority cargo searches[b]
Tier 3	Upon validation that member demonstrates sustained commitment to maintaining measures and practices that exceed Tier 2 guidelines	No time frame specified, but may be done as part of Tier 2 validation	May include: • expedited release of cargo in U.S. ports at all threat levels designated by the Secretary, Homeland Security • further reduction in cargo examinations • priority cargo examinations • further reduction in the Automated Targeting System risk score for importers • inclusion in joint incident management exercises, as appropriate

Source: GAO.

[a] An examination is an inspection of cargo to detect the presence of misdeclared, restricted, or prohibited items that utilizes nonintrusive imaging such as x-ray and detection technology.

[b] A search is an intrusive examination in which a container is opened and its contents are unloaded and visually inspected for the presence of misdeclared, restricted, or prohibited items.

S. Government Accountability Office, *Supply Chain Security: U.S. Customs and Border Protection Has Enhanced Its Partnership with Import Trade Sectors, but Challenges Remain in Verifying Security Practices* (GAO-08-240, 2008), 20.

designated land borders. C-TPAT, which applies across all transportation modes, is a component of CBP's multifaceted approach for overseeing the security of container-ized cargo and the international supply chain—the flow of goods from foreign man-ufacturers, suppliers, or vendors where such shipments originate to retailers.[37]

Table 3.1 sets forth the minimum security requirements for C-TPAT par-ticipation for the trade sectors. The ebb and flow of commerce still needs to be maintained, but, if a company wants to protect its supply chain, more robust security is necessary.

As the GAO report aptly states,

[t]he growing interdependence of nations requires policymakers to recognize the need to work in partnerships across boundaries to achieve vital national goals. For this reason, CBP has committed, through its strategic planning process, to promote an international framework of standards governing customs and related business rela-tionships in order to enhance supply chain security.

The market is no longer contained within certain geographical boundaries—it is universal. Negotiating with foreign governments and companies is now a must. C-TPAT, which has tiered levels as set forth by structure under the SAFE Port (Security and Accountability for Every Port) Act of 2006, exchanges certain types of compliance for reduced levels of scrutiny and examination for that importer's containerized cargo. Table 3.2 summarizes the structure of the act.

Even when there are near picture-perfect programs implementing all gov-ernment requirements and meeting all regulations, shareholders need to real-ize two important facts: (1) programs are only as effective as they are implemented and enforced—every time and every day, and (2) meeting gov-ernment standards alone means the company is doing the bare minimum. The 2008 GAO report states that there has been difficulty in "determining the deterrent effect of security practices" as well as in validating that the C-TPAT members are maintaining consistent security practices according to the minimum guidelines. At bottom line, policies are being put in place to address, deter, and catch vulnerabilities, but the security practices process is ongoing, and the government prescribes the bare minimum—and even that is not consistently in place.

Federal regulation is not the only force that drives a company's supply chain security plan; the industry standard may be the company's best prac-tices. The International Organization for Standardization (ISO) is a network of nongovernmental national standard organizations for 157 companies, with a system coordinator in Geneva, Switzerland. It is a blend of both the private and public sectors, including organizations with a hand in government oper-ations and those that are solely in the private sector. The organization's aim is to facilitate a blend or compromise between the needs of society and the business sector. Because the ISO is a voluntary international organization, its standards do not carry the authority of law. But if a company cannot operate at industry standard, its vulnerabilities will pose risks to its shareholders and to others throughout the industry. In 2007, the ISO released a new series of supply chain management standards to address the entire supply process in order to reduce risks associated with piracy, fraud, and terrorism. The series includes provisions to

> establish, implement, maintain and improve a security management system; assure conformity with security management policy; demonstrate such conformity; seek certification/registration of conformity by an accredited third party organization; or make a self-determination and self-declaration of conformity.[38]

A company's own experience, as well as industry experience, will also contribute to the implementation, maintenance, and revision of the supply chain security practice. Unfortunately, when companies are not forced (through federal regulation) or motivated (by best practices), they often implement risk control devices only after experiencing a breach in supply-side security. Companies tend to focus on the bottom line at the expense of security if the prevention of an issue has not been a major topic for discussion to date. Furthermore, because security vulnerabilities are not always apparent, security is an easy target for budget cuts and other shortcuts. These tendencies encourage a reactive response, not proactive prevention—but only proactive organizations will reap consistent preservation of shareholder value.

Shareholders have a unique position within a company but often feel powerless to make any changes. Instead, shareholders simply sell their stock and invest in another company, often suffering a loss. But shareholders can sometimes voice their concerns through shareholder proposals, which are regulated under section 240.14a-8 of Title 17 of the Code of Federal Regulations. In order to submit a proposal—or, more technically, a "recommendation or requirement that the company and/or its board of directors take action, which [shareholders] intend to present at a meeting of the company's shareholders" (17 CFR 240.14a-8(a), revised April 2008), shareholders must meet certain requirements.

> In order to be eligible to submit a proposal, [shareholders] must have continuously held at least $2,000 in market value, or 1%, of the company's securities entitled to be voted on the proposal at the meeting for at least one year by the date [shareholders] submit the proposal. [Shareholders] must continue to hold those securities through the date of the meeting. (17 CFR 240.14a-8(b))

Additional requirements for proposals limit submissions to one proposal per shareholder per meeting, with a maximum length of 500 words, and with specific deadline requirements. Even if a shareholder properly follows the requirements, the proposal may still be rejected if the subject matter is not proper under state law, is a violation of law or proxy rules, or involves a personal grievance. Additional reasons for exclusions can be found at 17 CFR 240-14a-8(i), revised April 1, 2008.

A shareholder proposal relating to supply chain security was the subject of a 2007 Wal-Mart shareholder proposal. The proposal stated,

As long-term shareholders of Wal-Mart Inc., we support policies that apply transparency and accountability to corporate spending on political activities. Such disclosure is consistent with public policy and in the best interest of shareholders . . . . However, its payments to trade associations, such as the Retail Industry Leaders Association (RILA), used for political activities are undisclosed and unknown. RILA has taken the position that, "The government should not rush to require the use of "smart containers" or "electronic seals." (Statement submitted by RILA, Subcommittee on Crime, Terrorism and Homeland Security of the House Judiciary Committee, 3/15/05 Hearing). We believe our Company's support of RILA puts it in the perverse position of hindering national security improvements, putting our shipments at risk and U.S. citizens' well being in jeopardy, which reflects poorly on our commitment to customers.

Wal-Mart responded by requesting that the proposal be denied because "the proposal falsely and misleadingly implies that Wal-Mart, through its contributions to trade associations, is 'hindering national security improvements, putting our shipments at risk and U.S. citizens' well being in jeopardy . . . .'" Wal-Mart further replied,

Wal-Mart is committed to the highest standards of safety and security throughout its supply chain worldwide. Wal-Mart actively participates in programs that help ensure the security of cargo delivered into the United States, such as the Customs-Trade Partnership Against Terrorism ("C-TPAT"), which is a voluntary program of the Customs and Border Protection Agency and private industry. While there is no single method for ensuring supply chain security, Wal-Mart continually evaluates the security of its worldwide supply chain, supports legislation such as the Safe Port Act, and independently and collaboratively tests technology and systems that improve security and safety in Wal-Mart's supply chain and beyond.[39]

Even if shareholder proposals fail—and most do—they can still be powerful tools for calling attention to issues, drive change, make the public aware of supply chain security, and put management on notice regarding vulnerabilities.

The secretary general of the International Standards Organization (ISO) perhaps said it best: "Threats in the international market-place know no borders, and limits in potential losses."[40] The September 11, 2001 attacks stand as a painful reminder of the costs to shareholders. The airlines paid nothing to their victims; they were insulated from financial responsibility by Congressionally conferred immunity. Yet shareholders' value in most airlines was completely destroyed—not by the costs of compensating victims, but by the failure to appreciate the widespread market reaction and industrywide destruction of value that follow a security breach. Thus, even if a breach in supply chain security does not result in crippling financial liability occasioned by the damage done by the breach, the damages from supply chain security breaches are often not contained within the breaching company but spread to damage entire industries and perhaps nations, wiping out shareholder value across entire industries as well as across national borders.

NOTES

1. Dan Fletcher, "A Brief History of the Tylenol Poisonings," *Time*, February 9, 2009, www.time.com/time/nation/article/0,8599,1878063,00.html.

2. Spencer Davidson and Raji Samghabadi, "A Replay of the Tylenol Scare," *Time*, February 24, 1986, www.time.com/time/magazine/article/0,9171,960693,00 .html.

3. Dan Fletcher, "A Brief History of the Tylenol Poisonings," *Time*, February 9, 2009, www.time.com/time/nation/article/0,8599,1878063,00.html.

4. The History Channel, "This Day in History: September 29, 1982, The Tylenol Murders," *The History Channel*, www.history.com/this-day-in-history.do?action= Article&id=52868#.

5. James Burke, *A Career in American Business (B)* (Boston: Harvard Business Publishing, 1989).

6. Spencer Davidson and Raji Samghabadi, "A Replay of the Tylenol Scare," *Time*, February 24, 1986, www.time.com/time/magazine/article/0,9171,960693,00.html.

7. Rachael Bell, "The Tylenol Terrorist: Copycat Criminals," *truTV Crime Library Criminal Minds and Methods*, www.trutv.com/library/crime/terrorists_spies/ terrorists/tylenol_murders/4.html.

8. George J. Church, Lee Griggs, and Rita Healy, "Copycats Are on the Prowl," *Time*, November 8, 1982, www.time.com/time/magazine/article/0,9171,925827,00 .html.

9. Rachael Bell, "The Tylenol Terrorist: Copycat Criminals," *truTV Crime Library Criminal Minds and Methods*, www.trutv.com/library/crime/terrorists_spies/ terrorists/tylenol_murders/4.html.

10. Union Carbide, "Bhopal Information Center: Chronology," Union Carbide, www.bhopal.com/chrono.html.

11. International Organization for Standardization, "New Suite of ISO Supply Chain Management Standards to Reduce Risks of Terrorism, Piracy and Fraud," *International Organization for Standardization*, October 25, 2007, www.iso.org/iso/ pressrelease.htm?refid=Ref1086.

12. Rick Weiss, "Tainted Chinese Imports Common: In Four Months, FDA Refused 298 Shipments," *The Washington Post*, May 20, 2007, www.washingtonpost .com/wp-dyn/content/article/2007/05/19/AR2007051901273.html.

13. Felix Kessler, "Tremors From Tylenol Scare Hit Food Companies," *Fortune*, March 31, 1986, http://money.cnn.com/magazines/fortune/fortune_archive/1986/ 03/31/67329/index.htm.

14. William A. Klein and John C. Coffee, Jr., *Business Organization and Finance, Legal and Economic Principles*, 10th ed. (New York: Foundation Press, 2007), 139–140.

15. Johnson & Johnson, "Investor Relations," Johnson & Johnson, www.investor .jnj.com/investor-relations.cfm.

16. The History Channel, "This Day in History: September 29, 1982, The Tylenol Murders," *The History Channel*, www.history.com/this-day-in-history .do?action=Article&id=52868#.

17. Union Carbide, "Bhopal Information Center:Chronology," Union Carbide, www.bhopal.com/chrono.html.

18. U.S. Postal Service, "The United States Postal Service: What We Can Do to Make the Mail Safe," *USPS News: Press Releases*, October 23, 2001, www.usps.com/news/2001/press/pr01_1023safe.htm.

19. U.S. Department of Homeland Security, "Chronology of Changes to the Homeland Security Advisory System," U.S. Department of Homeland Security, www.dhs.gov/xabout/history/editorial_0844.shtm.

20. Federal Bureau of Investigation "Headline Archives: FBI 100: The Unabomber," Federal Bureau of Investigation, April 24, 2008, www.fbi.gov/page2/april08/unabomber_042408.html.

21. BBC, "1972: Parcel bomb attack on Israeli embassy," *BBC, On This Day*, http://news.bbc.co.uk/onthisday/hi/dates/stories/september/19/newsid_2523000/2523027.stm.

22. Associated Press, "Letter Bombs Mailed from Egypt Found," *Daily News (Los Angeles, CA)*, January 3, 1997, www.thefreelibrary.com/_/print/PrintArticle.aspx?id=83850466.

23. Andrew R. Thomas, ed., *Aviation Security Management: Volume One: The Context of Aviation Security Management* (Westport, CT: Praeger Security International, 2008), 142–260.

24. U.S. Centennial of Flight Commission "Aviation Security," U.S. Centennial of Flight Commission, www.centennialofflight.gov/essay/Government_Role/security/POL18.htm.

25. U.S. Centennial of Flight Commission "Aviation Security," U.S. Centennial of Flight Commission, www.centennialofflight.gov/essay/Government_Role/security/POL18.htm.

26. U.S. Centennial of Flight Commission "Aviation Security," U.S. Centennial of Flight Commission, www.centennialofflight.gov/essay/Government_Role/security/POL18.htm.

27. Andrew R. Thomas, ed., *Aviation Security Management: Volume One: The Context of Aviation Security Management* (Westport, CT: Praeger Security International, 2008), 169.

28. By act of Congress, they are absolved form paying damages.

29. IATA, "Simplifying Air Cargo: Cargo Security Strategy 2006/07: Year 1," IATA, www.iata.org/NR/rdonlyres/33F4CD02-03E1-478C-A42A-F9778BA7F547/0/IATA_Cargo_Security_Strategy_Year1.pdf.

30. Microsoft Encarta Online Encyclopedia, "Industrial Revolution," Microsoft Encarta Online Encyclopedia, 2008, http://encarta.msn.com/encyclopedia_761577952/Industrial_Revolution.html.

31. Guy Norris and Mark Wagner, *Boeing 777: The Technological Marvel* (Osceola, WI: MBI Publishing Company, 2001), 23.

32. U. S. Government Accountability Office, *Supply Chain Security: U.S. Customs and Border Protection Has Enhanced Its Partnership with Import Trade Sectors, but Challenges Remain in Verifying Security Practices* (GAO-08-240, 2008).

33. U. S. Government Accountability Office, *Offshoring of Services: An Overview of the Issues* (GAO-06-5, 2005), 5.

34. U. S. Government Accountability Office, *Offshoring of Services: An Overview of the Issues* (GAO-06-5, 2005).

35. U.S. Department of State, "The U.S. Electronic Passport," U.S. Department of State, http://travel.state.gov/passport/eppt/eppt_2498.html.

36. Bill Gertz, "Outsourced Passports Netting Govt. Profits, Risking National Security," *The Washington Times*, March 26, 2008, www.washingtontimes.com/news/2008/mar/26/outsourced-passports-netting-govt-profit-56284974.

37. U.S. Government Accountability Office, *Supply Chain Security: U.S. Customs and Border Protection Has Enhanced Its Partnership with Import Trade Sectors, but Challenges Remain in Verifying Security Practices* (GAO-08-240, 2008), 1.

38. International Organization for Standardization, "New Suite of ISO Supply Chain Management Standards to Reduce Risks of Terrorism, Piracy and Fraud," *ISO*, October 25, 2007, www.iso.org/iso/pressrelease.htm?refid=Ref1086.

39. Wal-Mart Watch, "Shareholder Proposals," Wal-Mart Watch, http://walmartwatch.com/img/blog/wmt_shareholders_proposals_2007.pdf.

40. International Organization for Standardization "New Suite of ISO Supply Chain Management Standards to Reduce Risks of Terrorism, Piracy and Fraud," *ISO*, October 25, 2007, www.iso.org/iso/pressrelease.htm?refid=Ref1086.

CHAPTER 4

Supply Chain Security Performance Measures

Yuko J. Nakanishi

Securing the supply chain is significantly more complex than securing one transportation mode or facility, since it is comprised of multiple modes and transfer facilities owned and operated by public agencies and private companies in the United States and in foreign nations. Therefore, the supply chain is as secure as the weakest link.

The supply chain also poses an enormous threat to U.S. homeland security since the highest-impact threat materials such as nuclear/radiological weapons are likely to enter the United States through the supply chain. To address these threats, federal security legislation such as the Maritime Transportation Security Act of 2002 and the SAFE Ports Act of 2006 have been enacted.

Performance measures can enhance supply chain security by altering the behavior of teams and individuals. When fashioned and implemented properly, they can move entire organizations toward achieving particular goals. At the same time, when poorly done, performance measurement programs can have negative, unintended consequences, including unwanted behaviors and outcomes.

The first step in the development of performance measures is to determine the primary goals of supply chain security strategies. Once the goals have been determined, objectives are identified, and for each objective, performance measures and targets are established.

The primary goals of counterterrorism strategies are as follows:

- Decrease likelihood of an attack
- Decrease vulnerability of critical assets

- Increase likelihood of threat detection
- Decrease likelihood that an attack will be successful should one occur
- Mitigate the consequences of an attack should one occur

While the first goal is impossible to measure accurately, the other goals may be translated into objectives from which performance measures can be developed. In addition, it is easy to make the case for causal linkages between accomplishing these goals and decreasing the likelihood of an attack. For instance, decreasing the vulnerability of a critical asset will increase the effort needed to undertake and successfully carry out an attack and thus will decrease the likelihood of an attack.

Supply chain security goals are related to these primary counterterrorism goals, but more specifically focus on securing the transport of goods and transfer/storage facilities.

Challenges of creating a successful performance measurement system include understanding and resolving conflicting goals. At a very fundamental level, the goals of supply chain security and efficient goods movement are at odds with each other. To address these conflicting goals, a goal that takes both into account might be created: "Improve Supply Chain security while limiting its impact on efficient goods movement."

In addition, the many stakeholders and entities—private and public, domestic and international—involved in the supply chain each have their own agendas, perspectives, and missions. There are differences between the missions of the Department of Homeland Security (DHS) versus that of a private shipper versus that of a foreign port located halfway around the world. The private shipper is more concerned about costs per shipment and speed than about the security of the goods being transported. DHS is understandably more likely to expend resources to enhance security, while foreign ports may be more interested in getting containers into and out of their facility efficiently. These multiple, sometimes conflicting viewpoints need to be considered during the development of a performance measurement system.

This chapter, while trying to take into account multiple viewpoints, is written primarily from the viewpoint of DHS and other relevant federal agencies, such as the U.S. Maritime Administration.

PERFORMANCE MEASURES: AN OVERVIEW

An effective performance measurement system "can help agencies select and distill key data items in order to better understand how things are working and to more readily identify areas needing improvement."[1]

Key management uses of a performance measurement system include performance monitoring, evaluations of economic performance, support of management functions (e.g., how close the organization is to achieving a specific goal), identifying and addressing weaknesses, internal communications, and external communications.[2] Key characteristics of effective performance-measurement systems include[3]

- *Stakeholder acceptance*: All stakeholders need to buy in to the performance measurement system and agree upon performance measures included in the system. Stakeholders include port operators and owners, federal/state/local agencies, shippers, carriers, truckers, longshorepersons, other port personnel, airlines and airports, and airline and airport personnel.
- *Linkage to goals*: Since performance measures are the primary means of assessing whether goals are being met, they need to be clearly linked to desired goals. The viewpoints and goals of multiple stakeholders need to considered.
- *Clarity*: For measures to have the desired impact on behavior and performance, their purpose, definition, measurement procedure, and so forth need to be clear and understood by relevant audiences.
- *Reliability and credibility*: Reliability of performance measure results depends on the data collection and analysis methodologies, sample size, and objectivity of the individuals or unit charged with performance measurement.
- *Variety of measures*: If a comprehensive measurement system is sought, it should include measures that evaluate past, present, and future performance and should address a broad range of relevant issues.
- *Number of measures*: Having too few measures means that not all relevant issues will be covered—but any more than 20 measures will be difficult to track.
- *Level of detail*: The level of detail addressed by a measure should be commensurate with the audience. For example, senior management may be better served by an overall picture of port security than by a detailed view of the performance of individual elements of the facility.
- *Flexibility*: Performance measurement processes will likely change over time based on changes in external and internal environments. Therefore, flexibility should be built into the system.
- *Realism of targets*: Targets should be attainable, though slightly out of reach. Targets that are unrealistic may discourage workers.
- *Timeliness*: Timely reporting of results allows immediate action to investigate and address weaknesses.
- *Integration into decision making*: Results of performance measures should be analyzed and used to improve and expand upon existing security measures and strategies.

THREATS AND VULNERABILITIES

The primary threat to the supply chain is the smuggling of WMDs and other dangerous materials and contraband into the United States. Carriers with passengers on board can be especially vulnerable. A plane carrying passengers and cargo containing threat material such as a biological weapon can cause significant loss of life and serious injuries if the plane crashes in a populated area. A similar type of threat exists when a truck or rail route is located near a populated city.

Not all elements and modes within the supply chain are equally vulnerable to attack. Cargo inside containers weighing 30 tons each will likely be secure on a transatlantic cargo ship. However, cargo being transported by truck can be more vulnerable to tampering and pilferage. Cargo also becomes more vulnerable during intermodal transfers, and while it is stored in any type of storage facility.

The supply chain is only as secure as its weakest link. This means that the cargo that is secure in the cargo hold of an airplane becomes vulnerable once it reaches its transfer point if there are vulnerabilities not addressed in the transfer process. A significant vulnerability is transportation workers and others who may come into contact with the shipments. Terrorists may resort to identity theft by stealing or making counterfeit IDs, badges, and uniforms. Because much of the needed paperwork is electronic, cyberthreats also need to be addressed. A terrorist illegally accessing the electronic manifest system could alter the weight or contents of a U.S.-bound container in order to smuggle threat materials into the country. Furthermore, disgruntled employees and employees vulnerable to blackmail or bribes may be persuaded to assist terrorists with their mission.

Therefore, an advanced identity management system is an important element in ensuring the security of supply chains.

THE CUSTOMS-TRADE PARTNERSHIP AGAINST TERRORISM (C-TPAT) PROGRAM

The C-TPAT program led by the U.S. Customs and Border Protection (CBP) Agency seeks to improve supply chain security by engaging the private sector on a voluntary basis. The program focuses on combating terrorism and targeting high-risk goods and travelers. Companies passing C-TPAT evaluation are designated "low-risk" so that their cargo can be processed at border facilities faster and more efficiently, allowing cargo shipped by other companies to receive more attention. This expedited processing is seen as a major benefit of C-TPAT for member companies. The entire supply chain of validated companies is examined for potential weaknesses, including the point of origin (which may be located in a foreign nation).

CBP has had a results-oriented focus, recognizes the need for appropriate performance measures, and has been developing performance measures to improve the efficiency and effectiveness of its programs. CBP acknowledges the difficulties in measuring the deterrence effects of its programs and the direct impact on unlawful activity.

C-TPAT has been using the following key measures to assess the success and impact of the C-TPAT program:

- Percent of sea container cargo transported by C-TPAT carriers
- Percent of value imported by C-TPAT importers
- Percent of C-TPAT importer entry volume

- Compliance rate for C-TPAT members with the established C-TPAT security guidelines
- Average CBP exam reduction ratio for C-TPAT member importers compared to non–C-TPAT importers
- Time savings to process U.S./Mexico Border FAST lane transactions
- C-TPAT validation labor efficiency rate

The first three indicators reveal information about the scope of the C-TPAT program, although the direct security impacts are not addressed with these measures. The fifth and sixth measures address benefits for C-TPAT members in terms of reductions in inspections and faster transaction times. These measures also provide information on CBP's ability to shift resources from low-risk supply chains to unknown or high-risk supply chains. The final measure is an indicator of labor efficiency for C-TPAT validations.

PROTECTIVE MEASURES AND PERFORMANCE MEASURES

In addition to the security initiatives implemented through the C-TPAT program, there are a wide range of protective measures including technologies and security tactics that can be implemented at any point in the supply chain. Several key protective measures are identified in this section. For these protective measures, key vulnerabilities, performance evaluation methods, and relevant performance measures are provided.

Identity Management

The Transportation Worker Identification Credential (TWIC) is a common, tamper-resistant identification credential integrating a biometric identifier for all transportation personnel requiring unescorted access to secure areas. Ports were the first transportation facilities to begin TWIC implementation. As of April 2009, almost 900,000 TWIC Cards had been issued, and almost 1.1 million persons—including merchant mariners, port employees, longshorepersons, and truck drivers—enrolled in the TWIC program. The access control system, which is expected to include biometric readers, has not yet been implemented. Once it has been fully implemented, all workers will have their identities verified using the readers. The system would be automated to ensure minimal delays in port operations. Currently, manual checks and random checks using biometric readers are being conducted.[4]

Key Vulnerabilities

- Spoofing identities and biometrics
- Unauthorized access to central database containing TWIC information

Performance Assessment

- Likelihood of unauthorized individuals gaining access to secure areas
- Likelihood of an ineligible worker obtaining a TWIC card
- Likelihood of unauthorized access to TWIC database

Performance Measures

- Percentage of test subjects gaining access to secure areas
- Percentage of test subjects obtaining a TWIC card by presenting false information
- Percentage of successful hacking attempts

Additional performance criteria with regards to biometrics in particular are described in Nakanishi and Western, cited above, and are summarized here:

- *False acceptance rate (FAR)* is the probability of incorrectly verifying a person's identity, which would allow that person to gain entry into the transportation facility.
- *False rejection rate (FRR)* is the probability that a person that should match the original enrollment template does not match. Increasing FRR will increase costs due to the additional processing effort it will require.
- FAR and FRR are interrelated; tradeoffs occur based on the selected acceptance/rejection threshold criterion. The intersection point of the FAR and FRR at which the error rate is equal represents the crossover accuracy of the biometric system.
- *Failure to enroll rate* is the probability that a person will be unable to enroll due to insufficiently distinctive biometric sample(s). The need to perform exception processing for these persons will increase the overall costs of the system to the transportation agency.
- *Failure to acquire rate* is the proportion of attempts for which the system is unable to capture or locate a usable image.
- *Ability to verify rate* is the likelihood that a deployment will require exception processing and is measured by the following formula:

$$(1 - \text{Failure to enroll rate}) \times (1 - \text{False non-match rate})$$

- High ability to verify reduces costs associated with exception processing, while low rates may indicate a difficult-to-use system.

Surveillance Strategies

The objective of surveillance strategies, which are typically comprised of both security personnel and technologies (such as CCTV, intelligent video, and sensors), is to detect and deter unauthorized individuals attempting to gain access to secure areas or unauthorized individuals already in secure areas. Key vulnerabilities of technologies such as CCTV, intelligent video systems, and sensors have to do with accuracy and reliability. They include the inability to detect unauthorized individuals as well as false positives and equipment downtime.

Performance Assessment

- Likelihood of detecting unauthorized individuals
- Likelihood of false positives
- Likelihood of equipment failure

Performance Measures

- Percentage of test subjects representing unauthorized individuals detected by the system
- Percentage of test subjects representing authorized individuals incorrectly flagged by the system
- Downtime per 1,000 hours of operation

Cargo Management

Electronic freight manifests (EFMs) have as their goal the creation of a "message portal that enables access to shipment information to all supply chain partners in real time."[5]

Key Vulnerabilities

- Unauthorized access to the manifest system in order to alter information contained in the system

Performance Assessment

- Likelihood of unauthorized access of the manifest system

Performance Measures

- Percentage of successful hacking attempts using test subjects

Container Security Initiative

The Container Security Initiative, developed by the CBP, seeks to evaluate and secure cargo containers before they reach U.S. soil—in fact, at their points of origin. This requires significant cooperation by foreign governments to ensure that their ports meet specific security standards and comply with security protocols. There are currently fifty-eight ports in Europe, Asia, Africa, the Middle East, and North and South America that are CSI-compliant. These ports cover 86 percent of U.S.-bound containerized cargo. Containers are evaluated before leaving the port, and high-risk containers receive security inspections using detection technology such as X-ray scan and radiation scan.[6] Electronic seals protect the integrity of containers by providing a clear indication of any tampering that may have occurred.

Key Vulnerabilities

- Noncompliant ports and/or workers
- Falsification of worker identities
- Worker bribes and disgruntled employees
- Ineffective detection technology, including high false positive rates and inability to detect true positives
- Ineffective evaluation procedure to identify high-risk containers
- Ineffective electronic seals

Performance Assessment

- Compliance with CSI protocols
- Ability to verify worker identities
- Ability to identify high-risk employees
- Ability to identify high-risk cargo and containers
- Ability to rapidly and accurately scan containers
- Ability of electronic seals to secure containers

Performance Measures for Each Port

- Percentage of containers inspected according to CSI protocol
- Percentage of test subjects correctly verified as high-risk job applicants
- Percentage of workers correctly verified
- Percentage of containers using electronic seals that (1) are resilient to tampering attempts and (2) indicate tampering occurred when in fact it did occur

Vehicle Tracking/Fleet Management

License plate readers can alert law enforcement with regards to locations of stolen or otherwise wanted vehicles, and the use of RFID tags can transmit information about vehicles with expired registrations and other permits, as well as locations of vehicles that may be considered to be high-risk. GPS systems are used by shippers with larger fleets for fleet management purposes including calculation of delivery time, determination of optimal routes, labor management, and accident response.

Key Vulnerabilities

- Inability of system to accurately locate vehicles in fleet
- Susceptibility to unauthorized access and tampering

Performance Assessment

- Performance of these technologies can be measured by evaluating the accuracy with which the systems provide locations of vehicles within the fleet.
- Test vehicles whose locations during test runs are precisely known should be used for the evaluation.
- Hackers should be hired to test the security of the system.
- Systems should also be reliable, operating whenever needed.

Performance Measures

- Percentage of accurate test vehicle locations
- Percentage of successful hacking attempts
- Downtime in 1,000 hours

CONCLUSION

This paper discussed performance measures for C-TPAT, identity management, surveillance strategies, cargo management, container security, vehicle tracking, and fleet management. There are many other categories of measures that can and should be considered and implemented.

Although securing the supply chain is challenging, a well-executed performance measurement system can help a diverse group of stakeholders move toward and attain important security-related goals and objectives. Performance measures can also help managers and staff monitor performance, identify trends and weaknesses, and help in internal and external communications.

NOTES

1. TCRP Report 88: "A Guidebook for Developing a Transit Performance-Measurement System" (sponsored by the Federal Transit Administration, Transportation Research Board, National Research Council, Washington, D.C., 2003).

2. TCRP Report 88: "A Guidebook for Developing a Transit Performance-Measurement System" (sponsored by the Federal Transit Administration, Transportation Research Board, National Research Council, Washington, D.C., 2003).

3. Nakanishi, Yuko and George F. List, "Regional Transit Performance Indicators: A Performance Measurement Model" (Rensselaer Polytechnic Institute Working Paper, 2000).

4. Nakanishi, Yuko and Jeffrey Western, "An Evaluation of Biometric Technologies for Access Control at Transportation Facilities and Border Crossings" (Transportation Research Board 84th Annual Meeting CD-ROM, 2005), online at http://twicinformation.tsa.dhs.gov/twicinfo/.

5. Hartman, Kate and Mike Onder, Electronic Freight Mgt Initiative Presentation.

6. Nakanishi, Yuko and Jeffrey Western, "An Evaluation of Biometric Technologies for Access Control at Transportation Facilities and Border Crossings" (Transportation Research Board 84th Annual Meeting CD-ROM, 2005), online at http://twicinformation.tsa.dhs.gov/twicinfo/.

CHAPTER 5

Identification of Potential Target Locations and Attractiveness Assessment due to Terrorism in the Freight Transport

Dimitrios Tsamboulas and Panayota Moraiti

Terrorist attacks, such as the recent ones in the United States, Spain, and the United Kingdom, have established a threat of extreme severity posed by international terrorism. The attacks and the response they have elicited have long-lasting implications. In addition, further terrorist attacks remain a prominent danger, as several subsequent thwarted attempts testify.

Apart from casualties, a terrorist attack can lead to significant economic losses, both as a direct consequence of the attack as well as through the secondary effects within and around the affected region. In the case of transport, it is widely recognized that mobility represents one of the prerequisites that enables and fosters economic activity at local, regional, national, and international levels. Threats to mobility, on the other hand, have a direct impact on economic performance.

The freight sector, although less attractive to the terrorist than the passenger transport sector, demands equal attention. Nevertheless, it has not received the same attention in the research field as the passenger sector has, since the latter is directly related to human casualties. But because supply chains play the key role for global commerce and constitute an attractive target for terrorism, policymakers are taking steps to improve the security of transportation systems and of the supply chain.

Protecting the supply chain and its associated critical infrastructure represents an enormous challenge nowadays. Threat and risk assessments are widely recognized as valid decision support tools for establishing and prioritizing security program requirements. A threat analysis, the first step in determining risk, identifies and evaluates each threat on the basis of various factors, such as its capability and intent to attack an asset, the likelihood of a successful attack, and the lethality of such an attack. Risk management is the deliberate process of understanding "risk"—the likelihood that a threat will harm an asset with some severity of consequences—and deciding on and implementing actions to reduce it. Risk management principles acknowledge that (1) although risk generally cannot be eliminated, it can be reduced by enhancing protection from validated and credible threats; (2) although many threats are possible, some are more likely to occur than others; and (3) all assets are not equally critical, and all locations are not equally attractive victims for attack.[1]

The main objective of this paper is to draw the general principles of an attractiveness evaluation methodology as part of a concept for supply chain security enhancement, addressing the risk derived from a threat of terrorists using surface transportation freight means in order to carry out significant attacks. A methodology is presented that incorporates a number of relevant indicators to identify potential target areas for freight for which additional security measures can be recommended in times of heightened threat. The methodology will be based on a multicriteria analysis and will be used by the decision maker as a practical and flexible tool to enable swift activation of predefined risk mitigation measures for the controlling of freight movement in response to both prolonged and imminent threats in areas of increased risk.

BACKGROUND

Threat to Freight Transport

The terrorist threat to the freight transport network gains far less attention than passenger transport, since few terrorist organizations have made a serious attempt to either target major freight networks or use freight as their means of attack. Nevertheless, any serious attempt at assessing the risk must look beyond past experience; hence, this paper is set out to examine for a number of locations their perceived attractiveness to the terrorist through the following types of predicted attacks: (1) freight transportation mode/network as means of attack and (2) using freight itself as weapon.

The key issues with regard to the freight sector lie in gaining a thorough overview of its key components—that is, the means of freight delivery, freight contents, and the operational system that controls and regulates it. Figure 5.1 depicts the challenges for terrorism attacks faced by the supply chain network.[2]

One reason why the freight system might be attractive to terrorism relates to targeting the supply chain itself, which is an open system and inherently vulnerable to attacks, with the scope to paralyze, disrupt, and destroy the economic and social resources of the society.

Alternatively, terrorists could smuggle weapons through the supply chain to facilitate attacks not directly involving the supply chain. Terrorists follow the path of least resistance. One international expert commented that "if

Figure 5.1
Supply Chain Network—The Challenges

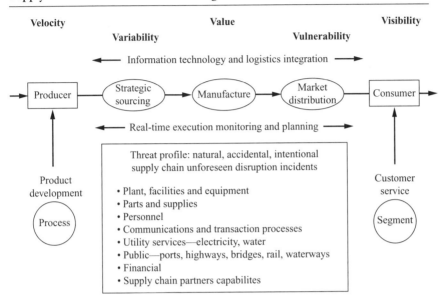

[terrorists] don't feel they have an 85% or better chance of success, they will switch to a softer target."[3] Trucks can often gain access—or come very close—to office buildings, making them softer targets than other highly defended potential targets of interest, as can been seen in Figure 5.2.

Moreover, the freight network could prove attractive due to the nature of some of the goods it carries: particular types of hazardous cargo, such as

Figure 5.2
Risk by Type

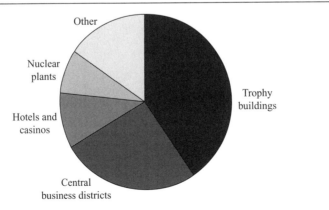

noxious chemicals, poisons, flammable fuels, radioactive materials, and nuclear waste that are regularly transported along both roads and railways. The theft or diversion of any such freight could lead to a situation in which it could be "weaponized" and immediately or ultimately exploited by terrorists, either as a form of blackmail or through actual use. Another significant concern is cargo contamination in agricultural and food commodity transportation.[4]

Additional factors favoring the probability of attack are as follow:[5]

- The small percentage of containers actually physically inspected
- Theft and smuggling
- The major investments needed in a low-margin industry (an issue of ownership)
- Lack of clearly defined responsibilities and liabilities of actors in the chain
- Conflicting, unclear, and overlapping jurisdictions of national and international regulatory and oversight authorities
- Lack of uniformity in the rules and their application for making transactions in different parts of the world and its nations
- Lack of standards (technological and operational)
- The missing link between security and throughput
- Increasing security enhancements in the passenger transportation sector deterring terrorist activity

Finally, a survey carried out among relevant stakeholders in Texas indicated that about half of trucking companies and half of freight forwarders felt that containers were a security concern.[6]

Critical Infrastructure

A fair amount of work has been carried out with regard to identifying and protecting critical infrastructure. According to Executive Order 13010,[7] critical infrastructure is defined as "Infrastructures so vital that their incapacitation or destruction would have a debilitating impact on defense or economic security." According to the executive order, the definition for transport is as follows:

Transportation: Physical distribution systems critical to supporting the national security and economic well-being of this nation, including the national airspace systems, airlines, and aircraft, and airports; roads and highways, trucking and personal vehicles; ports and waterways and the vessels operating thereon; mass transit, both rail and bus; pipelines, including natural gas, petroleum, and other hazardous materials; freight and long haul passenger rail; and delivery services.

Table 5.1 illustrates how the criteria and components of critical infrastructure have expanded over time.[8] On the horizontal axis, the table depicts

Table 5.1
What Constitutes Critical Infrastructure over Time

	Criteria for Being Considered Critically Vital to . . .			
	National Defense	Economic Security	Public Health and Safety	National Morale
Telecommunications information networks	×	×		
Energy	×	×		
Banking/finance		×		
Transportation	×	×		
Water			×	
Emergency services			×	
Government			×	
Health services			×	
National defense	×			
Foreign intelligence	×			
Law enforcement			×	
Foreign affairs	×			
Nuclear facilities in addition to power plants			×	
Special events				×
Food/agriculture			×	
Manufacturing		×		
Chemical			×	
Defense industry	×			
Postal/shipping			×	
National monuments/icons				×

the expansion of the national functions that began with national defense and economic security and finally include national morale. Similarly, the vertical axis illustrates the expanded list of sectors that have been identified specifically as critical infrastructures.

Risk Analysis

Although governments and policymakers are taking significant steps in protecting against terrorism, it is important to recognize that complete protection is unrealistic as well as economically unfeasible. The implementation of a number of security initiatives have also placed an increased burden in terms of processes and costs for all the players in global supply chains. In order to benefit from efficient and effective global supply chains, the security related activities incurred must be completely synchronized with the requirement of global supply chain management.[9]

Thus, in order to allocate limited resources, there is need for a systematic approach to the identification of the significant risks from terrorism and the development of effective measures to manage such risks. In the case of transportation risk management, security threats and vulnerabilities are now considered explicitly. Risk prioritization and followthrough is a process-oriented, iterative activity involving (1) identifying critical transportation facilities, (2) performing risk assessments, (3) developing risk management control strategies (prevention and deterrence, preparedness, response, recovery), (4) implementing control strategies, and (5) monitoring performance.[10]

Several risk analyses have been carried out based on the above model, the majority of which, focus on either identifying "attack scenarios" based on the attributes and perceived behavior of terrorist groups[11, 12, 13] or on passenger/public transportation risk assessment.[14] The latter is due to the fact that surface transportation systems are in general easy and effective targets for terrorists, being as they are very public, convenient, and accessible.[15] The outcome of this work is targeted to the development of a threat level matrix with its response threat counterpart.[16]

There is the common question of whether the application of any forms of risk analysis can contribute to the reduction of immediate or longer-term impacts of future terrorist attacks. Analyzing the risk of terrorism to critical infrastructures requires an understanding of the relationship between the attack and the consequences. In addition, the increasing complexity and interdependencies among the various systems/segments of the supply chain and the various sectors of the economy require systemic and quantitative risk modeling, assessment, and management efforts.[17] The type of risk analysis needed is one that covers multiple sectors in an integrative manner. Adding this type of risk analysis to the risk decision processes now used cannot help but make for better policymaking, decision making, and option selection.[18]

Vulnerability is defined as the "manifestation of the inherent sites of the system (e.g. physical, technical, organisational, cultural) that can be exploited by an adversary to harm or damage the system."[19] Therefore, it entails both an indication of how attractive a particular location is to terrorists, as examined in this paper, as well as an analysis of the consequences of the attack. Threat assessment is usually carried out by intelligence agencies based on foreign and domestic threat data, whereas the identification of vulnerabilities presents a more complex analytical problem.

Relevant research on the above topic has been carried out by Paté-Cornell and Guikeme,[12] who presented a high-level screening model, whereas Garrick et al.[13] proposed a scenario-based methodology known as probabilistic risk assessment (PRA) to identify, quantify, and manage terrorist threats. Apostolakis and Lemon[19] propose the use of PRA combined with multiattribute utility theory (MAUT) to screen terrorism scenarios that would affect infrastructure services to specific targets. Patterson and Apostolakis[20] took this work one step further to present a possible approach to ranking geographic regions that can influence multiple infrastructures.

Contrary to the research presented in the sources above, which focuses mainly on the passenger side, this paper presents a simpler and straightforward screening methodology, based on the multicriteria theory, for identifying and prioritizing potential target locations, given the scenario of freight transportation use as either means (whether by smuggling people or weapons [whether incendiary, nuclear, biological, or chemical] or as a base for weapons launch or other attack) or weapon.

Both macro- and microscale screening are proposed—that is, screening at two distinct levels: the national level and subsequently the regional/local level. The proposed methodology is designed to systematically identify and evaluate a particular location in terms of its attractiveness as a target of terrorist objectives. For example, this could involve, as a first step, the identification of a particular city and subsequently the most attractive regions/locations within the identified city boundary (i.e., a particular building or neighborhood). It is aimed at the decision maker and authorities to use in a preliminary vulnerability assessment.

METHODOLOGY

Overview

The proposed methodology aims at identifying the attractiveness of a specific area as a terrorist target (being a city or any other large production area, or a specific area/location within a city), and to accomplish this, criteria are introduced that are considered to influence the attractiveness of target to terrorists. Furthermore, weights are established for each of these criteria, as well as associated indicators for their measurement. Hence, the methodology introduces an analytical hierarchy process for the relation between criteria and indicators for each criterion in order to facilitate their weighting and measurement. Finally, the overall degree of attractiveness is computed by adding the resulting weighted scores. In this way, associated indices can be produced for all potential locations that can be subsequently categorized by their measured degree of attractiveness. The values of these indices range between 0 (no attractiveness) to 1 (the highest attractiveness).

The above process is realized through a multicriteria analysis (MCA), a key feature of which is emphasis on the judgment of the decision making team in establishing objectives and criteria, estimating relative importance weights, and, to some extent, judging the contribution of each option to each performance criterion. The subjectivity that pervades this can be a matter of concern. Its foundation, in principle, is the decision makers' own choices of objectives, criteria, weights, and assessments of achieving the objectives, although "objective" and easily measurable data such as observed prices can also be included. However, MCA can bring a degree of structure, analysis, and openness to classes of decision.[21]

Steps of the Proposed Methodology

The specific MCA applied in this study, designed to derive a score evaluating the degree to which a specific location presents a potential target to terrorism activity (attractiveness index), comprises of the following steps:

Step 1: Setting clearly the assessment objectives and their way of measurement. The criteria of the multi-criteria evaluation method are the indicators (quantitative and qualitative) in each assessment category.

Step 2: Weighting of the criteria. The weighting technique includes the criteria-related weights (criteria will be weighted against each other). This step is to determine the priorities of elements at each level. There are several approaches related to the weighting of criteria, ranging from simple techniques to more sophisticated mathematical routines. For the purpose of this analysis, one of the options is the paired comparison approach, a scaling approach employed in order to derive criteria weights by answering the question "Is this criterion more important than such-and-such another?"

Step 3: Estimation of criteria levels in physical scale. The scores for each criterion are estimated. Criterion scores can be derived in many different ways and can be expressed in qualitative or quantitative terms depending on the nature of the criterion. For the quantitative criteria, the physical scale of performance is measured in the units that define the criterion. For the qualitative criteria, the scale of performance is measured in a "verbal" scale with two or more discrete points.

Step 4: Estimation of criteria/impact levels in artificial scale. To make the various criterion scores compatible in order to facilitate their aggregation, it is necessary to transform them into one common measurement unit: for example, forcing each criterion score to take values between 0 and 1 by making use of the so-called utility functions of the following form:

$$U_{Cj} = \begin{cases} +P_{Cj}/A, & \text{if } P > 0 \\ 0, & \text{if } P = 0 \\ -P_{Cj}/B, & \text{if } P < 0 \end{cases} \tag{1}$$

where

j = criterion number

C_j = criterion j

P_{Cj} = physical (real) performance of criterion j (an absolute value)

U_{Cj} = artificial (after transformation) performance of criterion j

A, B = constant variables that either depend on measurement thresholds or that are set by the relevant decision makers

The qualitative criteria scores are derived by ranking the "verbal" physical performances from worst to best and then assigning the values of artificial scale respectively from the lowest to the highest values (values between these are possible):

−1	No impact
0	Low

+0.25   Moderate

+0.5   High

+1   Extreme

Step 5: Aggregation. Aggregate the weighted values (using criteria-related weights) of each criterion. That will provide a total score of the system's overall performance. Weighted summation of criterion scores takes place by applying MAUT.[21] The final score is calculated by the following equation, using the results of Steps 2 and 4:

$$T.P. = \sum_{j=1}^{J} W_j * U_j$$

where

j = criterion number

W_j = criterion weight

U_j = artificial performance of criterion j

$T.P.$ = total performance (attractiveness index)

Selection of Criteria and Indicators

The criteria and subcriteria are the measures of performance by which each candidate location will be assessed and prioritized. Collectively, these factors reflect the conditions, concerns, consequences, and capabilities that might cause a particular location to be considered an attractive target.[22] A large proportion of the value added by a formal MCA process derives from establishing a soundly based set of criteria against which to judge the different locations. The criteria chosen should be directly and objectively measurable.

It can be helpful to group together criteria into a series of sets that relate to separate, distinguishable components of the overall objective for the decision. The main reasons for grouping criteria are (1) to help the process of checking whether the set of criteria selected is appropriate to the problem, (2) to ease the process of calculating criteria weights in large applications for which it can sometimes be helpful to assess weights first within groups of related criteria, then between groups of criteria, and (3) to facilitate the emergence of higher-level views of the issues, particularly of how the options realize tradeoffs between key objectives.[23]

Five sets of general criteria were selected for the purpose of assessing the attractiveness to terrorism activity, related to freight transportation, hereby named *assessment criteria.* These are partly based on relevant work by the European Commission related to critical infrastructure (COM 702/2004). The proposed criteria are

1. Public impact

2. Economic impact

3. Social and political impact
4. Infrastructure
5. Newsworthiness

The above are analyzed in detail in the following in conjunction with the relevant indicators proposed by the authors for their assessment. Each indicator is assigned a value based on the importance of the factor in assigning such a label to a location. The criteria, the indicators, and their values, as well as a description for each indicator, are listed in Tables 5.2 and 5.3 for the national and regional/local levels, respectively. These will serve as guidelines for scoring and ranking the all-inclusive list of locations.

Public Impact

The impact on the life and wellbeing of the population exposed is one of the key elements that could attract a terrorist attack, as well as a key factor in determining the consequences—that is, the amount of population exposed and affected, the loss of life, medical illness, or serious injury. The following indicators were selected:

At a national level:

• Population
• Exposure (degree of damage/km^2)
• Number of tourists

At a regional/local level:

• Population density (people/m^2)
• Exposure (degree of damage/km^2)
• Duration of exposure (hrs/day)
• Existence and type of evacuation/response plans (proximity to fire stations, police stations, army camps, hospitals)

Economic Impact

This relates to the impact a terrorist action would have on the economic scale—that is, on the financial and business activities, the significance of economic loss and degradation of products or services, the effect on the gross domestic product (GDP), and so forth. The following indicators were selected for both national and (insofar as they apply) regional/local levels:[24]

• Country GDP
• Industrial production
• Agricultural production
• Energy production

Table 5.2
Assessment Categories and Related Indicators at National Level

		National Level	
	Indicators	Criterion Number	Description
Public impact	Population (number)	NC_1	What is the population that would determine the casualty risk?
	Exposure (degree of damage/km²)	NC_2	How dense is the exposure per surface area?
	Tourists (number/year)	NC_3	Is there significant tourism activity?
Economic impact	GPD of country (€/per capita)	NC_4	What effect would the damage have on the means of living, resources, and wealth of the nation?
	Industrial production (€/year)	NC_5	
	Agricultural production (€/year)	NC_6	
	Energy production (€/year)	NC_7	
	Oil refineries production (€/year)	NC_8	
	Services (€/year)	NC_9	
	Tourism turnover (€/year)	NC_{10}	
	Passenger throughput if the city has a major passenger hub (number of passengers/year); otherwise, the value is 0	NC_{11}	Is the number the passenger throughput high enough to attract an attack?
	Freight throughput if the city has a major freight hub (tons/year); otherwise, the value is 0	NC_{12}	Is the number the freight throughput high enough to attract an attack?
Social/ political impact	Degree of importance of governmental/ administrative buildings (scale 0–5, with 5 having the highest importance)	NC_{13}	Are there governmental/ administrative buildings of particular importance? What is their role on government continuity?

(Continued)

Table 5.2

(Continued)

	Indicators	Criterion Number	Description
		National Level	
	Degree of importance of monuments and national symbols (scale 0–5, with 5 having the highest importance)	NC_{14}	Are there such assets of symbolic importance? How important are they, and at what level?
	Degree of importance of religious symbols (scale 0–5, with 5 having the highest importance)	NC_{15}	Are there such assets of religious importance? How important are they, and at what level?
	Degree of importance of iconic symbols (scale 0–5, with 5 having the highest importance)	NC_{16}	Are there such assets of iconic importance? How important are they, and at what level?
	Degree of importance of international organizations' buildings, if any (scale 0–5, with 5 having the highest importance)	NC_{17}	Are there such buildings of political importance? What is their role on government continuity?
Infrastructure (for freight)	Transshipment centers (number of major ones with throughput 1 million tons/year)	NC_{18}	Are there such assets that provide direct accessibility to freight?
	Ports (marine and hinterland) (number of major ones with throughput 1 million tons/year)	NC_{19}	
	Freight villages (number of major ones with throughput 1 million tons/year)	NC_{20}	
	Storage sites (number of major ones with throughput 100,000 tons/year)	NC_{21}	
	Degree of importance for international freight corridors going through the city area	NC_{22}	Do these constitute nodal points in international freight corridors?

Table 5.2
(Continued)

		National Level	
	Indicators	*Criterion Number*	*Description*
Newswor-thiness	Degree of consequence (scale 0–5, with 5 having the highest importance)	NC_{23}	How will the event affect people? Does it matter, or is it unimportant?
	Degree of proximity (scale 0–5, with 5 having the highest proximity)	NC_{24}	Does the event closely affect the region in which it will be published/broadcast?
	People involved or affected (number)	NC_{25}	The more people involved or affected in an event, the more newsworthy the event is.
	Degree of prominence (scale 0–5, with 5 having the highest importance)	NC_{26}	Is the nation/city well known or in the public eye?

- Oil refinery production
- Services
- Tourism turnover
- Passenger throughput (in the case of major passenger hubs)
- Freight throughput (in the case of major freight hubs)

Social and Political Impact

This relates to the damages incurred in the social and civil activities, in the psychology of the population, and in the confidence in the ability of the government. The following indicators were selected for both national and regional/local levels:

- Number/importance of governmental/administrative buildings
- Number/importance of monuments and national symbols
- Number/importance of religious symbols
- Number/importance of iconic symbols
- Number/importance of international organizations

Infrastructure (for Freight)

This general criterion relates to the presence and number of critical infrastructure elements as these have been identified according to the guidelines mentioned in the previous section. The common denominator, in this case, is accessibility to freight.

Table 5.3
Assessment Categories and Related Indicators at Regional/Local Level

	Regional/Local Level		
	Indicators	*Criterion Number*	*Description*
Public impact	Population density (people/km²)	RC$_1$	What is the population density that would determine the casualty risk?
	Exposure (degree of damage/km²)	RC$_2$	How dense is the exposure in a particular area? (For example, a shopping mall vs. a residential area.)
	Time length of exposure (hrs/day)	RC$_3$	Is there a particular time of day that the impact would be more significant in that particular area?
	Existence and well known evacuation/response plans (scale 0–5, with 5 having the highest value)	RC$_4$	Are there emergency response actions in place? What are their capabilities?
Economic impact	GPD of the area considered (€/capita)	RC$_5$	What effect would the damage have on the means of living, resources, and wealth of the particular region/location?
	Industrial production, if any, of the area considered (€/year)	RC$_6$	
	Agricultural production, if any, of the area considered (€/year)	RC$_7$	
	Energy production, if any, of the area considered (€/year)	RC$_8$	
	Oil refineries production, if any, located in the area considered (€/year)	RC$_9$	
	Services, if any, of the area considered (€/year)	RC$_{10}$	
	Tourism turnover, if any, of the area considered (€/year)	RC$_{11}$	
	Passenger throughput if there is a major passenger hub in the area considered (number of passengers/year), otherwise, the value is 0	RC$_{12}$	Is the number the passenger throughput high enough to attract an attack?

Table 5.3
(Continued)

	Regional/Local Level		
	Indicators	*Criterion Number*	*Description*
	Freight throughput if there is a major freight hub in the area considered (tons/year); otherwise, the value is 0	RC_{13}	Is the number the freight throughput high enough to attract an attack?
Social/ political impact	If in the area considered there are governmental/administrative buildings, the degree of their importance (scale 0–5, with 5 having the highest importance); otherwise, value is 0	RC_{14}	Are there governmental/administrative buildings of particular importance? What is their role on government continuity?
	If in the area considered there are monuments and national symbols, the degree of their importance (scale 0–5, with 5 having the highest importance); otherwise, value is 0	RC_{15}	Are there such assets of symbolic importance? How important are they, and at what level?
	If in the area considered there are religious symbols, the degree of their importance (scale 0–5, with 5 having the highest importance); otherwise, value is 0	RC_{16}	Are there such assets of religious importance? How important are they, and at what level?
	If in the area considered there are iconic symbols, the degree of their importance (scale 0–5, with 5 having the highest importance); otherwise, value is 0	RC_{17}	Are there such assets of iconic importance? How important are they, and at what level?
	If in the area considered there are international organizations buildings, the degree of their importance (scale 0–5, with 5 having the highest importance); otherwise, value is 0	RC_{18}	Are there such buildings of political importance? What is their role on government continuity?

(Continued)

Table 5.3
(Continued)

		Regional/Local Level	
	Indicators	*Criterion Number*	*Description*
Infrastructure (for freight)	Presence of critical infrastructure in the area considered (value is 1 if present); otherwise, value is 0	RC_{19}	Are there such assets (transshipment centers, freight villages, ports, etc.) that provide direct accessibility to freight?
	Throughput (tons/year)	RC_{20}	Is it a busy freight transport facility of particular importance? Can someone conceal cargo easily?
	Proximity to the border (distance in km)	RC_{21}	Will a border close connection enhance the attack?
	Type of goods, commodities (scale 0–5, with 5 representing the highest potential of being "weaponized")	RC_{22}	Are hazardous goods transported with the potential to be "weaponized"?
	Accessibility to container routes (scale 0–5, with 5 having the highest accessibility)	RC_{23}	Are there any standard routes used for freight transport (e.g., railway line connecting a maritime port to its hinterland counterpart, truck rest stops)?
	Degree of surveillance (scale 0–5, with 5 having the highest degree)	RC_{24}	Are their security rules and regulations in place? What type of surveillance/technology is in force?
	Information (scale 0–5, with 5 having the highest availability)	RC_{25}	How is information made available?
Newsworthiness	Degree of consequence (scale 0–5, with 5 having the highest importance)	RC_{26}	How will the event affect people? Does it matter, or is it unimportant?
	Degree of proximity (scale 0–5, with 5 having the highest proximity)	RC_{27}	Does the event closely affect the region in which it will be published/broadcast?

Table 5.3
(Continued)

		Regional/Local Level	
	Indicators	*Criterion Number*	*Description*
	People involved or affected (number)	RC$_{28}$	The more people involved or affected in an event, the more newsworthy the event is.
	Degree of prominence (scale 0–5, with 5 having the highest importance)	RC$_{29}$	Is the region/area well known or in the public eye?

At a national level:

- Transshipment centers
- Ports, both marine and hinterland
- Freight villages
- Storage sites
- Degree of importance of international corridors transiting the area

At a regional/local level:

- Presence of any of the above
- Throughput (tons/yr)
- Proximity to national border
- Type of goods and commodities
- Accessibility to container routes
- Degree of surveillance of transport means
- Information

Newsworthiness

It is worthwhile to consider the impact of a terrorist attack with regard to its newsworthiness—that is, the amount of potential a story about an event in a particular location has. The newsworthiness could be rated based on criteria/indicators developed for the media; the ones proposed are

- Degree of consequence of the event
- Degree of proximity

- Number of people involved or affected
- Degree of prominence (of location)

It is recommended that each of the indicators in the above list be rated on a scale of 0 to 5.

APPLICATION

For purposes of demonstrating the application of the methodology, and in order to test the feasibility of the assessment method and criteria chosen, the proposed methodology was applied at a national level among nine of the most significant compartments/regions of a European country in order to assess the attractiveness of its cities/large economic or production centers. The evaluation results are presented in Table 5.4. The anonymity of the country and related compartments are omitted to avoid any controversy and undesirable ramifications. For the same reasons, only final results are presented.

By applying the methodology to the chosen number of regions, utilizing the same criteria and subcriteria, as well as their corresponding weights (provided by the NTUA study team), a prioritization was achieved for the degree of attractiveness of these regions within the country chosen. Data availability was poor and inconsistent as regards the reference years, but the results obtained demonstrated that of the regional compartments studied, the one corresponding to its capital city presents the highest attractiveness index (0.891), rendering it the most attractive region for potential terrorist attack. The rest of the regional compartments considered presented a significantly lower attractiveness index.

By applying the methodology to a number of locations, utilizing the same criteria and subcriteria, as well as their corresponding weights, a prioritization can be achieved for the degree of attractiveness of locations in a country and the areas within a city.

CONCLUSIONS

The terrorist threat to the freight transport network gains far less attention than passenger transport, since there are no known incidents of terrorist attacks using freight transport as direct means to stage a terrorist event. However, the nature of the current terrorism threat commands a more rounded approach to transportation risk management. Furthermore, it is believed that freight networks will become more attractive to the terrorist as the continuous security enhancements on passenger networks limit terrorists more and more.

This paper provides a straightforward methodology assessing the attractiveness of particular locations to terrorist activity through the use of the

Table 5.4
Evaluation Results

Crit No.	Weight of Group	Weight within Group	Country Compartments								
			1	2	3	4	5	6	7	8	9
Public impact											
NC_1	0.3	0.2	0.000	0.008	0.060	0.004	0.006	0.014	0.010	0,018	0,026
NC_2		0.7	0.004	0.000	0.210	0.001	0.000	0.006	0,001	0,002	0,002
NC_3		0.1	0.001	0.001	0.030	0.001	0.002	0.001	0,000	0,007	0,004
Economic impact											
NC_4	0.2	0.3	0.012	0.009	0.060	0.000	0.010	0.000	0.010	0,013	0,018
NC_5		0.1	0.000	0.003	0.020	0.001	0.002	0.002	0,003	0,006	0,011
NC_6		0.01	0.000	0.001	0.002	0.001	0.001	0.001	0,001	0,002	0,002
NC_7		0.07	0.000	0.002	0.014	0.001	0.005	0.001	0,001	0,003	0,008
NC_8		0.2	0.000	0.000	0.000	0.000	0.000	0.000	0,000	0,000	0,000
NC_9		0.2	0.000	0.005	0.040	0.003	0.004	0.003	0,004	0,012	0,014
NC_{10}		0.1	0.001	0.001	0.020	0.001	0.002	0.001	0,000	0,005	0,003
NC_{11}		0.01	0.000	0.000	0.002	0.000	0.000	0.000	0,000	0,001	0,001
NC_{12}		0.01	0.000	0.000	0.002	0.000	0.000	0.000	0,000	0,001	0,001
Social/political impact	0.1										
NC_{13}		0.1	0.000	0.000	0.000	0.000	0.004	0.000	0,000	0,000	0,000
NC_{14}		0.5	0.000	0.000	0.050	0.000	0.000	0.000	0,000	0,000	0,000
NC_{15}		0.18	0.000	0.000	0.018	0.000	0.000	0.000	0,000	0,000	0,000
NC_{16}		0.2	0.000	0.000	0.000	0.000	0.000	0.000	0,000	0,000	0,000
NC_{17}		0.02	0.002	0.000	0.001	0.000	0.000	0.000	0,000	0,000	0,001
Infrastructure	0.1										
NC_{18}		0.3	0.000	0.005	0.012	0.000	0.000	0.026	0,017	0,050	0,000
NC_{19}		0.3	0.003	0.004	0.040	0.002	0.004	0.012	0,003	0,007	0,011
NC_{20}		0.2	0.010	0.000	0.010	0.010	0.000	0.010	0,000	0,000	0,010
Newsworthiness	0.3										
NC_{21}		0.3	0.018	0.018	0.090	0.000	0.000	0.000	0,000	0,009	0,009
NC_{22}		0.2	0.060	0.060	0.060	0.060	0.060	0.060	0,060	0,060	0,060
NC_{23}		0.1	0.006	0.006	0.030	0.000	0.000	0.000	0,000	0,003	0,003
NC_{24}		0.4	0.000	0.000	0.120	0.000	0.000	0.000	0,000	0,000	0,000
TOTAL SCORE			0.117	0.122	0.891	0.086	0.099	0.136	0.109	0.199	0.183

freight transport network, either as means of launching an attack or by "weaponizing" the cargo itself. The methodology is based on a multicriteria theory and is performed at the national as well as regional/local level. The result is a ranking of potential target locations, whether cities or areas within a city that could be expressed in a graphical form on a map. This will aid decision makers and authorities in allocating of countermeasures to better protect the society.

The proposed methodology allows for decision makers to decide which criteria call for greater consideration based on their subjective judgment, especially if these criteria considered do not have a common scale of measurement—or, in some cases, are intangible with no existing scale of measurement. Therefore, in order to overcome the inherent subjectivity of this method, it is proposed that it be carried out at a group decision making level. The broad assumptions involved in this methodology could be limited to a minimum using expert opinions in order to provide a realistic analysis.

It is believed that the proposed methodology will provide added value to transportation risk management, and that it will be able to act as the primary step in identifying and prioritizing the various characteristics and impacts that may lead terrorists to select a particular location as target. The latter, in conjunction with the identification of the locations' security vulnerabilities, will enable the application of appropriate countermeasures and mitigation strategies for the protection of such locations.

NOTES

1. United States Government Accountability Office (GAO), "Combating Terrorism: Threat and Risk Assessments Can Help Prioritize and Target Program Investments," report to Congressional requesters, 1998.

2. D. Closs and E. McGarell, "Enhancing Security throughout the Supply Chain," Special Report series, IBM Center for the Business of Government, 2004.

3. Risk Management Solutions, "Countering the Terrorist Threats to Corporations: Using Computer Models to Prioritize Risk Management Decisions," Risk Management Solutions, Inc., 2004.

4. R. M. Brewster and R. LeVert, "Identifying Vulnerabilities and Security Management Practices in Agricultural and Food Commodity Transportation," Transportation Research Board CD-ROM, Annual Meeting, Washington, D.C., 2005.

5. M. Van de Voort, H. Willis, D. Ortiz, S. Martonosi, and A. Rahman, "Policy Considerations in Securing the Global Containerized Supply Chain," presentation at Risk Management Tools for Port Security, Critical Infrastructure and Sustainability, Venice, Italy, 2006.

6. J. Prozzi, K. Spurgeon, and R. Harrison, "Secret Lives of Containers Evidence from Texas," Transportation Research Record 1833, Transportation Research Board, Washington, D.C., 2003.

7. The President, *Critical Infrastructure Protection*, Executive Order 13010 (1996). Federal Register 61 (138).

8. J. Moteff, C. Copeland, and J. Fisher, "Critical Infrastructures," *What Makes an Infrastructure Critical?* Report for Congress, No. 31556, Congressional Research Service, The Library of Congress, 2002.

9. R, Banomyong, "The Impact of Port and Trade Security Initiatives on Maritime Supply-Chain Management," *Maritime Policy Management* 32, nos. 1–3:14–26.

10. M. D. Abkowitz, "Transportation Risk Management: A New Paradigm," Transportation Research Board CD-ROM, Washington, D.C., 2003.

11. Y. Shahar, *Toward a Target-Specific Method of Threat Assessment* (Heidelberg, Germany: Springer-Verlag Berlin Heidelber, 2005).

12. M. E. Paté-Cornell, and S. Guikema, "Probabilistic Modelling of Terrorist Threats: A Systems Analysis Approach to Setting Priorities among Countermeasures," *Military Operations Research* 7: 5–20.

13. B. J. Garrick, J. E. Hall, M. Kilger, J. C. McDonald, T. O'Toole, P. S. Probst, E. Rindskopf Parker, R. Rosenthal, A. W. Trivelpiece, L. A. Van Arsdale, and E. L. Zebroski, "Confronting the Risks of Terrorism: Making the Right Decisions," *Reliability Engineering and System Safety* 86:129–176.

14. A. Eder, "After September 11, How Transit Agencies Prepare for the Threat of Terrorism," Transportation Research Record, No. 1927, Transportation Research Board, Washington D.C., 2001, 92–100.

15. C. N. Y. Fink, "Antiterrorism Security and Surface Transportation Systems Review of Case Studies and Current Tactics. Transportation Research Record," No. 1822, Transportation Research Board, Washington, D.C., 2003, 9–17.

16. Threat Advisory System Response (TASR), "Guideline Considerations and Potential Actions in Response to the Department of Homeland Security Advisory System," ASIS International GDL TASR 09, 2004.

17. Y. Y. Haimes and T. Thomas Longstaff, "The Role of Risk Analysis in the Protection of Critical Infrastructures against Terrorism," *Risk Analysis* 22, no. 3:17–29.

18. P. F. Daisler Jr, "A Perspective: Risk Analysis as a Tool for Reducing the Risks of Terrorism," *Risk Analysis* 22, no. 3:45–57.

19. G. E. Apostolakis and D. M. Lemon, "A Screening Methodology for the Identification and Ranking of Infrastructure Vulnerabilities due to Terrorism," *Risk Analysis* 25:361–376.

20. S. A. Patterson and G. E. Apostolakis, "Identification of Critical Locations across Multiple Infrastructures for Terrorist Actions," *Reliability Engineering and System Safety* 92:1183–1203.

21. DTLR, *Multi-Criteria Analysis Manual* (London: DETR, 2000).

22. B. Huang, "A GIS-AHP Method for HAZMAT Route Planning with Consideration of Security," *Environmental Informatics Archives* 2:818–830.

23. S. Rowshan, M. C. Smith, S. J. Krill, J. E. Seplow, and W. C. Sauntry, "Highway Vulnerability Assessment: A Guide for State Departments of Transportation," Transportation Research Record 1827, National Academy Press, Washington, D.C., 2003, 55–62.

24. "Country Indicators for Foreign Policy: Indicators Descriptions," CIFP Risk Assessment Indicators Definitions, http://www.carleton.ca/cifp/docs/RiskAssessmentIndicators_FullDescriptions.pdf.

CHAPTER 6

A Model for Supply Chain and Vessel Traffic Restoration in the Event of a Catastrophic Port Closure

Hector Guerrero, David Murray, and Richard Flood

The threat of a terrorist attack on an American port has received considerable attention since 9/11. Stephen Flynn, Senior Fellow at the Council on Foreign Relations, has written extensively on the topic[1] and has presented testimony to numerous federal committees concerned with the vulnerabilities that persist.[2] In his testimony he describes an imaginary scenario of a container originating in Indonesia and bound for Chicago. The container has been compromised by an al Qaeda sympathizer and contains a dirty bomb. The major outcomes associated with such an event are clear: (1) a potential loss of life and injury, (2) harm to the environment, (3) initial uncertainty as to where the compromise of the supply chain has occurred, and (4) long-term deleterious effects on the efficacy of the current transportation security system.

Outcomes 1 and 2 should lead to an immediate *terrorism response* as specified by the Maritime Transportation Security Act of 2002.[3] Outcomes 3 and 4 will require a thorough long-term investigative effort by federal agencies and will certainly lead to a review and reconsideration of policy. Yet there is another relatively short-term outcome that remains to be considered. For the event as described above, it is very probable that the port of entry of the container will be closed indefinitely—that is, until the port is returned to a secure and safe state. This is likely regardless of whether the event occurs *at* the port or whether the container simply *passes through* the port. Thus, the inevitable port closure will result in a disruption of the associated supply chains and the necessity to reroute the ocean carriers with scheduled stops at the port to other convenient and capable ports. Additionally, the primary mission of a terrorist attack will be achieved—severe economic disruption.

The policy questions arising from this event are numerous. Some deal with the port closure decision, and others with issues of how the disruption effects will be dealt with. In Table 6.1 we present a summary of some of the important policy questions and related issues. This study concentrates on outcomes 3 and 4 and was funded by a grant from the Transportation Security Administration (TSA) under the title Operation Restore. The title reflects the projects emphasis on the restoration of the supply chain by rerouting ocean vessel traffic to alternative ports once a port closure has occurred. Although restoration of vessel

Table 6.1
Relevant Port Closure Policy Issues

Policy Question	Related Issue
1. What type of event constitutes a basis for a port closure?	These are complex decisions and must be dealt with on an individual basis. Some events result in the obvious need for action; others are not as obvious and can lead to false alarms.*
2. What agency, local or federal, has, or should have, authority to declare a port closed to cargo vessels and other traffic?	This is usually the domain of the Coast Guard Captain of the Port, but other agencies will often insist on also being involved; for example, depending on the type of incident, the FBI and local law enforcement.
3. How will the many stakeholders associated with the supply chain be involved, and how will the scheduled vessel arrivals at the closed port be rerouted to other ports?	There is persistent tension between industry and government as to how decisions for rerouting ocean traffic will be accomplished. This contentious issue is centered on the vital public interest to maintain access and control of many important cargo types (pharmaceuticals, heating oil, fuels, etc.) versus industry's desire to avoid governmental intrusion from agencies such as the DHS, the Coast Guard, the TSA, MARAD, the DOT, and so forth.
4. Assuming that a governmental and private industry consensus *can* be reached, how can we most efficiently deal with the disruption and restore the supply chain and vessel traffic?	There are a number of decision making and collaborate tools that come together as decision support systems (DSS) and executive support systems (ESS) that can be used to accommodate the needs of the diverse stakeholders. These are very complex information technology systems and require a great deal of data gathering, coordination of effort and communication, and highly structured command and control.

*On January 7, 2007, the Port of Miami experienced a major security incident when operators of a tractor trailer were detained in the port for lack of credentials and for bypassing a security checkpoint. Later the port authorities insisted that the port was not closed, although this is disputed in some accounts.

traffic is tangentially concerned with the restoration of ports (the sooner a port can be restored, the sooner a restoration strategy can be eliminated and vessel traffic normalized), port restoration was not of primary interest in this study.

In the next section, we discuss the TSA's motivation for Operation Restore. Next, where we discuss the twenty-five ports that were considered in the study. Then, we introduce our basic model and the extension of the model to consider the entire supply chain, origin to destination. After this, we provide details of how users of the model are engaged in decision making. Finally, we conclude with lessons learned, conclusions, and a discussion of future directions.

BACKGROUND

The issues addressed by Operation Restore were identified by the TSA in 2002 and related to the National Strategy for Homeland Security.[4] These issues evolved in a political and governmental climate that was becoming increasingly concerned with terrorist threats to the U.S. and world economies, particularly since there was a lessened economic distinction between them. We seek to develop a methodology and prototypical tool that will provide efficient reassignment of scheduled ocean carriers to alternative ports in the event of catastrophic closure of a major U.S. port. Additionally, we considered both natural and terrorist events as causes of port closure. The consideration of natural catastrophe was largely due to Hurricane Katrina, which occurred during the course of the grant and led to the closure of the Port of New Orleans, one of the ports of interest.

The project began in mid-2004. As mentioned earlier, there was a keen awareness of the potential threats entering through ports, particularly those associated with the millions of containers that enter the United States annually. In the initial phase, a prototype planning tool was quickly developed and demonstrated as a model for restoration of maritime traffic. This early model, which focused only on the ocean link of the supply chain, set the foundation for future work. The tool was a decision support system that incorporated (1) data gathering, (2) stakeholder collaboration, (3) an analytical engine for rerouting based on large-scale integer programming, and (4) a secure Web-based infrastructure for coordinating all of the above. As awareness of the vulnerability of the *entire* supply chain (beyond just the maritime) became clear, our attention was refocused to incorporate not only the oceanside link, but also port operation and inland intermodal transportation links. The consideration of the expanded supply chain resulted in the analysis of a vastly more complex problem than originally defined.

PORT SELECTION

The ports for our study were selected based on their economic and strategic importance and were limited to a relatively small number (twenty-five), although they represent the vast majority of economic activity of the U.S.

Table 6.2
Operation Restore Ports of Interest

East Coast	Gulf Coast	West Coast
New York/New Jersey	Houston	Los Angeles
Boston	New Orleans	Long Beach
Philadelphia	Beaumont, TX	Oakland
Wilmington, DE	Corpus Christi	Tacoma
Baltimore/Cove Point	Texas City	Seattle
Norfolk/Newport News	Lake Charles, LA	Portland
Wilmington, NC	Freeport, TX	
Charleston		
Savannah		
Port Everglades, FL		
West Palm Beach		
Miami		

maritime economy. Although the ports in Table 6.2 are categorized by region, they can also be categorized by cargo capacity and cargo handling capability. For example, some ports are capable of unloading crude oil and liquefied natural gas, some ports tend to specialize in container and bulk cargo, and some are relatively broad in their capabilities. This is obviously an important factor in the selection of alternative ports, because there may be very small number of ports that are capable of processing specific rerouted vessels. For example, petroleum capable ports are often colocated within ready access to refining facilities.

Additionally, there are considerable differences in individual port capacities. The combined 2006 container traffic of the ports of Los Angeles and Long Beach was 14.2 million TEUs.* By contrast, the Port of Charleston, South Carolina, which ranks consistently in the top ten container ports, processed approximately 1.98 million TEUs. The combined container traffic at Los Angeles/Long Beach and New York/New Jersey is approximately equal to the traffic of the remainder of the top twenty-five container ports. Thus, a catastrophic event at Los Angeles/Long Beach would lead to extreme capacity constraints for container traffic throughout the United States.[5] Although reported port traffic may not represent maximum port capacity, it is likely that they represent a substantial fraction of capacity.

In many cases, the alternate use of ports will also be limited, though not restricted, to geographical regions. Container traffic destined to the West Coast is likely to be diverted to other West Coast ports; alternatively, the vessels may be directed through the Panama Canal if they do not exceed the maximum physical specifications for negotiating the canal.[6] During the ten-day ILWU lockout of Los Angeles/Long Beach in late 2003, the economic disruption of trade and associated backlog was approximated

---

*The twenty-foot equivalent unit (TEU) is the standard measure for intermodal shipping containers that travel by truck or rail.

at $6.28 billion. The disruption prompted shippers to consider all possible alternative routes, including diversion through the Panama Canal (for Panamax carriers) and some Suez Canal–routed traffic to the East Coast. Further complicating supply chain risk are the new supercontainer (7,600+ TEU) vessels beginning scheduled for service to both the West Coast and East Coast. For these vessels, there are draft limitations at many ports; thus, without extensive redesign of entry channels at ports, rerouting choices will be reduced further.

Ultimately, the decision to reroute a ship to a port will require the understanding of the many physical constraints discussed above, and also important economic constraints. Economic constraints will appear in the form of higher costs associated with additional logistical handling to deliver cargo to the desired destination. For example, shippers and owners of cargo will attempt to deliver goods to ports that do not require substantial increases in inland logistical handling costs for things such as intermodal transport, terminal access and availability, and distribution center transshipment.

THE EXTENDED SUPPLY CHAIN

The major determinate of rerouting complexity in a supply chain network is the associated breadth and depth of the network. A rerouting problem that focuses only on maritime or oceanside restoration, although complex, is far more manageable than consideration of the entire cargo origin-to-destination supply chain. Beyond the required addition of port operation for the extended supply chain, there is also the consideration of landside infrastructure to transport cargoes to their final destination. Thus, the vessel and port capacity must match available pipeline, rail and truck, or terminal and storage facility capacity and capability if cargo is to flow efficiently.

The expanded supply chain focus resulted in a substantial change in scope for Operation Restore. In particular, we extended our analysis to a tripartite model of the supply chain as shown in Exhibit 6.1: (1) oceanside vessel

Exhibit 6.1
Tripartite Model

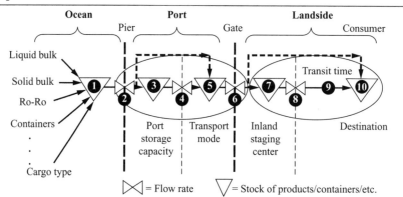

movement, (2) port operation, and (3) landside intermodal cargo movement. As would be expected, the complexity of the model increased dramatically, with greater data requirements, greater sophistication in solution procedures, and a more extensive coordinated decision making structure.

Of special interest in the tripartite model is the necessity to reroute while considering the capacity constraints at all stages of the supply chain. The flow between stages is represented by the bow tie symbol shown in Exhibit 6.1. It became clear that our original use of large-scale integer programming, which simultaneously considered capacity constraints at all stages, would not be a practical solution technique due to the need for a very rapid decision making process. Thus, less complex rule-based heuristics were explored and found to be quite efficient, and readily acceptable to stakeholders. Stakeholders made it quite clear that their involvement with Operation Restore would be based on three essential requirements: (1) the transparency of the solution technique and process, (2) the collaborative nature of the system, and (3) the need for flexibility should conditions and stakeholder positions change.

STAKEHOLDER/MODEL TASKFORCE INTERACTION PROCESS

We developed a general process for stakeholder and model taskforce interaction, reflecting the need for a process that remains flexible and that can be adapted as evolving policy defines the specifics of interaction. The process acknowledges two types of users: the *model taskforce* (which is composed of a relatively small group of decision makers with immediate access to the decision model) and a much larger *stakeholder* group (composed of other interested parties such as vessel owners, shippers, terminal operators, port authorities, etc.).

Central to the process is a secure Web portal we call HMS. HMS permits us to coordinate data acquisition, manage the dissemination of results, and collect stakeholder feedback for Operation Restore. The system is proprietary to our corporate partner in the grant, CIBER, Inc. Exhibit 6.2

Exhibit 6.2
Decision Process Activities for Restoration Model

1. Event occurs
2. Dynamic schedule and positions data automatically collected
3. Run model-produces preliminary solution for recovery
4. Advisory group reviews solution results and provides feedback
5. Iterative manual changes made to model results if needed
6. Disseminate model results to all stakeholders
7. Stakeholder feedback incorporated
8. Iterate
9. Continued until acceptable plan achieved

Exhibit 6.3
Detailed Process Flow

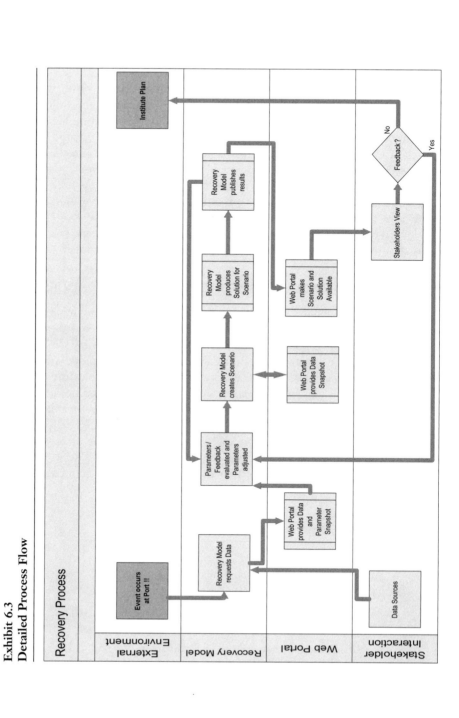

outlines the major activities of the decision process, and Exhibit 6.3 provides a process flow diagram that identifies the various domains of process activities. The process begins with notification that an *incident* has occurred. The model taskforce immediately initiates two types of data acquisition from the secure Web portal HMS: a *data snapshot* and a *parameter snapshot*. A data snapshot refers to the dynamic data used by the model: current vessels at sea, their location, physical characteristics, cargo, and so forth. A parameter snapshot refers to data that is collected on ports and vessels and that is more static in nature, but that can be changed—e.g., closing a port, changing the capacity of a port, and so forth. Furthermore, we use the term *scenario* to refer to a particular set of values assigned to the parameters for the model.

Scenarios provide a convenient mechanism for creating order from potential chaos, since they represent a structured way for the stakeholder team to ask *what-if* questions. In the context of the model, a what-if is an alternative set of values for the parameters, and therefore constitutes a specific scenario. When we solve the rerouting problem, we use a particular scenario (set of parameter values) and a particular data snapshot (dynamic data—usually the most current). The result is referred to as a *solution* to a particular scenario. Note that a single scenario can have several solutions, each associated with a particular data snapshot. A scenario–solution pair represents a set of vessel routings that has been produced by the model for a particular set of model parameters and a particular set of data conditions. Keeping track of these scenarios and their associated solutions is critical to making orderly progress toward the selection of a restoration plan for vessels.

As time progresses, data conditions will change, and the model taskforce will request a new data snapshot from HMS. A new solution incorporating the changed (or dynamic) data can then be obtained by solving a particular scenario with the new dynamic data. From time to time, the model taskforce will *publish* a scenario–solution pair by exporting the scenario and its solution back to HMS. It is then available for review and discussion by the broader stakeholder group via the Internet.

A collaborative forum on HMS then permits stakeholders to comment on scenarios–solutions and provide input. This feedback is used by the model taskforce to initiate possible parameter adjustments. For example, stakeholder feedback could suggest that a particular port can handle a higher level of capacity through the use of extended unloading shifts or redeployment of assets (portable cranes, etc.). It is also possible that the model taskforce might be informed directly of changes in the state of the system—e.g., a current change to port capacity due to planned maintenance. When the model taskforce determines that a new scenario is required because of these inputs, a new solution is created for the new scenario, and the new scenario–solution pair can be published. This process is repeated until an implementable solution is achieved.

Many scenarios can be produced and examined by the stakeholder team. This is why it will be very important to maintain a system that manages the evolving set of scenarios. Our process is able to maintain order and organize the effort of movement toward a solution that incorporates all important elements of interest with reasonable flexibility.

CONCLUSION AND FUTURE DIRECTIONS

This paper presents a summary of a working, prototype tool for vessel restoration. In some areas we exceeded our mission: inclusion of landside modeling and design flexibility to permit alternate uses for the model, for example. Our conclusions are summarized in Exhibit 6.4 and are categorized as *technical* and *policy* issues.

Technical issues are those associated with data sources/availability, and the question of *how much* modeling is adequate for efficient decision making. Data is undoubtedly the most important and problematic issue. Without access to real-time, reliable data, robust modeling is impossible. It became very apparent during our efforts to locate data sources that great concern was raised when governmental organizations were approached about sharing, or even discussing, their data. This was especially true in the case of U.S. Customs data—a vital source of cargo data. Without a resolution of this issue, the development of better models will be impossible.

Related to the data issue is the question of model adequacy. Greater detail in data permits more detailed models. Yet, it is conceivable that a model that is too complex will have adverse effects on the interaction between the task-force and the stakeholder teams. A careful balance must be drawn between complexity and acceptance of a model.

Policy issues range from defining an appropriate governmental response to effects on international trade. Throughout our study, we were constantly challenged by industry participants to explain or defend the anticipated policy that surrounded our efforts. The most contentious issue was the degree of government involvement in restoration activities that have traditionally been handled in a decentralized manner by private industry.

Another policy issue is the challenge of managing the effects on domestic and foreign shipping, railroad, and trucking firms. Organizations such as the World Shipping Council, Association of American Railroads, and American Trucking Association take great interest in the policy implications for their constituencies. It is important that their affiliates clearly understand the lines of authority in the event of a closure of a major port. Thus, they argued for a clear mandate and the specific intentions that the TSA and other agencies might have for vessel restoration.

Besides the resolution of issues stated in Exhibit 6.4, which should lead to better conditions for creating a workable restoration model, we also believe that alternative uses of the model also offer potential value. The model's

Exhibit 6.4
Issues

Technical Issues

1. Where are the data?
   - Will we have access to disparate data sources?
   - What will it take to receive access to these data?
   - Are there forms of automation in place to deliver data?
2. What level of detail (or granularity) in modeling is appropriate?
   - As the complexity of the model increases, will model value follow?
   - Will greater detail lead to a more or less efficient stakeholder collaboration process?
   - The land-side modeling complexity is particularly difficult to deal with-should a separate model be developed for this element of the rerouting?

Policy Issues

3. Are we focusing on the right events: terrorism, natural disaster, both?
4. When does the federal government step in to take control of restoration?
5. What are the resources that must be marshaled to make restoration possible?
   - Clear command and control/authority
   - Communication/cooperation
   - Understanding of resources, capacity, and capabilities
6. How do we deal with the domestic/foreign transportation community?
   - Are governmental interests the same or difficult?
   - What sway does the TSA have on foreign firms?
7. What are critical cargos?
   - Crude oil, fuel oil, LNG, and diesel
   - Lawn furniture and the latest fashions (or so Target and Wal-Mart think)
8. What are the chances that government can work with government?
   - We have seen some problems between agencies.
   - But we have also seen cooperation-solutions are possible.
9. What are chances that industry and government will work together?
10. What are chances that industry will work with industry?
    - The evidence from Katrina looks as if the chances are good.
11. How will response/recovery and restoration interact?
12. What we do in response/recovery affects restoration (short-term and long-term)—how can we accommodate these issues?
13. What are the lessons of Hurricane Katrina/Rita and other natural events?
    - Are worst-case preparations always advisable?
    - How do we balance our need to react with possible overreaction?
    - Does this difficult choice argue for better regional planning for ports and other stakeholders?

capability to perform capacity analysis may have many uses. A number of these uses are

1. Planning the capacity needs of individual ports: standard operating capacity and surge capacity.
2. Planning the regional rationalization of capacity: are new ports worthy of consideration, or is redistribution of capacity worthwhile?
3. Reconfiguration of port/intermodal assets at ports.

Vessel and supply chain restoration remains a very complex problem. The management of supply chain risk is not a new issue for supply chain stakeholders[7] or ports.[8] But it must be of vital interest to all stakeholders if we are to avert the economic damage that will certainly result from a catastrophic port closure. We believe that the cooperation between government and private industry during these events will determine the success or failure of a restoration effort. The technological tools that are required to construct a coordinated and effective system for restoration are available and within reach.

NOTES

This study was conducted under a grant from the Transportation Security Administration: Operation Restore HSTS04-O4-G-RED909.

1. S. Flynn, *America the Vulnerable: How Our Government Is Failing to Protect Us from Terrorism* (New York: HarperCollins, 2004); S. Flynn, *The Edge of Disaster: Rebuilding a Resilient Nation* (New York: Random House, 2007).

2. S. Flynn, "The Limitations of the Current U.S. Government Efforts to Secure the Global Supply Chain against Terrorists Smuggling a WMD and a Proposed Way Forward," written testimony before a hearing of the Permanent Subcommittee on Investigations, Committee on Homeland Security and Governmental Affairs, United States Senate, on "Neutralizing the Nuclear and Radiological Threat: Securing the Global Supply Chain," 2006, http://hsgac.senate.gov/index.cfm?Fuseaction=Hearings.Detail&HearingID=335.

3. Public Law 107-295, "Maritime Transportation Security Act of 2002," Washington, D.C., 2002.

4. "National Strategy for Homeland Security," Office of the President of the United States, 2002, http://www.whitehouse.gov/homeland/book/nat_strat_hls.pdf.

5. "Unclogging the Ports," *Journal of Commerce* (January 17, 2005): 12–14.

6. "Can Ports Handle Expected Increases in Container Volume?" *Journal of Commerce* (March 14, 2005): 12–14.

7. S. Chopra and M. Sodhi, "Managing Risk to Avoid Supply-Chain Breakdown," *MIT Sloan Management Review* 46, no. 1:53–61.

8. American Association of Port Authorities, "Current Issues Facing the Industry," http://www.aapa-ports.org/industryinfo/currentissues.html.

CHAPTER 7

Maritime Security: Domain Awareness

*U.S. Government Accountability Office**

BACKGROUND

According to the Coast Guard, MDA (maritime domain awareness) is an effort to achieve an understanding of anything in the global maritime environment that can affect the security, safety, economy, or environment of the United States. The process of achieving MDA includes (1) collection of information, (2) fusion of information from different sources, (3) analysis through the evaluation and interpretation of information, and (4) dissemination of information to decision makers, with the goal of identifying risks and threats before they turn into catastrophic events. One of the important tasks needed to achieve MDA is vessel tracking. Through the collection of vessel position information, comparison of that information with historical movements of the same and similar vessels, and additional information related to the vessel—such as its ownership and history—the Coast Guard attempts to determine the degree of risk presented by each vessel.

Since the September 11, 2001, terrorist attacks, a number of improvements in maritime security and MDA have been provided for in three main statutory enactments.

- Maritime Transportation Security Act. MTSA provides for a wide range of security improvements to maritime systems, ports, and vessels. Among its provisions, MTSA requires the implementation of a system to collect, integrate, and analyze information concerning vessels operating on or bound for waters subject to the

---

*This chapter is adapted from the GAO report "Maritime Security: Vessel Tracking Systems Provide Key Information, but the Need for Duplicate Data Should Be Reviewed," (GAO-09-337).

jurisdiction of the United States. To help meet this requirement, MTSA initially authorized the development and implementation of a long-range automated vessel tracking system for all vessels in U.S. waters equipped with a global maritime distress and safety system or equivalent satellite technology. MTSA requires the system to be capable of receiving information on vessel positions at intervals appropriate to deter security incidents. MTSA further allows the use of existing maritime organizations, such as the IMO (International Maritime Organization), to collect and monitor tracking information under the system. In addition, MTSA requires that certain vessels, including commercial vessels over sixty-five feet in length, carry AIS (automatic identification system) technology that broadcasts information such as the vessel's name, location, course, and speed while operating in U.S. waters.

- Coast Guard and Maritime Transportation Act of 2004. This act includes a provision that amended MTSA to mandate the development and implementation of the long-range automated vessel tracking system for all vessels in U.S. waters. The act also calls for the Secretary of Homeland Security to submit to specific congressional committees a plan that, among other things, (1) establishes a lead agency within the Department of Homeland Security (DHS) to coordinate the efforts of other agencies within DHS in the collection of maritime information and to identify and avoid unwanted redundancy of those efforts, (2) identifies redundancy in the collection and analysis of maritime information by agencies within DHS, and (3) establishes a timeline for incorporating information on vessel movements derived through the newly required long-range tracking system and AIS into the system for collecting and analyzing maritime information. DHS delivered this plan on June 28, 2005.

- Security and Accountability For Every Port Act of 2006 (SAFE Port Act). This act further amends the MTSA provisions for a long-range vessel tracking system. It sets a deadline of April 1, 2007, for the development of the tracking system. The SAFE Port Act also allows the Secretary of Homeland Security to establish a voluntary long-range vessel tracking system for the period before regulations are issued for the mandated system.

To help implement these laws, the Coast Guard has issued rules relating to both long-range tracking and AIS. In October 2007, the Coast Guard issued a proposed rule entitled Long Range Identification and Tracking of Ships and in April 2008 issued a final rule that requires certain vessels, including U.S.-registered vessels and foreign-registered vessels traveling to or from the United States, to report identifying and position data electronically through a long-range vessel tracking system. These vessels consist of passenger vessels, including high-speed passenger craft; cargo vessels, including high-speed craft, of 300 gross tons or more; and mobile offshore drilling units while underway and not engaged in drilling operations. The Coast Guard also issued an interim rule in July 2003 and a final rule in October 2003 delineating AIS requirements. The vessels covered depend on whether they are on an international voyage or operating in a vessel traffic service or vessel movement reporting service area. The requirements to carry and operate AIS equipment for vessels on international voyages generally apply to (1) all self-propelled vessels sixty-five feet or more in length, other than passenger and fishing vessels, engaged in commercial service, (2) passenger vessels of 150 gross tons or more, (3) tankers, regardless of tonnage, and (4) other vessels of 300 gross tons or more on international voyages. The requirements for vessels operating in vessel traffic service or vessel movement reporting service areas generally cover self-propelled vessels engaged in commercial service of sixty-five feet or more in length but do not include fishing vessels and passenger vessels certified to carry 150 passengers or fewer. However, towing vessels in commercial service that are twenty-six feet or more in length with more than 600 horsepower engines and passenger vessels certificated to carry more than 150 passengers are also covered.

The Coast Guard issued a Notice of Proposed Rulemaking in December 2008 that would substantially change these requirements. If the final rule is implemented as proposed, more commercial vessels will be required to carry and operate AIS equipment in all navigable waterways of the United States. The vessels that are covered under the proposed rule include (1) self-propelled vessels of sixty-five feet or more in commercial service, (2) towing vessels of twenty-six feet or more and more than 600 horsepower in commercial service, (3) self-propelled vessels carrying fifty or more passengers in commercial service, (4) vessels carrying more than twelve passengers for hire and capable of speeds greater than 30 knots, (5) certain dredges and floating plants, and (6) self-propelled vessels carrying certain dangerous cargos.

The administration has also called for improvements to maritime security, primarily through Homeland Security Presidential Directive-13 (HSPD-13, also referred to as National Security Presidential Directive-41), issued on December 21, 2004. HSPD-13 directs the coordination of maritime security policy through the creation of a National Strategy for Maritime Security. The directive required the Secretaries of Defense and Homeland Security to lead a joint effort to draft the strategy, which was issued in September 2005. Additionally, HSPD-13 directed relevant federal departments and agencies to develop eight supporting implementation plans to address the specific threats and challenges in the maritime environment. One of these supporting plans was the National Plan to Achieve Maritime Domain Awareness, developed by the Department of Defense and DHS and issued in October 2005. This plan provides an approach for improving information collection and sharing in the maritime domain to identify threats as early and as distant from U.S. shores as possible. For example, in terms of enhancing information collections, the plan calls for coordinating with international organizations to expand information requirements for data such as the notice of arrival. The plan also recommends expanding the application of AIS to improve the identification and tracking of marine vessels and leveraging national and international commercial and governmental relationships to produce dependable AIS and other vessel tracking.

MARITIME DOMAIN AWARENESS: INTERNATIONAL REQUIREMENTS

The IMO is an agency of the United Nations whose main task is to develop and maintain a comprehensive regulatory framework for shipping. Under its purview are vessel safety, environmental concerns, maritime legal matters, technical cooperation, and maritime security. Amendments to SOLAS

(Safety Of Life At Sea), to which the United States is a party, contain two provisions that relate specifically to MDA.

Chapter V, Regulation 19-1, which generally became effective January 1, 2009, has phased in implementation for vessels requires cargo vessels of 300 gross tons or more, passenger vessels, and self-propelled mobile offshore drilling units to be equipped with technology enabling the automatic transmission of the identity of the vessel, its position, and the time and date the position was transmitted. The regulation also lays out what countries are authorized to receive this information, and when. This SOLAS regulation is the basis for the Coast Guard's LRIT (Long Range Identification Tracking) rule.

- The IMO also set performance standards and functional requirements for LRIT in a resolution of its Maritime Safety Committee. This resolution establishes the role of LRIT data centers and the international data exchange, which are central to the distribution of LRIT information. These data centers, which can represent a single country or multiple countries, have three primary roles.
- Data centers will forward LRIT information from vessels at sea to the international data exchange for transmission to authorized countries.
- When LRIT information is forwarded by the international data exchange to an authorized country, the data center representing that country receives the information.
- Data centers make requests for LRIT information through the international data exchange.

The international data exchange acts as a facilitator for the exchange of LRIT between vessels and countries. As discussed above, when a vessel transmits LRIT information to its data center, that data center will forward the information to the international data exchange. The international data exchange then forwards the vessel's LRIT information to the data centers representing the countries that are authorized to receive the LRIT information from that vessel.

Another regulation contained in SOLAS deals with AIS. In general, Chapter V, Regulation 19 requires certain vessels of 300 gross tons or more on international voyages, passenger vessels regardless of size, and cargo vessels of 500 gross tons or more not engaged on international voyages to be equipped with AIS. According to the regulation AIS shall provide information, such as identity and position, and monitor and track vessels.

EVOLUTION OF LONG-RANGE TRACKING SYSTEMS

The United States' history of using national technical means for remote tracking of vessels on the high seas goes back many years, but in the early days, Soviet warships—not than commercial vessels—were the target of such tracking. Such means have been continually in place since that time, but their mission has grown from tracking potential military adversaries to tracking a wide variety of vessels, both military and nonmilitary, that are of interest to the United States. The actual vessels tracked are not necessarily limited by size.

Similarly, the capabilities of LRIT and AIS have been expanded as their purposes have changed. LRIT was primarily envisioned to utilize long-range technology to facilitate search and rescue operations and assist oceangoing vessels in distress. In order to respond to such an emergency at sea, the technology automatically transmits the identity, position, and time of position of a vessel in distress. To increase the likelihood of assistance to vessels in distress at sea, in 1988 the IMO adopted phased-in requirements for vessels to install specific satellite and radio-telephone equipment capable of automatic distress alerting. The same equipment and technology can be used for LRIT, but in addition to reporting information on vessels in distress, vessels would send periodic position reports that would permit them to be tracked by authorized governments.

AIS technology was originally designed to improve maritime safety, including the prevention of collisions among vessels. The system was originally designed to transmit identification, location, and maneuvering information (1) between vessels and (2) between vessels and land-based stations that are typically within twenty to thirty miles of one another. IMO requirements for the installation of AIS equipment include passenger vessels irrespective of size, vessels that weigh 300 gross tons or more on international voyages, and cargo vessels of 500 gross tons or more not on international voyages. By using commercially provided long-range AIS, the Coast Guard hopes to greatly expand the distance it can receive AIS signals up to 2,000 nautical miles from the coast.

NUMEROUS STAKEHOLDERS ARE INVOLVED IN MARITIME SECURITY AND MARITIME DOMAIN AWARENESS

Although numerous entities are responsible for maritime security and MDA within the United States, the federal government has primary responsibility and shares this role with numerous other stakeholders in the state, local, and private sectors. For example, DHS—with its component agency, the U.S. Coast Guard, acting as executive agent—has the lead role in maritime homeland security, while the Department of Defense leads efforts to further integrate maritime intelligence and increase MDA. In addition, the FBI has a lead role in investigating domestic maritime terrorism incidents. As shown in Table 1, state and local governments and the private sector, as well as the federal government, have responsibilities for maritime security and domain awareness.

RISK MANAGEMENT

The 9/11 Commission pointed out that no amount of money or effort can fully protect against every type of threat. Rather, a risk management approach is often used that considers, among other things, the relative risks various threats pose when determining how best to use limited resources to prevent

Table 1
Maritime Stakeholders and Their Roles in Maritime
Security and Domain Awareness

Federal government: Department of Homeland Security

U.S. Coast Guard

• Conducts vessel escorts, boardings of selected vessels, and security patrols of key port areas.

• Ensures that vessels in U.S. waters comply with domestic and international maritime security standards.

• Reviews U.S. vessel and facility security plans and oversees compliance with these plans.

• Meets with foreign governments and visits foreign port facilities to observe security conditions.

• Shares responsibility for implementation and operationalization of MDA with the U.S. Navy.

Customs and Border Protection

• Has principal responsibility for inspecting cargo, including cargo containers that commercial vessels bring into U.S. ports.

• Detects and prevents the illegal entry of persons and goods into the country.

Federal government: Department of Defense

U.S. Navy

• Provides support to Department of Homeland Security as requested for maritime homeland security operations.

• Maintains a credible maritime interdiction capability to deal with identified hostile vessels at any location when authorized to do so.

• Builds relationships with partner nations' navies to enhance cooperation and information sharing.

• Shares responsibility for implementation and operationalization of MDA with U.S. Coast Guard.

Federal government: Department of Justice

Federal Bureau of Investigation

• Federal Bureau of Investigation Maritime Liaison Agents, stationed at key U.S. ports, help disseminate maritime intelligence to port stakeholders.

• Leads Joint Terrorism Task Forces.

• Leads investigations of maritime terrorism incidents.

State and local governments

Law enforcement agencies

• Conducts land-based patrols of port facilities.

Table 1
(Continued)

- If the agency operates a marine unit, it typically conducts water patrols and sometimes escorts larger vessels.

Private sector

Facility and commercial vessel operators

- Develops and implements facility or vessel security plans that meet MTSA standards.
- Provides security for the facility or vessel.

The public

General public, recreational vessel

- Reports suspicious activity, operators, and marina employees
- Respects security rules regulations, such as those governing security zones

threats where possible and to respond effectively if they occur. While the Homeland Security Act of 2002 and Homeland Security Presidential Directive 7 call for the use of risk management in homeland security, little specific federal guidance or direction exists as to how risk management should be implemented. In previous work examining risk management efforts for homeland security and other functions, we developed a framework summarizing the findings of industry experts and best practices. For tracking vessels, this effort requires identifying high-risk vessels as a priority and developing a layered system of security to reduce the risks associated with them. For example, the Coast Guard uses a risk management approach in its effort to determine which vessels bound for the United States may pose the greatest threat to the United States and which, given the limited resources available to the Coast Guard, should be boarded to determine if they pose an undue risk.

To track vessels up to 2,000 nautical miles from U.S. shores, the Coast Guard is currently using classified national technical means and developing the use of two additional unclassified technologies—LRIT and commercially provided long-range AIS. Coast Guard officials told us that they cannot depend on full-time access to information provided by national technical means. The Coast Guard does not control the tasking of these resources, and they may be redirected to priorities higher than Coast Guard or DHS missions. Although no more details are available about national technical means because of their classified nature, the information below describes the Coast Guard's plans for LRIT and AIS.

LRIT is an international system that uses onboard radio equipment to transmit identification and position information to satellites. From the satellites, the information is forwarded to ground stations and then on to recipient countries, including the United States. While the system requires cooperation from vessels (radio equipment must be turned on), it is a closed system in that only countries with rights to the information can receive it. The Coast Guard expects the LRIT program to cost approximately $5.3 million in fiscal year 2009, and about $4.2 million per year thereafter. See Appendix I for a full description of LRIT.

The regulatory framework for the LRIT system is in place. As previously mentioned, the Coast Guard issued a final rule on April 29, 2008, setting requirements for many U.S.-registered vessels to transmit their identity and location with LRIT equipment wherever they are located. This rule implemented domestic requirements set forth in MTSA, as amended by both the Coast Guard and Maritime Transportation Act of 2004 and the SAFE Port Act, as well as the IMO's international requirements as laid out in SOLAS. As well as implementing requirements for most U.S. vessels subject to the SOLAS regulation, the rule also sets specific requirements for foreign vessels traveling to or near the United States to broadcast their identification and location. For example, under the rule, foreign vessels bound for a U.S. port must transmit their identity and location once they have announced their intention to enter a U.S. port—typically 96 hours prior to their arrival (which equates to approximately 2,000 nautical miles from the U.S. coastline at speeds traveled by typical oceangoing vessels). It also calls for foreign vessels on international voyages to typically transmit their identity and location when they are within 1,000 nautical miles of the U.S. coast, even if they are not calling on a U.S. port. The requirements for both foreign and domestic vessels include the specific data items to be transmitted, the timetable for reporting, the types of equipment that can be used to report the information, and the capabilities of the reporting equipment. The rule exempts certain vessels, such as those that will be traveling exclusively within twenty nautical miles of the U.S. coastline and that are equipped with operating AIS.

In addition to setting U.S. requirements for LRIT, the Coast Guard is also taking on international responsibilities to help ensure that LRIT position information is available on schedule. To ensure the appropriate distribution of LRIT information, the IMO mandated the creation of an international data exchange to facilitate the distribution of this information to authorized countries. For example, if a vessel registered in China is sailing to a U.S. port, the Chinese data center would have to begin to send the LRIT information to the U.S. data center through the international data exchange when the vessel announces its intention to enter a U.S. port. However, the mandate did not address which country or international organization would be responsible for developing, operating, and maintaining the international data exchange, or how it would be funded. Because the United States and other SOLAS signatories were worried that the data exchange would not be operational when the rule took effect, and because no other country had agreed to set up the exchange, the Coast Guard has agreed to develop and operate the data exchange for an interim period from January 1, 2009, to December 31, 2010. As of February 2009, it was unclear who would operate the international data exchange after the expiry of this two-year period.

Although the Coast Guard expected to begin receiving some countries' LRIT reports on schedule, it acknowledged that not all countries would be ready to participate. Coast Guard officials told us that the international data exchange and the U.S. national data center (the facility that will receive all LRIT transmissions from U.S.-registered vessels and forward them to the data exchange) are operational. The Coast Guard also expected very few U.S.-registered vessels will need new equipment to transmit LRIT information, because existing requirements already mandate the installation of radio equipment capable of the required transmissions. In contrast, the Coast Guard recognized that not all countries may have operational national or multinational data centers to forward information to the international data exchange by the time the rule goes into effect. The final rule states that the Coast Guard will still hold vessels coming to the United States responsible for providing LRIT information at that time.

THE COAST GUARD IS PLANNING ON FULL CAPABILITY OF COMMERCIALLY PROVIDED LONG-RANGE AIS BY 2014

If the Coast Guard does not receive LRIT information from a vessel covered by the rule, it has a range of enforcement options available. In general, the Coast Guard plans to leave local captains of the port—the Coast Guard officials responsible for maritime safety and security in a port area—to decide how to address these situations on a case-by-case basis. Under their regulatory authorities, these officials have the authority to—among other things— level civil penalties for noncompliance as well as refer knowing and willful violations to the Department of Justice for criminal prosecution. The captain of the port will make a risk-based decision given the information he or she has available from existing sources and, depending on his or her finding, decide on a response ranging from the taking of no action to boarding the vessel at sea, setting fines, or denying entry.

To have an additional means for receiving vessel information that includes identification and location of vessels at sea, the Coast Guard is demonstrating another tracking system that uses commercially provided long-range AIS. AIS receivers take in a set of radio signals from equipment on board vessels and then forward them to the Coast Guard via the commercial provider. AIS is an open system, and anyone who has an AIS receiver can track vessels using AIS signals. (See Appendix II for a full description of AIS.) The Coast Guard's use of commercially provided long-range AIS is part of the NAIS, a comprehensive effort to track AIS-equipped vessels in U.S. coastal areas, inland waterways, and ports, and those as far as 2,000 nautical miles from the U.S. shore.

While the Coast Guard has made development of commercially provided long-range AIS a substantial part of its long-range vessel tracking efforts, the program has fallen behind schedule. In 2004, the Coast Guard signed a contract with a commercial communications company to demonstrate the ability of commercial AIS to receive and forward AIS broadcasts from vessels at sea. This demonstration, originally scheduled for mid-2006, did not occur until June 19, 2008. Coast Guard officials said the delays were primarily caused by difficulties the contractor experienced in obtaining needed services for the Coast Guard demonstration as well as technical issues.

As a concession for the delays, the contractor provided the Coast Guard access to vessel position data sent via AIS through other means. According to Coast Guard officials and to a filing made by the contractor to the Securities and Exchange Commission, terms of the contract state that once operational testing is completed, the Coast Guard will receive 90 days of AIS data to determine the characteristics of commercially provided long-range AIS, such as the amount of data that would flow from each source. The Coast Guard can also receive data from the concept demonstration for an additional two years, based on original contract options and pricing. If the Coast Guard wishes to continue to receive these data, it will have to pay additional fees to the contractor.

In spite of the two-year delay in the demonstration, the Coast Guard does not believe that its use of commercially provided long-range AIS will delay the full implementation of NAIS. Coast Guard officials stated that there were development issues related to using these AIS receivers that are different from those related to developing a land-based AIS network that will cover the U.S. coastline. According to the Coast Guard, the completion of its assessment of the commercially provided long-range AIS demonstration, including coverage areas, potential interference, and data rates will allow it to compare commercially provided long-range AIS with other long-range tracking methods or, as they become available, different commercial providers of long-range AIS services.

To track AIS-equipped vessels in fifty-five major U.S. ports and nine coastal areas, the Coast Guard has installed a widespread network of ground-based AIS receivers it uses to monitor those areas. In some of these locations, the Coast Guard also makes use of radar and cameras, installed by the Coast Guard and other maritime security stakeholders, to help track vessels not equipped with AIS.

The Coast Guard installed ground-based AIS equipment in fifty-five ports and nine coastal areas as the first increment of NAIS (Nationwide Automatic Identification System). Before Increment 1, AIS coverage in the United States was very limited. AIS-covered areas included vessel traffic service and vessel movement reporting service areas, AIS prototyping and testing locations, and the St. Lawrence Seaway. This level of coverage, however, left out some major ports. As of September 2007, this first NAIS increment reached full operating capability, allowing near real-time tracking of vessels carrying and operating AIS equipment in all fifty-five covered ports and nine coastal areas. In the coastal areas, the system generally provides coverage to within twenty-four nautical miles of shore. This tracking is performed by the local Coast Guard sector.

While AIS is capable of tracking AIS-equipped vessels in many ports around the United States, as previously stated, many vessels in U.S. waters are not required to install or operate AIS equipment. According to Coast Guard regulations in effect on February 1, 2009, outside of the vessel traffic service and vessel movement reporting service areas, only vessels that arrive from a foreign port are required to operate AIS equipment, regardless of size or cargo. Outside of the vessel traffic service and vessel movement reporting service areas, all vessels less than sixty-five feet in length and all noncommercial vessels less than 300 gross tons—except for tankers and certain passenger vessels—are never required to operate AIS equipment in U.S. waters. A Notice of Proposed Rulemaking issued by the Coast Guard in December 2008 demonstrates the Coast Guard's intention to expand these requirements.

At eight of the ten sectors we visited, the Coast Guard can use additional sensors, such as radar and video cameras, to complement AIS. In four of the eight sectors where these additional sensors are available, the local Coast Guard works directly with other port security stakeholders in the sector command center. For example, in some ports the Coast Guard has access to sensor feeds provided by the Navy. Similarly, in other ports, the Coast Guard has access to cameras installed by local governments and private industry. These were installed to monitor conditions at specific locations such as bridge abutments or entrances to secure facilities. Other Coast Guard locations are far less equipped. In some ports, local Coast Guard units are dependent solely on AIS technology to track vessels.

In part to help obtain this intelligence and expand their awareness of activities on the water, the Coast Guard and other port security stakeholders have engaged in outreach efforts with the port community. All of the Coast Guard locations we visited had longstanding relationships with local professional mariners, such as pilots and tug operators. The Coast Guard officials we spoke with thought these relationships were beneficial in enhancing MDA. For example, several Delaware River pilots alerted Sector Delaware Bay of two small armed vessels traveling at high speed from the Chesapeake and Delaware Canal into the Delaware River. Coast Guard boats responded to these craft on the basis of this information. The suspect craft turned out to be Navy Seals on an unannounced exercise, but the pilots provided the only notice to the Coast Guard. The Coast Guard has also implemented a nationwide program called America's Waterways Watch to engage all those who work, live, or recreate on or near the water to be aware and report suspicious activity that may indicate possible threats. This type of effort is a major recommendation in the DHS small vessel security strategy. The strategy considers the small vessel community as the single largest asset in addressing the threat from small boat attacks. Coast Guard sectors have also developed information-sharing agreements with state, local, and law enforcement agencies that are intended to increase awareness and cooperation. Some state and local outreach efforts are especially active. For example, the New Jersey State Police Maritime Security Initiative follows the America's Waterways Watch model but goes even further. State police officers make regular—sometimes weekly—proactive visits to locations such as marinas, boat ramps, and waterfront properties to ask individuals in these areas about any suspicious or out-of-place behavior they may have witnessed.

LONG-RANGE TRACKING SYSTEMS ARE POTENTIALLY DUPLICATIVE, WHILE SYSTEMS FOR VESSEL TRACKING IN U.S. COASTAL AREAS, INLAND WATERWAYS, AND PORTS PROVIDE COMPLEMENTARY INFORMATION THAT COVERS ADDITIONAL VESSELS

While current plans for vessel tracking systems lead to potential duplication in vessels tracked and information received, systems that track vessels in coastal areas, inland waterways, and ports are complementary in that they track different types of vessels and vary in their capabilities. The long range systems—LRIT, commercially provided long-range AIS, and national technical means—were initially developed independently of each other and for different purposes, but the Coast Guard was unable to provide evidence that the planning for the current and future use of LRIT and commercially provided long-range AIS was coordinated. Furthermore, the Coast Guard has yet to consider the costs and benefits of obtaining offshore vessel identification and tracking information from the multiple sources currently, or soon to be, available to the Coast Guard. In coastal areas, inland waterways, and ports, there are greater differences among the tracking systems. AIS provides extensive information, but its use is limited to larger vessels while radar and video cameras, sensors that are located in some ports, provide limited information but can pick up varied vessels. Additionally, cameras can be affected by environmental conditions, unlike AIS and radar.

OTHER DATA SOURCES ARE AVAILABLE TO PROVIDE COMMERCIALLY PROVIDED LONG-RANGE AIS'S EXPANDED INFORMATION

As a standalone system, commercially provided long-range AIS is to provide more information on vessels traveling to the United States than LRIT, but when the information from each is combined with other readily available sources, the information will be duplicative. Current plans have both commercially provided long-range AIS and LRIT providing information about vessels bound for a U.S. destination at 2,000 nautical miles from the U.S. coastline. At approximately this location, vessels bound for the United States are typically required to send an advance notice of arrival to the Coast Guard, providing detailed information about the vessel, its voyage, its cargo, and its crew. When AIS or LRIT information is combined with the information provided in the notice of arrival, the Coast Guard will have available much the same information regardless of whether it is using commercially provided long-range AIS or LRIT to track a vessel.

Other characteristics of the two planned systems vary. Ordinarily, commercially provided long-range AIS will transmit information much more often (from every two seconds to every six minutes, depending on the information) than LRIT (every six hours). However, if the Coast Guard needs location information more frequently, LRIT will allow it to remotely poll inbound vessels and receive an automatic reply for location reports up to every fifteen minutes. However, since vessels are being tracked while they are several days from port, the Coast Guard is unlikely to need this information more frequently. Additionally, while the vessel transmitters for both tracking systems can be turned off by the crew, Coast Guard officials we spoke with said it is easier to change the programming of onboard AIS equipment to transmit false position reports than it is to do the same using LRIT.

Although the Coast Guard says it wants both commercially provided long-range AIS and LRIT to detect anomalies such as vessels broadcasting false position reports or not broadcasting position reports at all, the Coast Guard has other sources to corroborate such information. For example, the Coast Guard can use national technical means along with either LRIT or NAIS to detect anomalies. While the capabilities and information provided by national technical means are classified, the Coast Guard is able to obtain important benefits from the use of these means. According to the Coast Guard, to obtain the full benefit provided by national technical means, Coast Guard analysts track that information over time and combine it with information provided by other sources, such as notices of arrival and commercial reporting. Through analysis of the information available from national technical means, the Coast Guard should be able to provide sufficient information to verify the identification and location of vessels provided through LRIT or commercially provided long-range AIS.

As explained earlier in this report, each system in place in coastal areas, inland waterways, and ports has limitations, but these limitations can be mitigated with different sensors. In locations where all these sensors are available, their complementary nature allows for almost a complete picture of the port and surrounding area. For example, in one port, the Navy and local agencies have installed a wide array of sensors that cover 90 percent of the port and much of the coastal area. There, radar can detect larger noncommercial vessels that do not carry AIS. Cameras that can operate in daylight, at dusk, and at night can follow smaller vessels that do not carry AIS and are difficult to pick up on radar. For vessels that do carry AIS equipment, the land-based AIS receivers can provide a wide range of information that neither radar nor cameras can. As stated earlier in this report, we saw similar capabilities in other locations where the Coast Guard worked directly with other maritime security stakeholders to track vessels in ports and multiple sensors were installed. While the presence of multiple sensors allows this broad coverage, these sensors are only available where other agencies have installed them. In other locations, few sensors beyond AIS are available. In these locations, tracking is limited to those vessels transmitting via AIS equipment.

CONCLUSIONS

Threats to the maritime transportation system include the use of large merchant vessels to transport weapons of mass destruction, the use of explosive-laden suicide boats as weapons, and the use of vessels to smuggle people, drugs, weapons, and other contraband. The importance and vulnerabilities of the maritime transportation system require that efforts be made to reduce the risk of a terrorist attack. The Coast Guard has acknowledged that it needs to close the gaps in maritime security, including long-range tracking of vessels and threats presented by small vessels. Knowledge of activities, such as vessel movements that take place within the system, is vital to reducing the vulnerability of the maritime transportation system. Classified national technical means to do so have been operational for many years, and LRIT—a statutorily required long-range tracking system—is now available to the Coast Guard to monitor the movements of larger commercial vessels at sea. Along with the notice of arrival, these systems provide a complete picture of larger commercial vessel movements and other pertinent information.

CHAPTER 8

Reliable and Effective Detection, Protection, and Repair System for Canadian Oil/Gas Pipeline System: Conceptual Development and Validation

A. O. Abd El Halim, Mohamed Elshafey, and O. B. Isgor

Structural failure or damage issues associated with pipelines can originate from operational or external factors. Pipeline systems are a major component of the energy infrastructure considered one of the critical infrastructures in Canada. With terrorist attacks on the rise globally, Canada is certainly not immune to such threats. Recently, a guerrilla group claimed responsibility for a series of bombings of pipelines operated by Pemex, Mexico's national oil company, and authorities moved quickly to protect the nation's oil and gas industry from further attacks. The oil infrastructure is a prime target of several terrorist organizations. The threat does not only come from al Qaeda, but may also come from other terrorist groups—and the threats go beyond the Middle East region into Asia, Africa, and South and North America. The losses due to these attacks run into the billion of dollars, in addition to possible loss of life and severe damage to the environment. Damage to pipeline systems is not limited to terrorist attacks. Most of the deterioration of pipelines during regular operation takes place due to different mechanisms of corrosion and foundation movements. While each of these issues represents a challenge, it is important that we recognize the influence of one form of deterioration on the other factors. It is expected that during the mitigation of issues associated with pipelines several operational and external deterioration processes can take place simultaneously. Thus, blast loading effects could become more destructive from presence of internal corrosion leading to sudden rise in internal pressures. Also, occurrence of fire as a result of gas or like leak will increase in cases in which corrosion exists on the internal/external surface of the pipeline.

Due to the geographic characteristics of gas/oil pipelines the risk, threats, and vulnerabilities associated with the safety and security of oil infrastructure are very high. Reducing the risks that oil pipelines are exposed to is one of the biggest challenges facing the energy-producing regions. Terrorist threats and attacks are not the only threat to the physical security of oil pipelines, but they are the ones that result in the greatest damage. Other sources of threats include vandalism, conflicts and wars, and technical engineering. There are also the natural threats from the environment, such as floods, windstorms, earthquakes, and so forth. The final outcome of these threats is the subject of this section, focusing on the major modes of failure of oil and gas pipelines and the different sources of vulnerabilities of the pipelines.

The research presented in this report deals with concept development and validation. More specifically, the main objectives of the research are to identify the main problems influencing the continuous and efficient flow of oil and gas through pipeline systems. Analytical investigation was performed on several scenarios to identify critical stress, strain, and energy conditions for a pipeline system subjected to internal and external threats. The successful completion of this phase is expected to provide sufficient data and information to carry out future work both for examination in the laboratory and for field prototypes and specimens used to verify and modify the developed concept.

PIPELINES AS A MEANS OF TRANSPORTATION

The main transportation modes for oil and gas are pipelines, rail, road, and water. The choice of mode depends on several factors, among them distances between origins and destination, geography, technology, and economics. Pipelines are the most efficient mode of transportation because of their ease of operation, minimal required labor and energy requirements, and low maintenance requirements. A large pipeline can transport around 2 million barrels of oil a day, the equivalent of 9,375 large semi-truck tankers, twenty-four 100-car trains, or ten fifteen-unit barge tows. The other modes consume fuel and congest transportation corridors. In addition, pipelines have a lower accident rate. Most crude oil is transported by pipelines from wells, which may be located in such remote regions as deserts, to refineries, which are normally built closer to ports and populated zones. For example, the U.S. pipeline grid is extensive, reaching from the Southwest and the Gulf of Mexico (where oil is produced) to the Midwest and Northeast (where most of the population and industries are concentrated). It gathers oil and gas at individual wells, transports it to refineries for processing, and carries these products to the end user markets. Probably the most significant crude oil pipeline in the United States is the Trans-Alaska Pipeline System, which carries 20 percent of the produced oil from Alaska's North Slope to the Port of Valdez, a distance of 1,300 kilometers. In November 2002, a fourteen-foot shift was caused by the 7.9 Denali Fault earthquake, which ruptured the ground under the zigzagging pipeline. The robust design of the pipeline saved the country from severe economic consequences (U.S. Geological Survey Fact Sheet 017-03).

CAUSES OF FAILURE

Generally speaking, failure analysis is an engineering approach to estimating and predicting the causes and modes of structural failure. Among several causes of failure are structural loading, wear and tear, corrosion, and latent defects. One of the main objectives of performing failure analysis is to understand the real causes of failure so as to prevent their occurrence in similarly designed systems. Describing how structures fail and predicting their leading causes makes it possible to determine and understand how systems fail and why. The oil/gas pipeline infrastructure includes several elements and components that vary in shape, function, and strength. Subsequently, there are many structural and operational causes that may lead to failure of one or more of the components constituting the entire pipeline infrastructure. Among those causes are

- Misuse or abuse
- Assembly errors
- Manufacturing defects
- Improper maintenance
- Fastener failure
- Design errors
- Improper material
- Improper heat treatments
- Unforeseen operating conditions
- Inadequate quality assurance
- Inadequate environmental protection/control
- Casting discontinuities

Gas and oil pipelines have established an impressive safety record over the years. However, failures have occurred for a variety of reasons. Some of the causes of failure are identified in a previous document by Abd El Halim and Hafez. Since the 1940s, all of the oil and gas transmission lines have been built by welding. In general, American Petroleum Institute (API) 5L specification steels are used in pipelines. Pipeline wall thicknesses are established for line pressure and for allowable hoop stress levels for the material. The allowable stress levels for gas pipelines vary based on the location of the pipeline and are regulated by the U.S. Department of Transportation (DOT). Pipelines are pressure-tested in addition to nondestructive testing prior to their being put into service. Normally, pipelines are hydrostatically stressed to levels above their working pressure, and near their specified minimum yield strength. This pressure is held for several hours to ensure that the pipeline does not have defects that may cause failure in use. Some of the causes of pipeline failures are

- Mechanical damage
- Fatigue cracks
- Material defects
- Weld cracks
- Incomplete fusion
- Improper repair welds
- Incomplete penetration
- External or internal corrosion
- Hydrogen blistering

Mechanical damage normally consists of gouges and dents, generally are created by excavation or handling equipment during construction. While pipelines are among the best-designed structures, at the present time, they are among the most vulnerable systems. They are susceptible to natural disasters or vandalism, because they are typically located in remote areas, cover vast terrains, and are unsecured. In addition, the larger the diameter and the higher the volumes of transported oil/gas through the pipelines, the more attractive they are to terrorists. Even though large parts of pipelines are usually buried, they are exposed at some parts, such as river crossings and when the cutting through rocky grounds. However, generally speaking, and for economic reasons, the burial depth of the pipes is shallow, and they are clearly marked with warning signs, making them easier targets to access.

The vulnerability and the risk factors depend on certain factors, including

- The produced fluid whether oil or gas, and whether there are toxic substances in the fluid.
- The diameter of the pipeline. Larger diameters are more vulnerable and cause greater effects when damaged than smaller ones.
- Whether the pipeline is buried or exposed in places. The length of exposed portions also increases the vulnerability.
- The material and design of the pipeline system

Regardless of the type of threat, gas/oil pipeline systems could fail due to several factors which could be divided into five categories

External Factors

There are many factors that lead to failure and one of the most critical is the external factor. However, the primary cause is third-party vandalism. As described earlier, pipelines are vulnerable to vandalism due to their presence in remote areas that are very difficult to secure. Energy sources, especially oil, are attractive targets for warring parties. Many wars and terrorist attacks cause intentional damage to oil pipelines. An example of such attacks has been the bombing of the Occidental Petroleum pipelines—around 950 times since 1986, causing shutdowns and costing the government around 2.5 billion dollars in lost revenues. Another example is the continuous failures of the Iraqi Oil pipeline system as a result of the war and terrorist attacks, and the use of explosives by guerrilla troops to blow up Colombian oil pipelines.

Other outside factors include accidents or human errors, such as excavation without proper planning and sufficient information. For example, in 1989, in Russia, sparks from two passing trains caused gas leakage from a LNG pipeline, killing 645 people. In another example, in June 1999, an oil pipeline ruptured and caught fire in Bellingham, Washington, causing several deaths and a year-and-a-half shutdown of the pipeline. This caused economic hardships to the Seattle–Tacoma Airport, which relied on the fuel supplied by the pipeline. Critical sections of oil/gas pipelines can also cause accidents due to defected joints, welded sections, and corrosion.

Environmental Factors

One of the main causes of failure of pipelines is corrosion. Corrosion could be through external or internal metal loss. Stress corrosion cracking is also a form of corrosion that may occur to pipelines. The U.S. Department of Transportation's Research and Special Programs Administration, Office of Pipeline Safety (RSPA/OPS) found that corrosion failure was the cause of 25 percent of pipeline failures in 2002 and 2003. Furthermore, the U.S. Office of Pipeline Safety (OPS) has counted 6,377 accidents between 1986 and August 2001. These incidents caused 376 deaths, 1,699 injuries, $1,140,697,582 in property damage, and a gross loss of 2,777,205 barrels of various oil fuels. (OPS is unable to quantify the loss of natural gas.) In August 2000, an explosion occurred in the gas pipeline near Carlsbad, New Mexico, killing twelve people; the explosion was caused by corrosion in the pipelines. Gas prices in California increased significantly due to this incident, and an electricity crisis also broke out.

Natural Force and Human Error Factors

Nature can cause serious damage to pipeline systems depending on the severity of the phenomenon. Natural disasters include earthquakes, floods, fires, storms, hurricanes, and so forth. Lightning, for example, can cause damage to pipelines, and ground movement can result in severe ruptures in pipelines. However, the probability of lightning events or ground movement causing damage to pipelines is very small. In August and September 2005, Hurricanes Katrina and Rita disrupted the flows of oil, natural gas, and electric power simultaneously, causing a vast energy disruption and power outage in North America. A good example of an oil pipeline accident that caused serious spillage is the accident that occurred July 2007 in Burnaby, B.C.

Material and Fabrication Defects

Although these modes of failure do occur, they are not of major concern, for they are detected early and at the beginning of a pipeline's life and can be addressed promptly. However there are crack-like weld defects that may grow and cause failure due to cyclic loading resulting from outside forces or fluctuations in internal pressure.

Operational Errors and Mechanical Component Failures

These include human errors due to incorrect operation. In oil pipelines, these errors constitute a very small percentage relative to the other sources of damage. The top causes of failure are excavation and corrosion damages.

CONSEQUENCES OF FAILURE

Damage to pipelines may vary in scale and in consequences. Mere damage to the pipeline itself could result, or an accident might become so serious as to claim human lives and cause significant economic losses. In general, the consequence of a failure can be divided into life safety consequences, environmental consequences, and economic consequences

Life Safety Consequences

Depending on the constituents of the produced oil transported by the pipeline, and whether it contains toxic substances, damage to the pipeline can cause fires, explosions, or release of toxic fumes. These events may cause injuries or even fatalities among people in close proximity. Table 8.1 reports data on industrial accidents resulting in more than twenty-five fatalities in Europe between 1971 and 2001. It should be noted that oil- and gas-related accidents resulted in the highest number of deaths, as indicated by 1988 North Sea, UK, and 1989 Acha Ufa, USSR.

Environmental Consequences

In addition to fatalities and economic losses, there are also environmental impacts. Environmental consequences include the long-term effect of damages of pipelines to the human health and to the environment. This may be due to the exposure to toxic substances or due to the exposure of ground surfaces or water sources to oil spills. It could also cause severe air pollution. For example, release of hydrocarbon liquids to surface waters and groundwater,

Table 8.1
Industrial Accidents Resulting in More Than 25 Fatalities[a]

	Location	Products Involved	Type of Accident	Fatalities
1971	Czechowice, Poland	Oil	Explosion	33
1971	English Channel	Petrochemicals	Ship collision	29
1973	Czechoslovakia	Gas	Explosion	47
1974	Flixborough, UK	Cyclohexane	Explosion	28
1976	Lapua, Finland	Gunpowder	Explosion	43
1978	San Carlos, Spain	Propylene	Fireball (road transport)	216
1979	Bantry Bay, Ireland	Oil, gas	Explosion (marine transport)	50
1979	Warsaw, Poland	Gas	Explosion	49
1979	Novosibirsk, USSR	Chemicals	Unknown	300
1980	Ortuella, Spain	Propane	Explosion	51
1980	Rome, Italy	Oil	Ship collision	25
1980	Danaciobasi, Turkey	Butane	Unknown	107
1982	Todi, Italy	Gas	Explosion	34
1983	Istanbul, Turkey	Unknown	Explosion	42
1984	Romania	Chemicals	Unknown	100
1985	Algeciras, Spain	Oil	Transhipment	33
1986	Chernobyl, USSR	Nuclear	Reactor explosion	31*
1988	Arzamas, USSR	Explosives	Explosion (rail transport)	73
1988	North Sea, UK	Oil, gas	Fire	167
1989	Acha Ufa, USSR	Gas	Explosion (pipeline)	575
1991	Livorno, Italy	Naphtha	Transport accident	141
1992	Corlu, Turkey	Methane	Explosion	32
1998	Donetsk, Ukraine	Methane	Explosion (mine)	63
1999	Zasyadko, Ukraine	Methane	Explosion (mine)	50
2000	Donetsk, Ukraine	Methane	Explosion (mine)	81
2001	Donetsk, Ukraine	Coal dust/ methane	Explosion (mine)	36
2001	Toulouse, France	Ammonium nitrate	Explosion	31
2002	Donetsk, Ukraine	Methane	Explosion (mine)	35

Note: Other events may have occurred that have not been widely documented.
* Number of fatalities related directly to reactor explosion.
[a] "Technological and natural hazards: Europe's environment—The third assessment," http://reports.eea.europa.eu/environmental_assessment_report_2003_10/en/kiev_chapt_10.pdf.

and release of gases to the atmosphere, are known outcomes. In Russia, more and more new pipelines are being constructed to transport oil and gas to the west from the new frontiers in the east, including in the Caspian region and Siberia. Another major type of hazard, in which the impact is predominantly environmental, is marine oil spillage, such as in the case of the famous *Prestige* disaster off the west coast of Spain.

Table 8.2
Countries with More than 2,000 km of Pipelines

United States 793,285	Egypt 12,664	United Arab Rep. 5,365
Russia 239,439	Pakistan 11,766	Chile 4,924
Canada 98,544	Spain 11,548	Syria 4,483
Algeria 95,999	Libya 11,088	Denmark 4,425
Mexico 53,004	Uzbekistan 10,051	Tunisia 4,367
Australia 34,295	Norway 9,607	Serbia and Montenegro 3,570
Iran 33,844	Saudi Arabia 9,413	Austria 3,534
Argentina 33,833	Belarus 9,352	Thailand 3,377
China 33,648	Nigeria 9,265	South Africa 3,353
Germany 32,985	Bolivia 9,200	Sudan 3,331
United Kingdom 32,832	Netherlands 8,629	Ecuador 3,220
Ukraine 28,778	Iraq 8,500	Georgia 2,956
France 22,145	Turkmenistan 7,944	Japan 2,949
Kazakhstan 21,733	Czech Republic 7,661	Bulgaria 2,947
Brazil 21,291	Malaysia 7,281	New Zealand 2,756
India 18,546	Slovakia 7,218	Burma 2,614
Italy 18,471	Oman 6,966	Slovenia 2,537
Indonesia 18,351	Turkey 6,739	Qatar 2,438
Ukraine 15,436	Azerbaijan 5,969	Belgium 2,178

Economic Consequences

The economic consequences are the monetary value of the damages. This sum is calculated by adding the direct costs of the damage to the pipeline to the hazard related costs after converting time and lives to money value. Direct costs include cost of line repair, cost of lost produce, and cost of interrupting the service. Hazard-related costs include costs of property damage, spill cleanup, and site restoration, and compensation of deaths and injuries. Table 8.2 shows the size of the constructed pipelines in the world. These pipelines and their critical assets have become the target of a new wave of terrorists, a trend expected to continue for several years into the future. As demonstrated earlier, the oil and gas pipeline infrastructure extends over thousands of kilometers within and across nations, making it accessible to anyone with bad intentions. Clearly, the damage to these assets can result in serious economic losses ranging from the immediate costs of repairing the damaged pipe and the loss of the wasted gas or oil to a sudden rise in the prices of oil and gas on international markets.

CONCLUSIONS

Over the past decade, several approaches have been proposed for improving the performance of oil/gas infrastructure that are subject to some of the risks faced by engineers and managers alike. Most recently, the research team at

Carleton University proposed an integrated approach that combined structural analysis with sensor technology to improve the overall security and safety of the pipeline assets. In this phase of the project, which deals with the structural analysis of the infrastructure, the emphasis is on the utilization of a newly developed material made of aluminum foam (AF) that has the properties of a foam structure. Two distinctive structural properties were identified as suitable for the research at hand: (1) the higher compressibility of the AF under impact loading and (2) the presence of cavities within the structure of the foam that could be utilized for positioning sensors for detection, identifying potential threats, and communicating critical information.

This research investigation is divided into a number of phases. This report presents the first phase of the study, which can be defined as "Concept Development and Validation." This phase deals with the identification of the main problems influencing the continuous and efficient flow of oil and gas through pipeline systems. A numerical investigation is carried out to identify critical conditions for a pipeline system subjected to internal and external threats. Finally, several proposed scenarios were analyzed in which the new AF was utilized as a layer that can absorb additional energy and minimize the residual energy harmful to property and persons. In this investigation, only the performance changes due to the use of AF are investigated, and practical aspects of this setup (e.g. flow, corrosion of the exposed surface, galvanic coupling between steel and AF) are not considered. The specific details and aspects of the proposed design will be addressed when the results have been verified experimentally.

More specifically, the investigation has led to the following conclusions:

- The use of AF to build composite sections produces pipes with better performance against internal and external blasts is a feasible and promising alternative solution.
- The sections supported with AF absorbed significantly larger blast energy for a longer duration than the sections produced only by steel with the same overall thickness.
- The use of AF in pipes also increased the blast resistance of the corroded sections.
- The use of AF, while improving the overall performance, also produced lightweight pipes, thus providing potential savings in terms of material and constructions costs.
- The utilization of the AF system would provide an opportunity to examine the inclusion of the sensors into the protection system of the oil/gas pipeline infrastructure.

The results and conclusions presented in this report led to the proposal of several recommendations for realizing the main objectives of the overall project. The first recommendation is to carry out an experimental study to test the validity of the concepts and analysis presented in this report. The experimental study should include determination for actual and accurate mechanical properties of the AF material and its behavior under different environmental and loading conditions. Second, the concept of utilizing sensor technology integrated into the AF layer should be put to test when the mechanical properties are determined. Third, small-scale prototypes of the analyzed sections should subjected to explosive loads to verify the major findings of this research work, especially as regards resilience energy and failure modes.

NOTES

The authors would like to express their deepest gratitude to Ms. D. Said, Ms. N. Rashwan and Mr. O. Ibrahim, and Mr. A. Aglan for their contribution and assistance during the completion of this report.

BIBLIOGRAPHY

P. Heuper, "Fundamentals of Energy Infrastructure Security: Risk Mitigation in the International Environment," *Business Wire* (September 1, 2005), http://findarticles.com/p/articles/mi_m0EIN/is_2005_Sept_1/ai_n15336922.

N. Adams, "Terrorism and Oil," PenWell Corporation, Tulsa, Oklahoma, 2003.

"Pipeline Safety: Hazardous Liquid Pipelines Transporting Ethanol, Ethanol Blends, and Other Biofuels," *Federal Register* 72, no. 154, http://thefederalregister.com/d.p/2007-08-10-E7-15615.

A. O. Abd El Halim and R. Hafez, "Sensor Systems for Canadian Oil/Gas Pipeline Monitoring and Protection," final report submitted to NRCan Canada, March 2008.

M. Nessim Stephens and Q. Chen, "Risk-Based Optimization of Pipeline Integrity Maintenance Activities: Project 1-Methodology," Project 94006, Centre for Frontier Engineering Research, December 1994.

A. Farrell, H. Zerriffi, and H. Dowlatabadi, "Energy Infrastructure and Security," *Annual Review of Environmental Resources* 29:421–469.

"Pipeline Failure Causes," http://www.corrosion-doctors.org/Pipeline/Pipeline-failures.htm.

Yergin, D. "Ensuring Energy Security." 2007. http://dev.foreignaffairs.org/20060301faessay85206/daniel-yergin/ensuring-energy-security.html.

Wikipedia, "Pipeline Transport," http://en.wikipedia.org/wiki/Pipeline_transport.

Parfomak, P. "Pipeline Security: An Overview of Federal Activities and Current Policy Issues" (CRS Report for Congress, 2004), http://www.fas.org/sgp/crs/RL31990.pdf.

"Significant Pipeline Incident Details" http://primis.phmsa.dot.gov/comm/reports/safety/SigPSIDet_1987_2006_US.html#_all.

"Petrodollar Recycling and Global Imbalances," International Monetary Fund, http://www.imf.org/external/np/speeches/2006/032306a.htm#P39_5092.

"Energy Information Administration", http://www.eia.doe.gov/oiaf/economy/energy_price.html.

"Technological and Natural Hazards, Europe's Environment: The Third Assessment," http://reports.eea.europa.eu/environmental_assessment_report_2003_10/en/kiev_chapt_10.pdf.

Guy Pluvinage and Mohamed Hamdy Elwany, "Safety, Reliability and Risks Associated with Water, Oil and Gas Pipelines," NATO Science for Peace and Security Series, Springer Netherlands, December 14, 2007.

S. Bajpai and J. P. Gupta, "Securing Oil and Gas Infrastructure," *Journal of Petroleum Science and Engineering* 55, nos. 1–2:174–186. Pipeline Accident Report, Natural Gas Pipeline Rupture and Fire near Carlsbad, New Mexico, August 19, 2000, National Transportation Safety Board, Washington, D.C.

CHAPTER 9

Innovations in Trucking Security

Jarret Brachman

POST-9/11 SECURITY

The collective shock caused by the September 11, 2001, terrorist attacks spurred governments and companies around the world to think harder about their security protocols. Government agencies prioritized and expanded efforts for identifying tactical vulnerabilities in America's critical infrastructure and transportation sectors. Private industry invested billions of dollars into reviewing and updating existing protocols, developing new technologies, and interfacing in dynamic ways with new partners. Even university-based transportation research and education programs emerged dedicated to focusing the topic securing transportation infrastructure, assets and operations.

The trucking industry, like other transportation sectors, has wrestled with finding innovative and cost-effective solutions to address the security challenges facing it. Whereas most innovations within the trucking industry emerge in reaction to economic pressures, there is a growing awareness within the industry about the important social responsibility it also plays in keeping the country safe. There has been a growing internal recognition that trucking companies must protect expensive assets and inventory; prevent misuse, abuse, and theft of their equipment; and scrutinize the backgrounds of their personnel not just for profitability but for national security. The challenge is that the trucking industry needs to accomplish all of this and more while keeping costs manageable and maintaining efficiency in operations.

Many of the responses to 9/11 from both inside the trucking industry as well as from outside actors have been tactical in nature. In other words, the industry has focused many initiatives on short- to medium-range countermeasures, which are meant to limit an adversary's options or mitigate immediate physical damage. Questions like "How should the trucking industry best protect against the unauthorized use of its assets or theft of its hazardous cargo?" are tactical in nature. A number of steps have been taken to bolster the security situation of the industry. Companies have increased the overall level of scrutiny on access, credentialing, and oversight. The trucking industry, working in conjunction with government partners, has also sought to implement some strategic-level programs that concentrate on shoring up the long-term security of America's trucking system. These programs have included the Highway Watch program and the Trucking Security Program, both overseen by the Department of Homeland Security. Many of these programs, however, including the two aforementioned programs, have fallen by the wayside due to lack of interest, funding, or results.

Static and Dynamic Approaches to Security

There are at least two competing ways to think about how to secure a system. One is the more conventional understanding of security that views it as protecting "stuff" from "damage." The way that securitization of target assets or infrastructure is most often accomplished is through tactical solutions. In other words, this approach to security is focused more on physical protection and linear solutions. These solutions generally focus on restricting access and mitigating damage. The other model of security, however, is developing grounded in a nonlinear approach. In other words, this approach views the process of security as being rooted in networked solutions, in technology, and in communication. It presupposes that no static defense is more effective than dynamic, information-driven and integrated solutions.

The trucking industry differs, in many ways, from other forms of transportation in the United States. Whereas airports, rail yards, and maritime ports have all increased physical security of inventory and assets, the trucking system is an inherently open one. The industries primary assets, trucks, are almost always in motion. Open systems, like the trucking system, often have a variety of internal elements interacting dynamically with one another as well as with their environment. Because of the number and dynamism of the interactions in open systems, they are notoriously difficult to secure thinking in conventional ways. Static approaches simply do not work to secure dynamic, open systems. In other words, thinking about the trucking system as a front that needs to be defended is doomed to fail from the outset. There are simply too many openings for potential areas and opportunities for exploitation that it is impossible, even with the most advanced technology ready to mount an impenetrable defense.

This reality does not mean, however, that the trucking industry is destined to remain undefended. Rather, the most innovative advancements in the field vis-à-vis securitization have been those that approach security itself from a networked-based perspective. Rather than seeking to implement command decisions, for which security is considered to be defense, new approaches to trucking security view security from a control-based viewpoint. Steering mechanisms device command mechanisms are gaining popularity because they are driven by information and communication, all of which is made possible by emerging technology.

Trucks have been and will likely continue to be an instrument of choice for nefarious actors, in large part because of how multifaceted they are. Trucks can serve as intermediary delivery instruments in that they help to clandestinely transport cargo like explosives or explosives-related materials, hazardous materials, and other items from one place to another. Trucks can also be weaponized. In other words, by hijacking or illicitly seizing control of a truck, they can be driven into targets, packed with explosives and detonated, used for other such purposes. Although a multiplicity of security challenges faces the trucking industry today, there has been an equally dramatic diversity of innovations that have emerged in response to these challenges. This chapter will deal with touching on the exciting innovations affecting trucking security across three broad categories of interest for the trucking industry: cargo, assets and personnel. There have been notable advancements in each of these three fields since 9/11, both in terms of collective understanding as well as technical innovations.

TRUCKING INDUSTRY INITIATIVES

There has been a decisive prioritization of thinking about security across all spheres of the trucking industry in recent years. One positive metric is that the industry visibly and proudly recognizes its own accomplishments with regard to innovative thinking and practice with regard to trucking security. The Security Council of the American Trucking Associations (ATA), for instance, presents its "Security Professional of the Year" and "Excellence in Security Award" annually.[1] The ATA Security Council consists of professionals from the transportation security industry that represent motor carriers and organizations with a vested interest in trucking. The group's mission is to conduct relevant research, teaching, conducts training and facilitates dialogue across the industry. In 2008, the ATA bestowed the "Security Professional" award to the Knight Transportation, Inc.'s Corporate Security Director and the "Excellence in Security Award" to the Con-way Freight corporation.[2]

According to the ATA, these two awards are presented, "to the individual and company best demonstrating their ability to design, implement and manage a successful security program that not only addresses traditional threats to personnel, truck and cargo, but also encompasses anti-terrorism and emergency preparedness programs."[3] Richard Martin, who was awarded the 2008 Security Professional of the Year recognition, for example, was selected for managing an "extensive security program including employee screenings and training, cargo theft interdiction, investigations, as well as loss prevention and recovery."[4] Similarly, Con-way Freight was recognized as a company that had implemented a robust security plan designed to encompass both "traditional asset protection and innovative homeland security programs and training."[5] Jeanne Dumas, the ATA Security Council's director, said that "Con-way Freight led the way in examining, embracing and ably managing every available tool to better secure its employees, trucks and cargo."[6] It was Con-Way's initiatives aimed at furthering security protocols and understanding for their company as well as the overall national industry that, according to the ATA, was the basis on which they were given the prestigious recognition.

Although the trucking industry has pursued a number of efforts in recent years to increase security while maintaining efficiency, three particular innovations in how business is done stand out: running bonded freight, formalizing relationships with government agencies, and increasingly coordinating with trucking companies. Running bonded, or sealed, freight is by no means new for trucking companies. What has changed, however, is the ways in which freight moves, and the kinds of inspections the package may or may not be subjected to. The second point deals with the number of new government programs that have emerged since 9/11/2001 that are dedicated to harnessing cutting-edge technology in order to increase security without impacting, or at least minimizing the impact, on efficiency and throughput. The third point is that the trucking industry itself has adapted, finding ways innovative ways to share, coordinate and communicate with one another.

Tracking and Protecting Cargo

Wireless technology has revolutionized the way that most industries do business today. In fact, entire new industries have emerged due to the emergence and pervasive deployment of wireless technologies. It follows, then, that the trucking industry has found numerous ways to harness and customize these wireless tools. Many of these innovations in technology and protocols directly impact trucking security. The most significant advancements in wireless technology concern communication and tracking. In numerous ways, access to innovative wireless technologies as well as innovative use of existing wireless technologies have led to a more integrated security framework within the trucking industry. Wireless tracking technology affects everything from personnel access to inventory processes. In a security context, these innovations have led to better and more secure approaches to credentialing.

Communicating with assets and personnel is a key component of a networked-based approach to security within open systems. The trucking industry's use of communication tools has exponentially expanded over the past decade. There have been a number of technological innovations and refinements made in recent years that have dramatically increased the nature and scope of intersystem communication. Satellite-based and cellular-based communication, for example, have become the most common and pervasive. Offering wireless communication access that is virtually unbounded by geography, satellite phones, terminals, and cellular phones have given personnel and fleets unprecedented ability to communicate with one another. Real-time vehicle positioning tracking and stolen vehicle tracking systems have also offered new and continuously refined ways for owners to communicate with or know the geographic location of their assets in real-time.

Deploying such communication in the field, however, is not always without problem. Many states have begun implementing mandatory restrictions on cellular phone usage in vehicles without hands-free devices. In 2009, the New Jersey state senate's Law and Public Safety Committee voted to push a bill forward in the Senate that exempts truck drivers from the state's current restrictions on using cell phones and other two-way communication devices while driving. These kinds of technologies could, according to the proposed bill, actually be helpful for law enforcement in that it would empower truck drivers with the tools to readily communicate with law enforcement readily. In essence, it was painted as extending the eyes and ears of the New Jersey police. "New Jersey has invested significant training dollars in the private sector to educate the trucking industry on how to be an additional set of eyes and ears on our roadways when it comes to potential terrorist activity," Sen. Fred H. Madden Jr., D-Camden and Gloucester, said in a written statement.[7] The New Jersey trucking industry eagerly supported the bill. Doug Morris, Director of Security Operations for Owner Operator Independent Driver Association (OOIDA), said that, "using the eyes and ears of truckers is critical. Truckers are skilled communicators when it comes to watchdogging our nation's infrastructure."

With the aid of technological innovations, many of which are employed worldwide across sector, trucking is no longer an opaque system. On the contrary, networked-based communication innovations have made this open system more transparent than ever before. Some less pervasive but still popular communication technology innovations that have relevance to trucking security include in-vehicle Internet access, automated in-vehicle route guidance via global position, real-time traffic information, and even radar-based collision warning systems.

Radio frequency identification (RFID) technology has emerged in recent years as an effective and inexpensive way for companies to gain powerful levels of visibility over all aspects of their supply chains. The two categories of RFID in use today include active and passive. Passive RFID tags do not initiate transmissions to a source; in fact, they lack an internal or onboard energy source. Rather, they passively collect specific, targeted information, that can only be activated by a reader with sufficient access. These tags tend to be simple, inexpensive and even disposable.

The other kind of RFID tags, known as "active RFIDs," can be read like passive RFIDs but can also initiate their own transmissions of data back to a source. Although active tags tend to be more complex and expensive than passive RFID tags, they offer expanded range and capabilities. While RFID readers can monitor cargo containers even when they are in being shipped via ships and trains, companies often lose visibility over their inventory when it is moving via truck. "The lack of RFID readers near many remote highways creates an [intermodal black hole] where passive RFID chips cannot be read," says Rick Kessler, CIO of Horizon Lines.[8] Importantly, passive RFID tags have no internal power source, which means that the only way to transmit their data is to have them come in contact with RFID readers. The range of these readers tends to be limited to a span of several feet. On the other hand, active RFID tags are powered by an internal source. They can contact readers up to approximately 300 feet and can read data at speeds of up to seventy-five miles per hour.

Both active and passive RFID tags have greatly expanded the trucking industry's ability to monitor the status and security of its assets and cargo. RFIDs, for instance, have been deployed on cargo seals in order to passively or actively log tampering or breaches into specific areas. Competing with RFID seals are infrared seals, which rely on a close-proximity, line-of-sight infrared beam; contact seals, which require a physical link between the reader device and the seal; and remote reporting seals, in which each seal relays integrity data to its reader by way of satellite or cellular communications. These remote reader seals are more expensive but do significantly enhance global visibility thanks to built-in GPS capability and virtually global access enabled by the remote communications platform.

Government Initiatives

The trucking industry has both increased its focus on and expanded its understanding of trucking security. No longer is it sufficient to think about security in terms of conventional ways, encompassing things like loss prevention; now thinking must include homeland security programs and interaction with federal, state, and local government security, law enforcement, and emergency management agencies. To do that, however, the trucking industry has had to implement existing and emerging technologies and protocols in innovative ways as well as innovate new technologies and protocols. Part of this innovation in thinking has involved increasing partnerships with federal government agencies.

Schneider National, Inc., for instance, is one of several nationwide trucking companies who have sought to be at the forefront of thinking on trucking security. In their efforts, they have collaborated with a number of security agencies, including the Department of Homeland Security's Transportation Security Administration and the FBI. Schneider also participates on the Coordinating Council of the Highway and Motor Carrier Sector, and in the government Customs-Trade Partnership Against Terrorism (C-TPAT) program.[9] The C-TPAT is administered by the Customs and Border Protection agency, which is under the Department of Homeland Security. It is a program that is designed to develop and sustain relationships between government and private industry in order to enhance cargo and border security. By bringing together consolidators, importers, manufactures, and participants in the international supply chain, including the trucking industry, the C-TPAT program has been generally viewed as a key step forward for government-to-business collaboration in a post-9/11 security environment.

In short, the C-TPAT guidelines seek to streamline the process of cargo container movement and inspection. C-TPAT helps to ensure that trucking companies store containers in the proper way and try to enforce the correct implementation of container seals. It seeks to ensure that containers remain sealed once loaded. C-TPAT enforces shipping and receiving companies who deal with containers to establish and implement written protocols that articulate specific container seal handling. C-TPAT also requires that clear protocols are stated that explain how to handle container seal breaches or suspected tampering. The program forces companies to restrict access to specific employees within a company by limiting the distribution of container seals. In the C-TPAT program, each participating company receives a unique number for identification purposes. This "Status Verification Interface" (SVI) allows these companies to participate in other cargo transfer streamlining programs, including the Free and Secure Trade (FAST) program, another government-administered initiative designed to help shipping companies streamline their business while maintaining a high level of security. The program seeks to identify compliant and known companies importing into the United States from either Canada or Mexico by way of highway modes of transportation. Importantly, all trucks that are entering the United States from Mexico that seek to enter by way of the FAST program must be carrying goods manufactured by a C-TPAT-approved Mexican company. Additionally, the American company importing those goods must also be approved by the C-TPAT program. The highway carrier or trucking firm moving the goods must be both FAST-and C-TPAT-certified. Finally, the commercial truck driver needs to have been approved and must hold an up-to-date FAST license.

One of the important benefits of the FAST program is that it allows Customs and Border Protection (CBP) officers to dedicate their resources to higher-risk shippers and shipments. The programs target goal is to reduce the time-lag that CBP cargo inspections take, which serves to expedite the overall border clearance timeline. This is good both for the government inspection process and private industry, as border delays are bad for security and bad for business.

A number of other government-sponsored programs also seek to facilitate cargo movement domestically and internationally. The U.S. government encourages companies to increase their own security protocols vis-à-vis international suppliers through the National Customs Automated Prototype (NCAP) program and the Pre-Arrival Processing System (PAPS) program. The government runs a border cargo release program known as the Customs Automated Commercial System (ACS). Using bar code technology, the program seeks to increase the speed at which commercial shipments are released. The security measures are still in place, however, because of the complementary implementation of the Border Cargo Selectivity (BCS) and Automated

Targeting System (ATS) programs. Other government-sponsored programs includes the Transportation Security Administration's efforts to increase scrutiny and visibility over those drivers with access to hazardous materials. The TSA classifies hazardous materials as including "gasoline, explosives, radioactive and infectious substances, propane, chlorine, acids, ammonia and other poisonous gases."[10] The TSA reported in 2008 that it had completed fingerprint-based background checks on over 1 million truck drivers to ensure that commercial truckers applying for the Hazardous Material Endorsement (HME) on a commercial driver's license were of no security threat or risk to the United States.[11] TSA deputy administrator Gale Rossides said that "truckers are another set of eyes on the road and are part of the security network." According to Rossides, truckers "play a vital role in keeping our freeways, streets, counties and cities safe."[12]

Glitches in the System

Collaboration between business and government, and even between governments, has not been without some glitches. Recently, Canadian truckers doing business at ports in the United States have needed to obtain documentation known as transportation worker identification credential (TWIC) cards. The U.S. Congress mandated the TWIC program under the Maritime Security Act, making the TWIC card a requirement for commercial truck drivers and any other relevant personnel who require unescorted access into secure port areas. The frustration on the Canadian side is that even though the Free and Secure Trade (FAST) card requires background checks, Canadian trucker drivers must also obtain TWIC cards, something viewed by many as redundant and unnecessary bureaucracy. Making matters more frustrating, in order to acquire a TWIC card, drivers must appear in person at a TWIC enrollment center for an interview. The application process then takes up to one month. If accepted, the applicant must return to the same center to get their card. If it is rejected, there is an appeal process.

On June 1, 2009, the United States implemented a program called the Western Hemisphere Travel Initiative. This program mandated that anyone crossing into Canada through the United States be in possession of a valid passport, FAST card, enhanced driver's license, or other valid and acceptable form of identification. In response to the growing frustration with redundant identification mechanisms, background checks and time delays, the United States is seeking ways to consolidate and streamline security measures. A spokesman for the Transportation Security Administration, Greg Soule, said in 2009 that the TSA is "looking at ways to consolidate various certifications and background checks."[13]

On January 8, 2009, the inspector general of the Department of Homeland Security (DHS) released a review that examined the success of the Federal Trucking Industry Security Grant Program. The program had been awarded to, and was administered by, the American Trucking Associations' Highway

Watch program for three consecutive years. While the inspector general's report applauded the fact that the program enrolled more than 800,000 members, it faulted the program's enrollment strategy, its security incident documentation and its internal program tracking. In its formal response, the ATA stated, "From the time ATA first received federal funds in mid-March 2004 through mid-2008, ATA trained and enrolled well over 800,000 highway and motor carrier professionals in the domain awareness and reporting program." The ATA argued that it "successfully accomplished this [even though there were] difficulties posed by numerous changes in agencies responsible for overseeing the program, changes in government-dictated program priorities and management, and uneven DHS involvement in the cooperative venture."[14] The fact remains that even the best-intentioned collaborative efforts between the U.S. government and private industry in the field of trucking security can fail.

Emerging Cooperation

There have been numerous examples of instances in which trucking companies have sought to coordinate with one another in new and dynamic ways. For instance, Schneider National, Inc., recently held a customer security summit in April 2008 that focused on identifying new and useful procedures for implementing transportation security across the industry. The participants involved in the conference included leading rail and highway carriers, manufacturing companies, security agencies and companies, and representatives from the California Highway Patrol. The goal of the summit was for these groups to take a forward perspective on breaches in supply chain security. Schneider's director of enterprise security summed up the goal of the summit by saying, "Our customers depend on us to ensure their products are being received and delivered securely and efficiently. By coming together with leaders in the industry, we were able to identify shared security gaps and put in place best practices and procedures to ensure tighter security within the transportation supply chain."[15]

In 2008, the American Trucking Associations (ATA) released their ATA Certified Cargo Security Professional Resource Guidebook (CCSP). The 186-page guidebook offers an in-depth summary of motor carrier security from pickup to delivery. Its goal is to help its readers better manage risk and understand the kind of security protocols that are appropriate and necessary across physical, facility, information, computer, or personnel security. The CCSP guidebook reviews a number of case studies across sectors, including logistics, hazardous materials, emergency management, intermodal, border, and food security. The ATAs' president and CEO described the importance of the book by noting, "Securing the transportation infrastructure and supply chain against potential acts of cargo theft, natural disaster, organized crime and even terrorism is a critical piece of the homeland security effort. ATA established the CCSP Certification and accompanying CCSP Resource

Guidebook to address this vital need by expanding and unifying our industry's approach to security."[16]

RETHINKING TRUCKING SECURITY FUNDING AND EXPENSES

Federal funding to private industry and academic partners has been another post-9/11 innovation in the field of trucking security. Perhaps the most notable federal grant program had been the Trucking Security Program (TSP), sponsored by the Department of Homeland Security. In 2009, DHS awarded the TSP grant to a company called Total Security Services International, Inc. TSSI, serving as the prime contractor, worked in conjunction with TSA and Federal Emergency Management Agency (FEMA) officials, as well as with representatives of Hampton University and Allbaugh International, in order to develop deployable plans for bolstering speed and efficiency for transporting and distributing supplies and commodities during catastrophic events.[17]

Although the TSP grants were originally meant to aid in personnel training with regard to identifying and reporting security threats, the funds have been increasingly spent to buy, install, and upgrade physical infrastructure and assets. Because DHS lacked a sound methodology informed by a risk-based calculation for awarding TSP grants, the program was terminated after its 2009 program year.

FUTURE DIRECTIONS FOR TRUCKING SECURITY

Although trucks may be operating in the system the majority of time, they are not always in motion. When parked at truck stops so that truck operators can obtain the required amount of rest each day, trucks are notably susceptible to theft, vandalism, and other criminal activities. In March 2009, Jason Rivenburg, a truck driver resting at the site of a former gas station in South Carolina, was shot to death during a robbery attempt. As a result, U.S. Representative Paul Tonko (D-N.Y.), introduced a bill in Jason's memory aimed at providing grant money for bolstering security and the overall conditions of truck stops across the United Sates. "Jason's Law," as the proposed bill became known, was aimed at establishing a pilot program to last six years.[18] The program would fund up to $120 million for grants for which local governments and private companies could apply in order to deal with the shortage of parking for commercial vehicles on the National Highway System. The grants would also be aimed at providing funding for other efforts, including the construction of safety rest areas, capital improvements to public commercial motor vehicle parking facilities currently closed on a seasonal basis, and constructing turnouts along the National Highway System for commercial motor vehicles.

The Owner-Operators Independent Drivers Association (OOIDA) rapidly issued a public letter of support for the bill and alerted its 160,000 members, asking them to contact their representatives and urge them to pass the bill. OOIDA Executive Vice President Todd Spencer said, "Tonko's bill is a 'good one' that would benefit truckers who struggle daily to find secure truck parking."[19]

Other areas of concern that will need to be addressed in upcoming years include the issue of security in high-crime and high-violence areas. Mark Koumans, who was the deputy assistant secretary in the Office of International Affairs, testified before the House Appropriations Committee Subcommittee on Homeland Security Appropriations that (echoing the Homeland Security Secretary Janet Napolitano) "Mexico right now has issues of violence that are a different degree and level than we've ever seen before."[20] The nearly 6,000 drug-related murders that occurred in Mexico in 2008 were doubled the previous high. Nearly half of those murders occurred in three Mexican states: Chihuahua, Sinaloa, and Baja California. The fact is that the networks of organized crime operating along the U.S.–Mexico border are well funded and well armed. They now operate on both sides of the border, something that has led to calls for commercial truckers to stay on toll roads, which they are more protected, if possible. Drivers are also encouraged to continuously check their cell phone coverage, report in at all stops, call before and after deliveries, and establish a "duress code" that can be used if they are being threatened. These are preventive measures and useful protocols that may help to prevent some of the border violence being seen against truckers. It is, however, tactical in nature, and will not serve to stop the violence over time.

CONCLUSION

Since the terrorist attacks of September 11, 2001, the United States has sought to improve its level of security across all industries, and particularly in the transportation sector. All modes of transportation increased their awareness of, and dedication to, combating the threat of terrorism, among other threats to national security. Whereas much attention has been paid to the commercial aviation and maritime shipping sectors, less research and public focus has been placed on evolutions in trucking security.

This chapter sought to identify some of the important recent innovations with regard to trucking security. Some of these solutions were technical in nature. RFIDs and wireless communication have opened nearly limitless possibilities for trucking companies to increase their visibility on nearly every step of the supply chain, their assets, their personnel, and more. Other innovations discussed in this chapter focused on the process of doing business in a secure way. This process included new efforts from both within the trucking community as well as efforts to formalize and streamline interaction between the trucking community and the federal government. The chapter identified some federal programs that have been initiated and subsequently terminated due to lack of results. It also reviewed a number of important federal programs that relate to the credentialing of truck operators for national security reasons. Finally, the chapter highlighted several important issues facing the trucking community, particularly that of secure stopping and secure transborder driving.

NOTES

1. The American Trucking Associations' (ATA) Web site is available at http://www.truckline.com/Pages/Home.aspx.

2. The ATA's Security Awards Web site can be found at http://www.truckline.com/federation/councils/security/pages/securityawards.aspx.

3. The ATA's Security Awards Web site can be found at http://www.truckline.com/fedcration/councils/security/pages/securityawards.aspx.

4. The ATA's Security Awards Web site can be found at http://www.truckline.com/federation/councils/security/pages/securityawards.aspx.

5. The ATA's Security Awards Web site can be found at http://www.truckline.com/federation/councils/security/pages/securityawards.aspx.

6. "ATA's Security Council Honors Top Efforts in Field," *The Security Council of American Trucking Associations*, May 7, 2008, http://www.thetrucker.com/News/Stories/2008/5/7/ATAsSecurityCouncilhonorstopeffortsinfield.aspx.

7. "New Jersey Bill Seeks Help of Truckers in Reporting Suspicious Activities," *Land Line Magazine*, May 22, 2009, http://www.landlinemag.com/todays_news/Daily/2009/May09/051809/052209-01.htm.

8. Marc L. Songini, "Trucking Firm Turns to RFID to Fill Black Hole—Uses Active Tags to Track Containers to Alaska," *Computer World*, February 13, 2007, http://www.computerworld.com/action/article.do?command=viewArticleBasic&articleId=9011214.

9. "Vulnerability of High-Value Merchandise within the Supply Chain Raises Need for New Collaborative Security Solutions," *Schneider National Press Release*, April 15, 2008, http://www.schneider.com/news/News_Archive/UT_001120.

10. "TSA Completes Background Checks on Over 1 Million Truckers," *Transportation Security Agency Press Release*, December 29, 2008, http://www.tsa.gov/press/releases/2008/1229.shtm.

11. "TSA Completes Background Checks on Over 1 Million Truckers," *Transportation Security Agency Press Release*, December 29, 2008, http://www.tsa.gov/press/releases/2008/1229.shtm.

12. "TSA Completes Background Checks on Over 1 Million Truckers," *Transportation Security Agency Press Release*, December 29, 2008, http://www.tsa.gov/press/releases/2008/1229.shtm.

13. Tom Peters, "Security demands slow truckers: New TWIC Cards a Cash Grab, Industry Says." *The Chronicle Herald*, June 5, 2009, http://thechronicleherald.ca/Business/1125708.html.

14. Dorothy Cox, "OIG report critical of Highway Watch; ATA Defends Program's Success," *The Trucker*, January 23, 2009, http://www.thetrucker.com/News/Stories/2009/1/23/OIGreportcriticalofHighwayWatchATAdefendsprogramssuccess.aspx.

15. "Schneider National Security Summit Covers Supply Chain Solutions," *Security Solutions* (April 29, 2008), http://securitysolutions.com/news/schneider-security-summit-0429/.

16. "Trucking Cargo Security Guidebook Released for Truckers," *Government Security*, December 22, 2008, http://govtsecurity.com/news/trucking-cargo-guidebook/.

17. "TSSI Scores Homeland Security Grant," *Fleet Owner*, May 7, 2009, http://fleetowner.com/management/tssi-homeland-security-grant-0507/.

18. "New Jersey Bill Seeks Help of Truckers in Reporting Suspicious Activities," *Land Line Magazine*, May 22, 2009, p. 22.

19. "New Jersey Bill Seeks Help of Truckers in Reporting Suspicious Activities," *Land Line Magazine*, May 22, 2009, p. 22.

20. Testimony of Deputy Assistant Secretary Mark Koumans, Office of International Affairs, before the House Appropriations Committee Subcommittee on Homeland Security Appropriations, "Secure Border Initiative (SBI), Control of the Land Border, and DHS Response to Violence on the Border with Mexico," March 10, 2009, http://www.dhs.gov/ynews/testimony/testimony_1237218661657.shtm.

CHAPTER 10

Integrating Airport Operations into the Global Supply Chain

Mohammad Karimbocus

The importance of the global supply chain has grown substantially over the past decades in the wake of globalization and the ensuing recourse to outsourcing of economic activities. Civil aviation, an important facilitator of the global supply chain, has its own "internal supply chain" in the form of its various support services. Aviation's supply chain shares an interesting parallel with the global supply chain. The latter bears the strong influence of global variations in work culture, legislation, quality, and so on. In the same way, air transport's supply chain is affected by differing mindsets on the part of the various services, depending on their nature: safety, enforcement, or commercial.

AVIATION'S SUPPLY CHAIN: MYTH OR REALITY?

To the uninitiated, the existence of a supply chain in aviation might seem a superfluous idea. This is understandable, given that any form of linkage between the various services might not be apparent at first sight. However, a more analytical look clearly makes the link evident. In fact, each service can potentially impact on every other service. For instance, let us consider the following:

- Tedious processing, whether at check-in, security, or border control, can result in bottlenecks and slowing of the passenger flow, thus delaying boarding.
- Delay-inducing air traffic control (ATC) procedures may prolong flight times and delay flights.
- Cumbersome airside operations might adversely affect aircraft readiness for flight.

It becomes clear that each of the above inefficiencies (and many others as well) would reduce efficiency elsewhere. This can have the form of reduced gate availability, increased occupancy of active areas (runways and taxiways), prolonged use of terminals due to delayed boarding, and constraints to airline operations planning. Also, passengers could miss their onward connections, and the ripple effects could also be felt at destination airports, especially those where slots are at a premium. In fact, there can be endless examples of such induced reductions in efficiency and efficacy in aviation. And when the question is about inefficiency, we inevitably think in terms of added costs.

For the air transport industry to operate with maximum efficiency, it follows that its internal supply chain must be functioning as seamlessly as possible. In practical terms, this implies the existence of a collaborative culture across the whole aviation spectrum. But it seems that on this front, aviation has been the victim of its own phenomenal success over the past decades. In fact, the massive growth in demand for air travel has resulted in equally significant growth in workload for all support services, and collaboration needs have grown proportionately. Quite paradoxically, with more resources being required to tackle the higher workloads, lesser consideration has been given to interservice collaboration. In fact, in today's environment, the general perception is that almost every service is operating in a pseudo-standalone manner with little regard to other service providers.

As the growth of the aviation has surpassed even the most optimistic forecasts, considerable efforts have been made at every level to stem the tide of constantly growing workloads. However, as far as the long-term sustainability of the industry is concerned, all these efforts seem to be inadequate.

THE STATE OF THINGS IN AVIATION

Before trying to figure out ways and means to foster the viability of air transport in the long term, it is necessary to assess the state of things. The most notable observations are as follows:

- Aviation development requires very substantial resources, and equally long lead times.
- Thanks to the quantum leap in information technology (IT), there has been an ever-growing recourse to automation to stem the tide of constantly increasing workloads. Nowadays, automation is present across the whole spectrum of civil aviation; its capabilities increase by the day. A simple comparison between old and current systems (be it aircraft cockpits, passenger processing systems, or ATC tools) shows the massive transformation of service provision over time. In fact, new generation personnel would find it hard to conceive of past eras' manual provision of all services. However, the advent of automation has a very high cost, and another pertinent aspect is that very little has been done to foster any sort of collaboration between the various stakeholders.

- Various attempts at innovation are being undertaken by almost all services. For instance, measures such as common-use facilities, self-service and remote passenger registration facilities, and a host of others have been introduced over time. Similarly, massive improvements have been made to air navigation systems and ATC capability. These innovations have effectively offered the ability to handle ever-growing workloads and have resulted in substantial capacity increase.

- Air travelers are required to call in well ahead of their proposed departure times, but seem to spend most of the time queuing at various inevitable preflight processes, or idling around for long periods in sterile areas.

- Machine-readable recognition technology is gradually taking over from manual border control; impending biometric-based systems will further enhance this service.

- In the same way, attempts have been made to revamp aviation security (especially after the tightening up of security procedures in the aftermath of security events) with such elements as behavior pattern recognition (BPR), advance profiling, and so forth. But, here again, limited success seems to have been achieved in terms of reduction of inconvenience to the traveler. In fact, there appears to be a general acceptance that security processes cannot be hassle-free.

- Based on traditional assessments of capacity, the aviation infrastructure is unable to expand in a manner proportionate with the growth in demand because of the strong competition for land and other resources with other sectors, as well as ever-increasing concerns for the environment.

- In the same way, it would be impossible for human resource requirements to grow proportionately with the increase in demand for air travel.

- There has been raised awareness for the long-term sustainability of air transport from both the economic and environmental viewpoints. This has resulted in all services' showing better awareness of costs, and of the need to curb aviation's polluting ability.

- Time and again, aviation is at the receiving end of special attention that can prove very costly. Security and environmental issues have, for instance, inflicted additional costs.

RECONCILING DEMAND WITH CAPACITY

The above analysis makes it clear that the aviation industry is at a crossroads with regard to its long-term sustainability. On the one hand, the demand for air travel is bound to maintain its unrelenting growth for as long as can be foreseen (it could be argued that periods of economic downturn would affect growth, but if past occurrences are any indication, the industry would rebound robustly after every setback), but on the other hand, the industry would have to contend with constraints to airspace and airport capacity. This leads to very simple evidence: a more judicious use of infrastructure lies with increasing the fluidity of air traffic flow, so long as airport passenger flows are accelerated, airside operations are streamlined for efficient slot use, and ATC efficiency is increased (although with due regard for safety norms).

THE WAY FORWARD: RESTORING AVIATION'S INTERNAL SUPPLY CHAIN

Given the inherent linkage between the various services, it follows that the potential for significant efficiency gains in aviation lies through restoring its internal supply chain. This can be achieved through

- Reinstating the culture of close and high level collaboration between all stakeholders
- Keeping track of resource utilization
- Spreading the concept of advance information across the whole aviation spectrum

COLLABORATIVE CULTURE

Collaboration involves the sharing of pertinent data for the efficient provision of services. It is a fact that in these days of high workload, services would be unable to devote adequate human resources for data exchange, and at any rate manual collaboration would prove cumbersome. However, technological advances have allowed for the possibility of automated data interchange in a nonintrusive manner. The most evident illustration is the ATS interfacility data communications (AIDC) concept used in ATC for automated coordination between contiguous ATC units.

MONITORING THE USE OF FACILITIES

Here again the most appropriate reference would be the provision of ATC. This safety nature of this service inherently requires the monitoring of airspace. Constant real-time surveillance of air traffic provides the potential for improved capacity. In the same way, the notion of apron control would enable a real-time tracking of airport infrastructure.

ADVANCE INFORMATION

This concept has existed down through living memory, used by many services:

- Airline flight planning has always been done such that air crews have knowledge of navigation, weather, and other information ahead of operating a flight.
- ATC ensures that air traffic flows globally in a safe, efficient, regular, and seamless manner, thanks to advance flow of necessary navigation information among ATC providers through a process called coordination.
- As far as possible, aircraft operators do acquire advance data such as seat allocation, dietary preferences, and so on to properly plan their operations.
- Airlines are also increasingly making use of real-time aircraft and engine "health" monitoring such that maintenance crews are ready and waiting once the aircraft reaches the gate.
- Advance passenger data is required in some areas, though primarily for enforcement purposes.

Just as with the AIDC concept, "machine-to-machine" communications in data form is a reality nowadays. The Aeronautical Fixed Telecommunication Network (AFTN), Automatic Dependent Surveillance (ADS), Aircraft Communications Addressing and Reporting Systems (ACARS), and Departure Control Systems (DCS) are all vivid examples of automation in information dissemination. And the projected implementation of the Aeronautical Telecommunications Network (ATN) by the International Civil Aviation Organization (ICAO) should further streamline the global dissemination of data within the civil aviation spectrum.

THE CREATION OF AN AVIATION OPERATIONAL MANAGEMENT SYSTEM

It becomes clear that the sole way to foster a collaborative culture within the aviation industry is through the ability for information to flow seamlessly. Of course, it would be utterly impractical and costly to expect one-to-one contact between the various services. The most plausible idea would be to create a central aviation operational management system using the hub-and-spoke principle. Actually, this tool would provide the appropriate connection between the automated systems in use at each and every service. Through preset parameters, essential data such as landing estimates, passenger data, gate allocation, and many others would be automatically captured and disseminated. An interesting feature would be the possibility of real-time updates of such elements as estimates, delays, aircraft handling status, gate availability, passenger "position" in the terminal, and so on, would be fed into the system through connection to the very sources of the data. This would ensure that very reliable information is being exchanged in a timely manner and would definitely enhance provision of services. And FIDS would display constantly accurate and updated data in the same way as flight progress displays on in-flight-entertainment systems, which are being perpetually updated, being linked to the aircraft's navigation system.

The idea of automatic and advance dissemination of information within a network is not novel in itself. In fact, it could be benchmarked on the AFTN switching system, which has existed for years. In fact, the AFTN switching system is a very vivid example of advance flow of aeronautical data, though it is restricted to mostly ATC use.

Figure 10.1 depicts the structure of the operational management system.

THE AVIATION OPERATIONAL MANAGEMENT SYSTEM IN ACTION

- Advance Passenger Processing

Advance processing is primarily meant to enhance capacity, but at the same time can potentially alleviate the inconveniences to which travelers are generally subjected by making possible the notion of "one-stop" processing. The

Figure 10.1
The Aviation Operational Management System

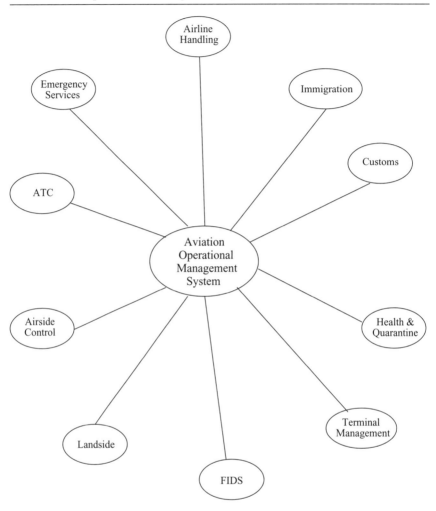

concept of advance processing would call for a rethink of the way services (especially enforcement ones) are provided. There would be higher "back room" activity and reduced "front line" presence.

The concept of advance processing would work on the premise that the only instance where the potential air traveler spends relatively significant instance would be at the time of booking for travel (whether it is online or at the travel agent's). It would operate based on the following steps:

Step 1: Essential personal information such as recognition data, travel authority, and so forth is acquired at time of booking and stored in the airline reservation system.

Step 2: At a preset time ahead of the scheduled departure of the flight under consideration, the passenger list, together with relevant data, is transferred to operational management system.

Step 3: Passenger list is relayed to services concerned. Due regard is given for cases of short-notice booking.

Step 4: Services concerned resort to advance processing of data supplied. This would, in practice, involve matching received data with available databases for authenticity verification, and so on. In this way, passengers in need of special attention, whether by customs, immigration, security, or any other service, would be identified ahead of being present at the airport.

Step 5: Each service sends a processing report to the operational management system, which in turn relays it to the airline handling facility for eventual use at passenger check-in.

Step 6: Check-in should in fact be a one-stop processing for most travelers. Input resulting from Step 3 would have identified those in need for specific processing. Passengers having already been given the "green light" at Step 3 would be given necessary guidance for onward flow, while others would be directed to the appropriate services for further processing. This would equally apply for both in-airport and remote check-in.

Step 7: The check-in phase would have now identified what can be termed as definite travelers, and the operational management system would relay the data supplied from the check-in process to all services concerned. Passengers targeted for more thorough security processing would have been identified, thus easing up the workload of aviation security. At this stage, it is pertinent to note that airline departure control systems inevitably call for all airline handling processes to be linked.

Step 8: In the same way, border control would have advance knowledge of the definite travelers, and this data would be available at immigration gates. Immigration processing would then be resumed to matching data of the traveler with the stored information. This would be especially convenient when an electronic recognition standard is adopted globally, and would lead to automated immigration gates (perhaps, automated access used in land-based mass transit systems could provide some inspiration in this respect).

Step 9: Border control functions coupled with interlining enable the real-time updating of passenger lists for each and every flight, thus facilitating the eventual boarding process.

Step 10: When boarding is complete, the airline handling station is supplied with final passenger list together with personal data for transmission to the destination station. That would include all interlining at destination.

Step 11: Upon reception of passenger list of an incoming flight, and at a preset time before scheduled arrival, the operational management system at destination would relay the data to all the services concerned so that, again, advance processing is effected.

The issue of short flights could be seen as a challenge for the timely dispatch of passenger data to destination airports in the sense that passenger data would be received closer to landing than for medium and long flights. However, it should be noted that mostly low- to medium-capacity aircraft are used for such flights. The smaller passenger count would mean shorter processing times and would thus significantly offset the time constraints in sending processed data to the arrival station. At any rate, the appropriate protocol would be in place for such situations.

Step 12: Given the prior filtering of passenger lists and identification of travelers requiring special attention, including transfer passengers, border control functions would be greatly enhanced for arrivals as well. The possibility for automated gates at arrival would also be real.

The principle guiding such processing would be that at the first stop in the departure terminal (check-in or baggage drop as appropriate), the necessary directions would be given, and services "down the line" updated on the status of the passenger.

A pictorial representation of advance processing, including the transmission of passenger data to destination stations is given in Figures 10.2A and 10.2B.

The underlying property of the operational management tool would be to ensure that information flow is seamless within the aviation system, and—more

Figure 10.2A
Advance Acquisition and Processing of Passenger Data

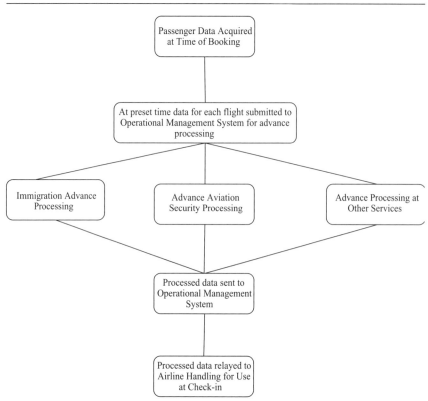

Figure 10.2B
Airport Passenger Handling and Transfer of Data

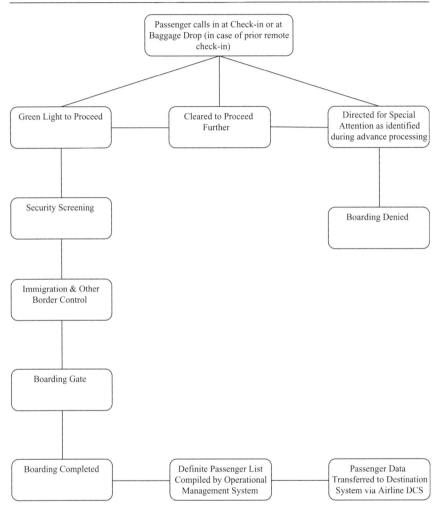

important—that it reaches the service provider ahead of the traveler, being present for pre- and post- travel processes. On the monitoring front, real-time tracking of airside handling status, and passenger flow in the terminal would be a major feature.

• Resource Management

Step 1: Estimates of arriving flights are input into the operational management system. The initial source of this information would be the airline handling agent through messaging from the departure station, and it would be subsequently updated by ATC.

Step 2: Based on established parameters, gate allocation would also be provided well ahead of time.

Step 3: Airside control ensures that the allocated gate is available in a timely manner by ensuring that it is free from previous occupancy. Its roving units are on the airside for monitoring.

Step 4: Airside control takes note of any ATC delay both in the air and on the ground in the event of congestion on maneuvering areas as it readies itself for the incoming flight.

Step 5: Flight enters gate and aircraft is on block.

Step 6: Airside roving unit maintains general oversight of airside activity, ensuring that handling is being effected with due respect to efficiency and safety criteria. It regularly sends situation reports to airside control and, on an ad hoc basis, notifies of any contingency. This enables all stakeholders to be aware of the state of things on the airside, especially when there is potential for delay (which would require alternate arrangements for ensuing arriving flights).

Step 7: At a preset time before the estimated time of departure from the gate, airside roving unit reports "flight status," with subsequent updates when necessary. This information is essential for both the assessment of gate availability, and for ATC to plan the flow of air traffic movement both on the ground and in the air. In this way, it would be possible to predict gate availability far enough in advance to optimize allocation.

The various steps on the monitoring and control function of the operational management system are detailed in Figure 10.3.

• Contingencies

Contingencies are part and parcel of any activity, and air transport is no exception. Admittedly, formidable technological progress now means that modern flying machines have a level of reliability that could not have been thought of at the infancy of modern civil aviation. These have significantly reduced emergency occurrence rates. However, risks of contingencies are real, and all stakeholders have devised emergency plans to cope with them.

During contingencies, there is an ever greater need for cooperation, and, ironically, services might be stretched and be unable to allocate sufficient resources for information interchange. Here again, the operational management system would prove very useful in providing the means for the automated dissemination of constantly updated data regarding the event at hand. It could also be the basis for better coordination in the deployment of resources for handling the emergency. Further, the prompt availability of information would definitely enhance the quality of emergency response, with ensuing consequences regarding risk attenuation.

For this function, and just as in all other automated networks, the operational management system would be "fitted" with appropriate aural and visual alarms to trigger for necessary attention at all services.

Figure 10.3
Airside Control and Monitoring

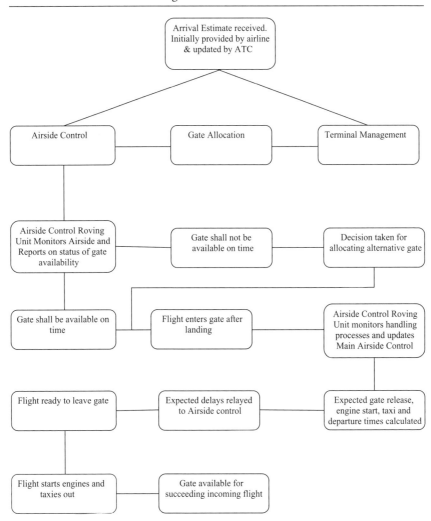

When the issue is about contingencies, this also implies the eventual return to normalcy. In order to maximize resource utilization, it would be necessary to predict (with reasonable accuracy) when normal operations would be reinstated. Through the operational management system, services would be in a better position to alleviate the disruptions triggered by the contingency event.

CHARACTERISTICS OF THE OPERATIONAL MANAGEMENT SYSTEM

• Accuracy and Conciseness of Data

From the beginning of modern civil aviation, great care has been taken for accuracy and conciseness in the dissemination of information. Appropriate codes have been devised at the very outset by ICAO and also user groups for making data concise. The operational management tool would follow the same rules regarding dissemination of data. And, since it would be the linkage between the various services, it would also have to provide the interface between different coding systems.

- Automated Data Flow

Since the system would establish a "machine-to-machine" link, information capture and flow would be automated, thus doing away with manual sharing of data.

- Ongoing Monitoring

Every operational aspect of airport activity would be the subject of constant real time monitoring. In fact, the operational management system, through its link with the various services, would disseminate highly accurate and constantly updated data such as status of passenger processing, landing estimates, status of aircraft handling on the airside, flights leaving the gate, taxiing and departing, and so on. It is evident that this would inject real benefits in terms of efficiency gains. It would also allow for the timely identification of any impediment to normal operations.

- One-Stop Processing

Air travel inevitably has a number of pre- and post-flight processes. Each service acquires and processes specific information and thereafter makes decisions that have a direct incidence on passenger flow. The airport management system, through its advance processing function, ensures that all appropriate decisions have been made and have been relayed to check-in so that the traveler is correctly directed to the next step based on whether or not he or she has been singled out for special attention beforehand. Consequently, for the average passenger, processing would be concentrated at check-in.

- Network Security

The tool would be basically a closed network with no link to the public domain. Thus the risks inherent to public-key systems would not be present

Transfers between different operational management systems would normally consist of actual passenger data once a flight has departed and should be effected via established links such as those used by departure control systems, which have sufficient protection from harmful interference. It is assumed that the projected ATN would also provide the required security.

However, the seamless flow of data within the system would be subject to the necessary protocols having been established between the various services for the nonintrusive capture of information.

• Human Resource Requirements

It must be admitted that with the advent of automation, competency needs of human resources have changed drastically. The operational management system would also change the role of the human element. Firstly, the need for advance processing would mean that there would be more background advance activity, while front line presence requirements could be reduced. Background activity would also include the management of the links with other stakeholders. It should however be noted that the system would operate like a messaging switch, and there should be constant monitoring of connected terminals.

The other human resource requirement would be the "know your neighbor" attitude. This mindset is very hard to find in aviation these days. The fostering of high-level collaboration is an imperative for the operational management system to deliver increases in efficiency. This can be achieved by expanding training beyond technical and operational aspects and exposing personnel to at least the basics of the provision of other services as well. Importantly, since check-in would provide a one-step processing for the normal passenger, adequate knowledge of security and border control would be an imperative for check-in personnel. Generally, there would also be the need to review competency levels upward for all services, especially with regard to fostering a collaborative culture.

While on the issue of human resources, it would be necessary to ensure that training is so designed for full appreciation that the human is at the center of aviation operations, and automation should never be perceived as taking over the human element's responsibility and accountability. In fact, the need for automation to be human-centered has long been identified by ICAO concerning safety-sensitive services such as flight operations and ATC. This should provide the necessary inspiration when considering that the operational management system would increase the general level of automation in the aviation industry.

• Real-Time Statistical Information

Regarding the storage of information, the operational management system would store data acquired in advance and updated in real time. Every element of information would be sent in to the system immediately upon action by a connected service. In addition to normal dissemination to other services concerned, this would allow for prompt data analysis operations when so warranted for tactical or even strategic reasons regarding the allocation and use of available resources. For instance, optimized resource deployment could be planned through the prompt analysis of activity levels, and the determination of peaks and troughs. Also, longer-term planning would be significantly enhanced due to the prompt availability of up-to-date information, and the ability for making timely safety and efficiency analysis.

DATA SHARING: SECURITY ISSUES

The primary role of the operational management system would be to ensure that the objective of safe and affordable air travel is being achieved with due regard for eliminating or at least attenuating any adverse impact on third parties. It would be the facilitator for seamless information exchange, which is the sine qua non condition for the aviation industry to be viable in the long term. The issue here is that there should be the necessary drive for data sharing.

It is necessary, however, to mention the issue of data sharing—or rather, the issue of the reticence to do so. Some services, especially enforcement ones, argue the question of security and data sensibility to justify such reticence, while the question of privacy of personal information is evoked by others. Such an attitude can only be unproductive, and hampers operational efficiency. The following example of an actual event shows the ripple effect of retaining information: A flight had just arrived, and at immigration processing, authorities decided that one passenger had to be deported by the same return flight. However, they withheld the information from the airline handler, citing issues of national security, until they realized that the flight was taxiing out for departure. They then requested ATC to have the flight return to its gate. While it was not bound to comply with this request, ATC did accommodate it, and redirected the aircraft back to its gate. This was not without consequences:

- Ground air traffic movements were disrupted.
- Due to the prolonged occupancy of the gate, incoming flights initially allocated that gate were directed elsewhere.
- The flight crew became concerned about duty time limitations, and was just within limit when the flight finally departed.
- Transfer passengers on the outgoing flight missed their onward connections at the destination airport and had to be accommodated at the airline's expense awaiting the next connections.
- The airline scheduling was also affected due to the late availability of the affected aircraft for subsequent flights.

This is ample evidence of the importance of timely data sharing. It should be understood within the whole aviation spectrum that information only flows within well-secured networks and never uses the public domain. It is thus inherently safe from unauthorized external access. The risk of sensitive information falling into wrong hands is thus minimal.

Lately, the issue of privacy of personal data has come to the fore. This should never have been raised in the first instance. Air transport is an international mode of travel, and ever since its inception, recognition data has always been used for identity control of the air traveler. Advance processing imperatives would only require the prospective air traveler to supply recognition data, travel authority, and any other relevant information earlier than under prevalent practices. Here again, the collected data would circulate within a well protected network, thus preempting any risk of public access to it.

DATA SHARING: PROTOCOL ISSUES

The other element of resistance to information sharing would be the perception of intrusion into an automation system. This would be unjustified in the sense that the concept has existed for quite some time and has been adequately proved to be nonintrusive.

Protocol issues should actually transcend over individual reservations. In a sense, the setting of the appropriate protocols for data sharing would be the initial step towards creating the collaborative culture.

INTERNATIONAL COOPERATION

Advance processing of recognition data would primarily be in the form of matching with appropriate databases. Immigration and security services would need to have access to data held by their external counterparts. This would imply the existence of a secure communication capability, or a system of international cooperation between such agencies.

However, the adoption of the operational management system concept on a large-scale globally would greatly ease the border control of incoming foreign nationals. In fact, based on the premise that appropriate verification would have been carried out at the initial departure station, services at the destination station would receive properly verified data, thus facilitating border control and greatly easing processing in case of air travel involving multiple legs.

When the use of biometrics for recognition systems becomes globally spread, it would be possible to create, under the aegis of a world body, a world passport database to which immigration agencies would have private key access. This would further enhance border control processes.

THE OPERATIONAL MANAGEMENT SYSTEM: JUST ONE MORE IT SYSTEM IN THE AVIATION JUNGLE?

It is a fact that automated systems abound in the air transport industry, and a cynical view would that the aviation operational management tool would be just one more addition to the myriad of IT systems available. However, this would be a very short-sighted perception. In fact, notwithstanding constant quality and capability enhancements, existing systems pay very little leverage to the need for collaboration between stakeholders. And for the industry to ensure its long-term viability there is one imperative: it should reinvigorate its internal supply chain. And this would only be possible through ensuring that information flows seamlessly within the aviation industry

CONCLUDING NOTE

Globalization is a reality, and interdependence between states is bound to keep on growing. Admittedly, time and again protectionist temptations would resurge, especially during periods of economic worry. However, such temptations would be short-lived, and globalization will always be prevalent.

The importance of air transport in fostering globalization is well understood, and thus the demand for air travel can be expected to maintain its significant growth despite occasional setbacks.

However, air transport is presently at a defining moment of its own. It is the subject of renewed environmental attention regarding its polluting capacity and is also having to continuously compensate for highly volatile fuel prices. The common trait of all the challenges affecting civil aviation is that the end result is always increased costs to the industry and, by extension, to users. Quite honestly, all the challenges facing aviation will only get tougher over time. But a fatalistic acceptance that nothing more can be done is most unwarranted.

It is reassuring to note that there is a widespread quest for efficiency, with all stakeholders devoting significant resources to this end. Unfortunately, even during these difficult times, there is inadequate appreciation that there needs to be strong collaboration among all the services. Up to now, several services have stayed in their own ivory towers. But the time has come for the demise of this attitude. Services can no longer operate without adequate regard to the effects of any inefficacy to the overall aviation scene.

Admittedly, state sovereignty needs to be secured, and adverse effects to the environment and other third parties need to be mitigated to the best possible extent. In this context, such elements as intelligence, behavior monitoring, and all enforcement techniques currently in place would continue to prevail. But, the aviation industry needs to couple them with a culture of collaboration so as to secure its long-term sustainability in the face of prevailing and forecast reality—indeed, it has the responsibility for paving the way for its future viability.

This can only be assured through restoring its internal supply chain and making collaboration the key word across the aviation industry. This is the key to making air travel affordable in the future.

CHAPTER 11

Regulation of Air Cargo Security at the International Level

Maria Buzdugan and Triant Flouris

The air cargo system is designed to provide fast and efficient shipment of goods across countries and across the globe.[1] Similar to other components of the aviation system, the efficiency of air cargo transportation impacts the economic vitality not only of the aviation industry, but also of the national and international high-value, "just-in-time"[2] supply chain that serves many other industries. In a fast-cycle logistics era environment, air cargo enables businesses to connect to global markets and global supply chains in an efficient, expeditious, and reliable manner. Due to increased market demands, in recent years the volume of cargo transported by air has grown significantly and—as will be shown below—is expected to continue to grow at a pace that will surpass, in the foreseeable future, the growth of the passenger air travel. In brief, transportation of goods by air has become an essential component of contemporary world economy. In this context, vulnerabilities in air cargo security place at risk the entire air transportation system and, if exploited, could prove extremely harmful to the global economy.

In the past, the main security measures in air cargo transport were focused on ensuring security to high-value shipments and taking special handling precautions with regard to dangerous and hazardous goods. However, since the Lockerbie[3] disaster and the terrorist attacks of September 11, 2001, the air cargo security is facing an entirely new array of security risks, such as placing explosives in cargo shipments or using the air transport equipment as a weapon in terrorist attacks. After September 11, the overemphasis on enhancing security of passenger air travel has left the air cargo system more vulnerable, and a likely target for terrorists.

While aviation security has preoccupied national and international for a number of years, leading to the adoption of several important air security conventions under the auspices of the International Civil Aviation Organization and the European Union, an increased need to address potential threats to aviation industry has more recently motivated the adoption of various security regulations, mostly at the national and regional level. Some of these measures deal with aviation security in general, while others address specific cargo transportation needs, with some focusing expressly on carriage of cargo by air. The global scope of air cargo transport and the threats to its security, however, raises the question of whether an international approach based on harmonized best cargo security practices would be both appropriate and feasible to adequately address the current and emerging air cargo security vulnerabilities rather than national and regional initiatives.

This chapter explores possible approaches to harmonizing air cargo security standards and potential implementation challenges that should be taken into account when designing such common approach.

Air carriers transport billions of tons of cargo each year. A lot of airlines are financially dependent on cargo transport, which carries, on average, higher profit margins than passenger traffic,[4] accounting approximately for 15 percent of total traffic revenue.[5] The volume of cargo carried by air is steadily increasing, despite the downturn in the aviation industry in recent years.[6] The worldwide air cargo traffic is estimated to reach 518.7 billion RTKs by 2023.[7] In this context, it should be noted that more than 77 percent of total air cargo traffic (measured in RTK) is carried by non-U.S. airlines, which have outpaced the growing rate of scheduled freight of U.S. carriers for quite some time.[8] A report by the U.S. Department of Transport anticipates that in coming years, the amount of freight transported by air will increase faster than the number of passengers, thus adding to the growing importance of air cargo.[9]

In terms of its structure, the air cargo system may be characterized as a complex distribution network that handles a vast amount of freight and links manufacturers and shippers to freight forwarders to airport sorting and cargo handling facilities where shipments are loaded and unloaded from aircraft. In addition to the air carrier, cargo transportation by air involves many participants, including manufacturers and shippers (some of whom are routinely engaged in international trade, others only occasionally), freight forwarders who consolidate shipments and deliver them to the air carriers, and providers of storage facilities that accommodate cargo until it is placed aboard an aircraft.

These air cargo industry characteristics provide an idea of why the air cargo system poses significant challenges for aviation security.

Numerous industry and government studies have identified vulnerabilities in the security procedures of some air carriers and freight forwarders, including the adequacy of background checks for persons handling cargo.[10] In addition, the air cargo system is vulnerable to a number of potential security threats, including hijacking or sabotage of the aircraft, criminal activities such as placing explosives aboard aircraft, smuggling, theft, illegal shipments of hazardous materials, and tampering with cargo during land transport from the point when freight leaves a shipper to the airport or at the cargo handling facilities of air carriers and freight forwarders.[11] Such security weaknesses in the system create serious risks and can have major economic impact. Breaches in transportation security in general already cost the global economy billions of dollars every year. In addition, a major terrorist attack involving a key element of transport infrastructure could have devastating consequences for the international economy (loss of life and property, interruption of trade, costs of diverting traffic).

This chapter concentrates only on two main types of risks against air cargo: placing explosive devices in air cargo and aircraft hijackings.

Given that cargo screening and inspection is currently not as extensive as is the screening of passengers and their luggage, the risk of undetected explosive devices placed in air cargo represents a major threat to aircraft security. The level of threat posed by this risk varies with the type of aircraft. Cargo carried aboard passenger aircraft may be especially at risk since such aircraft were targeted in the past.[12] In addition, most experts consider that placing explosives in all cargo aircraft may be less appealing to terrorists, because such an attack would not be likely to attract the media and public attention that a bombing of a commercial passenger aircraft would. However, according to *The 9/11 Commission Report*, al-Qaeda terrorists had an interest in placing explosives in all cargo aircraft prior to September 11, 2001, and were planning to bomb U.S.-bound cargo flights.[13] The current vulnerabilities in the air cargo system make this security threat an issue of particular concern. Placing a chemical or nuclear bomb on board an all-cargo aircraft and timing its detonation over a heavily populated area is a potential risk. However, it must be noted that rarely are the time schedules and routes of all-cargo aircraft made known well in advance, so it would be fairly difficult for a terrorist to anticipate the precise time when an aircraft will overfly a certain area.

A series of hijackings in the 1970s and 1980s served to concentrate security efforts on passenger threats rather than cargo. The September 11, 2001, attacks have highlighted a shift in focus of terrorist activities from hijacking to the total destruction of aircraft in flight. The emerging security measures aimed at preventing such hijackings are, however, overwhelmingly focusing on passenger aircraft, which could make all-cargo aircraft more vulnerable to terrorists action. As large all-cargo aircraft may carry considerable reserves of fuel, this may transform such aircraft into an appealing target for terrorists seeking to hijack large airplanes and use them as weapons. However, it must be kept in mind that, in general, it would be difficult to access the all-cargo crew area from the cargo hold.

METHODS AND TECHNOLOGIES FOR AIR CARGO INSPECTION

Cargo may be loaded on board aircraft in loose or bulk form (predominantly in the case of narrow-body aircraft) or in the form of containerized or palletized configurations (on wide-body passenger aircraft). Air cargo can vary in size and weight from less than 1 kg to several tons, and in type from perishables to human remains, with everything in between, from apparel and medical equipment to electronics, live animals, and so forth. Depending on the methods by which cargo may be offered to an air carrier for transport, which may involve unit-loading devices, wooden crates, or assembled pallets, there are a number of processing stages that the cargo goes through. Given the variety in the nature of air cargo and the type of air cargo operations, approaches to screening air cargo are logistically complex. From the outset, it must be noted that currently there is no single technology capable of efficiently and thoroughly inspecting all types of air cargo for a full range of threats, including explosives and weapons of mass destruction. In addition, one must keep in mind that different environmental conditions (such as extreme cold or heat) may have an effect on the performance levels of different types of technology.

Currently several technologies are used, either individually or in combination, to inspect cargo, such as explosive detection systems (EDSs), explosive trace detection (ETD), X-ray machines, computer-aided tomography, pulsed fast neutron analysis, radiation detection technologies, decompression chambers, and bomb-sniffing dogs. A brief review of what these methods entail and how they are used at various airports follows.

Explosive Detection Systems (EDSs) and Explosive Trace Detection (ETD)

EDS is a form of X-ray technology involving machines up to the size of a minivan and using computer tomography that generates three-dimensional scan images of objects to compare their density to the density of known objects in order to identify explosives.[14] An EDS machine costs in excess of $1 million. The explosives trace detection (ETD) systems, currently used to screen passenger baggage for explosive material, use a variety of technical principles to analyze the chemical composition of sample residue wiped from suspect articles and involve machines that are much smaller than the ones used for EDS screening. Government reports state that EDS provides an equivalent level of security to that provided by ETD technology, but EDS provides a higher level of efficiency.[15]

In 2004 the TSA conducted a pilot project that involved testing explosive detection technologies for inspecting air cargo. The main purpose was to determine the expected performance of the explosive detection system for inspecting outbound bulk air cargo onboard commercial air carriers for the threat of improvised explosive devices within the air cargo. The testing criteria included detection rates, false alarm rates, and throughput rates (i.e., the amount of cargo screened per hour). The results of this project suggested that EDS technology is well suited to inspect break bulk cargo under different environmental and climatic conditions.[16]

X-Ray Machines

The vast majority of air carriers use X-ray machines of various sizes to inspect air cargo. In most cases, large palletized cargo are broken down in order to make them fit through X-ray machines and then are repalletized before being loaded aboard the aircraft.

Computer-Aided Tomography

This technology involves a method of producing a three-dimensional image of the internal structures of an object from a large series of two-dimensional X-ray images taken around a single axis of rotation.

Pulsed Fast Neutron Analysis (PFNA)

The use of PFNA allows for the identification of the chemical signatures of explosives by measuring the reaction to injected neutrons and identification of elemental chemical signatures of explosives and other threats.

Radiation Detection Technologies

Radiation detection technologies are employed by some air carriers to inspect air cargo for potential weapons of mass destruction and other radiological items. These carriers inspect cargo shipments using radiation detection portals and handheld radiation detectors.

Decompression Chambers

This technology involves placing the suspicious items in a chamber that simulates the flight pressure conditions during takeoff, normal flight, and landing. Applying these conditions to the items will cause explosives attached to barometric fuses to detonate.

Hardened Cargo Containers

Hardened cargo containers that have potential of controlling the damage caused by an in-flight explosion by confining it to their walls.[17] Such containers are expensive, with an average cost of $15,000, as compared to a standard container, which costs about $1,000.[18] They also weigh about 150 pounds more than standard containers,[19] adding to aircraft fuel costs. Also, their lifespan is shorter than that of a standard container. If the hardened container is scratched or bumped during shipping, its life span can be reduced to less than one year (standard containers usually last eight years).[20]

Use of Certified Canine Teams

Certified canine teams are used to detect explosives in baggage as well as for air cargo inspection. These canine teams are employed to search narrow- and wide-body aircraft, terminals, and cargo warehouses in the airport environment.

Intrusion Detection Technologies

This type of technology includes devices that can be used to determine whether a package or container has been tampered with, by visual inspection (such as tamper-evident tape or seals)[21] or by emitting an alarm or notifying a central control station. Such are electronic seals that include a radio frequency device that transmits shipment information as it passes reader devices and transmits an alarm if a container has been compromised.[22] Such devices have the benefit of being a relatively inexpensive means to make tampering with cargo more difficult during transport by truck from the shipper to the airport and in cargo handling facilities. The cost ranges from under $1 per unit for tamper-evident tape to $2,500 per unit for electronic seals (but are reusable). The drawback is that all types of tape and seals are themselves vulnerable to tampering, given the appropriate tools.[23] In addition, experts point out that currently available electronic seals have a limited transmission range, which could lead to difficulties in identifying any signal of tampering.[24]

Emerging Technologies to Inspect Air Cargo

In the United States, the following technologies were selected by the TSA for further development and testing:[25]

- XR/PFNA X-ray combined with pulsed fast neutron analysis uses a beam of neutrons to excite common elements such as hydrogen, carbon, nitrogen, and oxygen in cargo. As a result, it generates a three-dimensional map of the elements from which explosives can be detected and located.
- Miniature explosive and toxic chemical detector utilizes sensors based on micro electromechanical systems (MEMS) technology aimed at detecting traces of explosives and toxic chemicals.
- Pressure-activated sampling system involves placing the items to be inspected inside a steel pressure vessel that is subsequently pressurized, allowing the air to be forced into the package contents. The air exhaust is then sampled and analyzed using an approved trace detector.
- Low-cost quadruple resonance (QR) explosives detection for containerized air cargo involves automatically moving a container placed on the transport mechanism into the scanning chamber, where it is positioned and examined by QR and trace detection technologies.

- Megavolt computed tomography for air cargo container inspection uses high-energy computed tomography to generate high-resolution, three-dimensional images of oversized boxes, palletized cargo, and cargo containers. It should be noted that this system is based on the same principles as those employed to inspect checked baggage, but is large enough to allow inspection of air cargo containers.

- Neutron resonance radiography for containerized cargo inspection involves an imaging system that uses medium energy neutrons to effectively measure the neutron absorption through thick objects and determine the relative concentrations of different materials from which explosives can be detected in air cargo containers with checked baggage as contents.

- Terahertz spectrometer-based trace detection system for cargo: it combines a particle and vapor sampling system with a terahertz detector, which is capable of analyzing trace residues based on their rotational spectra.

- Material specific explosives and nuclear material detection system for cargo is capable of accurately measuring the elements and their ratios in a container. The elemental densities are used to indicate the presence of explosives.

OVERVIEW OF OPERATIONAL PROCEDURES USED BY GOVERNMENTS AND THE INDUSTRY TO MITIGATE AIR CARGO SECURITY RISKS

To date, several regulatory initiatives to improve air cargo security have been undertaken at the international, regional, and national levels. Some of these measures expressly address security issues in air cargo transport, while others are of broader scope but contain provisions applicable to air cargo. At the international level, the security conventions and the more specific standards and recommended practices adopted by the ICAO in Annex 17, although useful in introducing several general principles (including the concept of "authorized importer") appear to be insufficient in keeping pace with the current needs in international air cargo security. The European Union provides a more comprehensive and aggressive set of measures dealing with aviation security in general and air cargo in particular. Since these regulations are already in force, it will be interesting to see how the EU will react to future proposals of international standards that might differ from the current European approach.

At the national level, some governments have taken steps to enhance aviation security through, *inter alia*, requirements for advance cargo information and providing for government–business partnerships in various forms. It is apparent that these initiatives are not pursued with equal determination by all states and have not followed sufficiently similar approaches allowing for an easy harmonization of air cargo in the near future. While certain initiatives, taken individually, may improve trade security in a particular sector or region, the lack of international coordination could lead to duplications of these requirements, translating into increased burdens on international traders. For example, the government–business partnerships entail different approaches to risk assessment of traders and shipments, as discussed below, making the mutual recognition of status of authorized trader at the present time less likely.

The Use of "Known Shippers" and "Regulated Agents"

The concept of "known shipper" or "known consignor" is emerging as one of the leading means to ensure security throughout the air cargo system and reduce costs and delays for regular shippers. The "known shipper" programs were created to establish procedures for differentiating between trusted shippers known to an air carrier or freight forwarder through prior business dealings, on the one hand, and unknown shippers who have conducted limited or no prior business with an air carrier or a freight forwarder, on the other. By using this system, shipments from unknown sources can be selected for additional screening and inspections. On the contrary, accredited service providers are considered to present a lower security risk and could benefit from less controls and delays.

Note that in many instances, this concept is frequently used in conjunction with the concept of "regulated agent" or "indirect air carrier"—referring to certified freight forwarders. The concepts of "known shipper" and "regulated agent" reconcile trade facilitation and compliance with security measures, leading to certain advantages for the traders in terms of expeditiousness of the secure chain. However, the adequacy and thoroughness of this system depends on how the criteria for shippers certification are actually defined, and how the regime is translated in practice.

The International Civil Aviation Authority (ICAO) in its Annex 17 to the Chicago Convention requires the contracting states to subject to appropriate security control cargo intended for carriage on passenger flights,[26] and to ensure that operators do not accept consignments of cargo on passenger flights unless their security has been accounted for by a regulated agent[27] or they are subjected to other security controls.[28] According to Annex 17, a "regulated agent" is defined as "[a]n agent, freight forwarder or any other entity who conducts business with an operator and provides security controls that are accepted or required by the appropriate authority in respect of cargo, courier and express parcels or mail."[29] A summary of ICAO applicable standards and recommended practices is provided in Table 11.1.

Various countries have adopted various criteria for identifying and validating "known shippers" or "known consignors." A brief overview of some of the regimes implemented in several countries follows.

"Known Shipper" in the United States

The "known shipper" program is defined in the United States as a protocol aimed at distinguishing shippers about whom security-relevant information is known to a freight forwarder or air carrier through prior business

Table 11.1
Summary Table of ICAO Standards and Recommended Practices Regarding Air Cargo Security

	Issue	*Core Provision*
Standard 4.1, Annex 9, Chicago Convention	Obligation of contracting states to adopt and implement appropriate national regulations and procedures	Contracting states to the Chicago Convention have the obligation to adopt and implement appropriate national regulations and procedures in such a manners as to prevent unnecessary delays of air cargo operations.
Standard 4.3, Annex 9, Chicago Convention	Obligation of contractingstates to consult with the parties concerned	Contracting states have the obligation to consult with air carriers and other parties concerned when adopting and implementing such regulations.
Standard 4.5, Annex 9, Chicago Convention	Cargo inspection	Main standards regarding cargo inspection: physical examination of cargo should not be the rule; instead use of risk management to determine which goods must be examined and the extent of that examination; also, use of modern screening or examination techniques is recommended.
Standard 4.9, Standard 4.11, Standard 4.15, Annex 9, Chicago Convention	Information required by public authorities	Information required releasing or clearing imported or exported goods must be limited to the one deemed necessary for these operations. See model cargo manifest. It must be accepted when presented in electronic format. Parties are encouraged to implement compatible systems.
Standard 4.20, Standard 4.21, Standard 4.25, Annex 9, Chicago Convention	Release and clearance of import and export cargo	States must limit their requirements for export clearance documentation to a simplified export declaration.

(Continued)

Table 11.1
(*Continued*)

	Issue	*Core Provision*
Standard 4.27, Recommended Practice 4.28, Annex 9, Chicago Convention	Goods imported by authorized person	Simplified customs procedures must be provided if the goods are imported by an authorized person and are goods of a specified type. Authorized importers who meet specified criteria: appropriate record of compliance with official requirements and a satisfactory system for managing their commercial records.
Standard 4.5, Annex 17, Chicago Convention	Security measures relating to cargo	States are required to ensure the protection of cargo, baggage, mail and operator's supplies being moved within an airport; to subject to appropriate security control cargo, courier, and mail intended for carriage on passenger flights; and to ensure that operators do not accept consignments of cargo on passenger flights unless their security has been accounted for by a regulated agent or they are subjected to other security controls.

dealings from unknown shippers who have conducted limited or no prior business with a freight forwarder or air carrier. This program has been a fundamental element of air cargo security since 1976 as part of the aircraft operator security programs.

The Aviation and Transportation Security Act[30] acknowledged that the Known Shipper program is a mechanism for screening cargo placed on passenger aircraft. Prior to September 11, 2001, cargo from unknown shippers was allowed to be placed on board passenger aircraft if it was screened by the freight forwarder or identified to the passenger aircraft operator so that the aircraft operator could inspect the cargo. After September 11, security directives and emergency amendments were issued to both freight forwarders and aircraft operators precluding the transport of cargo from unknown shippers aboard passenger aircraft. According to the current regime, the Known Shipper program requires all carriers to demonstrate two years of shipping history with a freight forwarder or shipper and to have made at least twenty-four shipments on behalf of that freight forwarder or shipper.

As part of the Known Shipper program, in February 2004, the TSA implemented a voluntary centralized Known Shipper database designed to streamline the process by which the identity of shippers and their status is made known to air carriers with whom they conduct business. Prior to this initiative, each air carrier and freight forwarder was in charge of maintaining its own information on shippers with whom it conducted business. As a consequence, each carrier had to go through the process of "certifying" a shipper as "known" although that particular shipper was already "known" to another air carrier. The centralized database allowed air carriers and freight forwarders to electronically verify the status of shippers unknown to them.

In May 2007 TSA adopted new regulations aimed at strengthening air cargo and enhancing the agency's Known Shipper program. For cargo to be loaded on aircraft in the United States, each aircraft operator and foreign air carrier using aircraft of a certain size and engaged in scheduled and public charter passenger operations or freight forwarder—designated "indirect air carrier" (IAC) under TSA regulations—that offers cargo to an aircraft operator satisfying the conditions above must have and carry out a known shipper program in accordance with its security program.

The program must:

- Determine the shipper's validity and integrity as provided in the security program
- Provide that the aircraft operator or the foreign air carrier or the IAC will separate known shipper cargo from unknown shipper cargo
- Provide for the aircraft operator or foreign aircraft or IAC to ensure that cargo is screened or inspected as defined in its security program

Under the new rules, when proposing a shipper for the Known Shipper program, an aircraft operator or foreign air carrier or the IAC is required to submit an application electronically to TSA for vetting against terrorist and law enforcement data. This information will then be stored in a central database along with the shipper's status in the program. Aircraft operators, foreign air carriers, and IACs are required to check a shipper's status on the system before accepting its cargo for transport on passenger aircraft.

Thus, according to the new regulations, participation of domestic operators, foreign air carriers, and freight forwarders in the TSA's centralized database is made mandatory. However, the process for validating known shippers was not revised, meaning that it remains the responsibility of freight forwarders and air carriers. Therefore, passenger and all-cargo carriers, as well as freight forwarders, will continue to have the responsibility of entering shipper information into the TSA's centralized known shipper database.

This system is not without its faults. One government report indicated that the fact that airlines and freight forwarders are the ones in charge with submitting electronic information to the TSA creates the risk of conflicts of interest, since air carriers who conduct business with shippers will also continue to have the authority to validate the same customer.[31] A BBC investigation carried out last year revealed major flaws in the system.[32] Captain Gary Boettcher, president of the U.S. Coalition of Airline Pilots Association (ALPA), was quoted saying: "There are approximately 1.5 million known shippers in the US. There are thousands of freight forwarders. Anywhere down the line, packages can be intercepted at these organizations. Even with reliable, respectable organizations, you really don't know who is in the warehouse, who is tampering with packages, who is putting parcels together."[33] The conclusion of the report was that the "known shipper" program is "probably the weakest part of cargo security today."[34]

"Known Consignor" in the United Kingdom

Perhaps one of the most respected programs in place is the one implemented in the United Kingdom. According to this regime, the UK Department of Transportation allocates the responsibility for assessing shippers to independent validators that the department selects based on their cargo security experience.[35] British traders involved in international air cargo transport may start the validation process by accessing online a list of appointed validators. The trader then contacts the validator of its choice to arrange a validation inspection. The validator advises the organization about what the inspection will involve and may offer, either free or for a fee, to carry out a prevalidation inspection.[36]

During the inspection, the validator considers the following aspects:

- The physical security measures in place at the site
- The staff recruitment and reference check procedures
- Staff security training procedures
- Whether any other organizations use the same site
- Access control to the site
- The point at which the cargo becomes air cargo
- The air cargo preparation procedures
- Air cargo packing procedures
- Storage of secure cargo
- Transport of secure cargo to security approved air cargo agent or airline[37]

It should be mentioned, among other requirements, that all staff who have access to air cargo must have received basic security training. Also, their recruitment procedure must request of written references, which will normally be expected to go back five years.[38]

Where security measures in place at trader's place of business are judged by the validator to be of a sufficiently high standard, a known consignor certificate (which provides confirmation to the security approved air cargo agent or airline that all the security requirements have been met) and a unique reference number (URM) are awarded. The company's site details are entered on a Web site so that regulated air cargo agents or airlines can verify the status.[39]

In case the validator finds the level of security unsatisfactory, it must give the company a report outlining where the business has failed to meet the security requirements. If the consignor decides that it will undertake a rectification action, a reinspection is possible.[40] An appeal of validator's decision is also available to traders in the case of an unsuccessful validation. Within seven days of the inspection, the consignor must write a letter to the Department for Transportation listing the grounds for the appeal and specifying the issues in dispute. The department will investigate the matter and issue a final decision. If the appeal is dismissed the consignor remains unknown, unless it decides to reapply for known status and is subsequently validated; if the appeal is accepted, the consignor will be added to the list of known consignors.[41]

The major benefit of acquiring a "known consignor" status is that the cargo shipped by such traders will not be screened before being flown and the known cargo will not have to pay the security charges levied by a listed agent or airline (as will have to do an unknown consignor).[42] Note that the role of the Department of Transportation is to oversee the validation system and, if appropriate, to remove a validator from the list. The department may send its own validators to accompany a validator on a visit to a site or may carry out no-notice spot checks of known consignor sites.[43]

"Known Consignor" in the European Union (EU)

The EU Regulation 2320/2002 on security in civil aviation and Regulation 622/2003 on implementation of common basic standards and procedures to maintain aviation security establish the common rules governing security in air cargo in Europe. These regulations establish a "known consignor" and "regulated agent" regime according to which a "known consignor" is defined as the originator of goods for transportation by air for its own account, who has established business relations with a regulated agent or airline, while a "regulated agent" is defined as an agent, freight forwarder, or other entity who conducts business with an airline, and provides security controls that are accepted or required by the appropriate authority with respect to cargo. A regulated agent must be designated, approved, or listed by the appropriate authority and subject to specified obligations as defined by the appropriate authority.

According to EC Regulation 2320/2002, a regulated agent or air carrier may recognize a consignor as a "known consignor" only if it

• Establishes and registers the identity and address of the consignor
• Requires the consignor to declare that it prepares consignments in secure premises, employs reasonably reliable staff in preparing the consignments, and protects the

consignments against unauthorized interference during preparation, storage, and transportation

• Requires the consignor to certify in writing that the consignment does not contain any explosives or incapacitating items and accepts that the package and contents of the consignment may be examined for security reasons

According to the EU regulations, air cargo companies from EU countries must ensure that 100 percent of their cargo is secure, whether it comes from a regulated agent or an unknown shipper. Note also that EU Regulation 831/2006, which came into force in EU member states in January 2007, requires regulated agents and airlines to acquire certain factual information (including financial information such as bank account details) from their "known consignors," and that the consignors consent to inspection by government compliance inspectors.

EU has developed an air cargo study that provides a EU-wide central air cargo database containing all regulated agents and known consignors. This database is intended to become the central accreditation and certification mechanism in the EU and also assist in the harmonization and mutual recognition of shippers databases with other counter parties. In fact, the TSA is currently negotiating with the EU the development of a database containing information on shippers and freight forwarders that will be shared between the United States and EU member states. The negotiations concentrate on issues such as how and what information in the database is to be shared.

A summary of the relevant EU Regulations provisions are included in Table 11.2.

Costs Associated with the Process of Validation of "Known Shippers"

The costs of overseeing the validation process and maintaining a "known shipper" database are quite onerous, and it would be unfair to impose them only on the government or only on the air cargo industry. The implementation of air cargo security must be based on a partnership in which each participant must bear its fair share of costs.[44] Some countries confronted with similar issues of funding impose a fee schedule to be charged to all shippers to cover costs associated with validation, maintenance of the shippers database, and regular inspections.

THE PATH TOWARD INTERNATIONAL UNIFORMITY

The global scope of air cargo transport and the threats to its security raises the question of whether an international approach based on harmonized best cargo security practices would be both appropriate and feasible to adequately

Table 11.2
Summary Table of EU Standards in Air Cargo Security

	Issue	*Core Provision*
Point 6.1, Annex 1, EC Regulation 2320/2002	Goods subject to security controls	All cargo intended to be carried on passenger or all-cargo aircraft
Annex, Definitions, EC Regulation 2320/2002	Concept of "regulated agent"	A "regulated agent" is defined as "an agent, freight forwarder or other entity who conducts business with an operator and provides security controls that are accepted or required by the appropriate authority in respect of cargo." Such agent must be designated, approved, or listed by the appropriate authority and subject to specified obligations as defined by the appropriate authority.
Article 6.3, paragraph 1, EC Regulation 2320/2002	Security controls	Cargo will be allowed for transportation by air only if (1) its reception, processing, and handling was performed by properly recruited and trained staff and (2) it was searched by hand or physical check or screened by X-ray equipment or subjected to other means, both technical and biosensory, so as to reasonably ensure that it does not contain any prohibited articles such as explosives or incapacitating items.
Article 6.3, paragraph 3, EC Regulation 2320/2002	Cargo exempted from security controls	Cargo received from a "known consignor" is a transshipment cargo (provided that it is protected against interference at the transit point), cargo whose origin and handling conditions ensure that it presents no security threat, or cargo subject to regulatory requirements providing for an appropriate level of security protection.
Article 6.4 and Annex, Definitions of EC Regulation 2320/2002	Concept of "known consignor"	A "known consignor" is defined as "the originator of property for transportation by air for his own account and who has established business with a regulated agent or air carrier on the basis of criteria detailed in [the annex]."

(Continued)

Table 11.2
(*Continued*)

	Issue	*Core Provision*
		A regulated agent or air carrier may recognize a consignor as a "known consignor" only if it (1) establishes and registers the identity and address of the consignor and the agents authorized to carry out deliveries on its behalf, (2) requires the consignor to declare that it prepares consignments in secure premises, employs reasonable reliable staff in preparing the consignments, and protects the consignments against unauthorized interference during the preparation, storage and transportation, and (3) requires the consignor to certify in writing that the consignment does not contain any explosives or incapacitating items and that it accepts that the package and contents of the consignment may be examined for security reasons.
Article 5, EC Regulation 2320/2002 EC Regulation 622/2003	National Aviation Security Programmes	The EU member states have established national aviation security programs that incorporate the community standards and ensure by means of established national quality control programs that the monitoring and implementation of the national aviation security programs is carried out properly.
Article 7, EC Regulation 2320/2002 EC Regulation 1486/2003	Monitoring compliance	Each member state must ensure that, upon request, commission have access to the national civil aviation security program, including the national civil aviation security training program, the national civil aviation security quality-control program, identified airports, and air carrier security programs.

address the current and emerging air cargo security vulnerabilities rather than national and regional initiatives.

Air cargo transportation in most instances has an international aspect, and so do most of potential security threats against it, such as terrorist attacks or other types of crime targeting air cargo. Thus it is only natural that a coordinated international approach should be adopted to effectively address emerging security threats to air cargo. The current patchwork of initiatives taken at the national and regional level is inadequate to properly address the transnational nature of security threats against air transport. In the absence of a uniform international approach, there it is the risk that different countries will adopt different standards and procedures—sometimes incompatible, other times duplicating—that will increasingly burden traders involved in international commence. Uniform standards regarding air cargo security and facilitation at a global level would promote certainty, uniformity, and predictability, as well as helping prevent unnecessary duplication of efforts and resources.[45]

A joint effort of national authorities would presumably improve the overall risk management and incident response techniques by allowing for sharing of information, expertise, and best practices in air cargo security. Also, because national authorities often must rely on security checks and procedures performed by other states on air cargo entering their countries, the existence of commonly agreed standards that are effectively and transparently applied would serve mutual security of air transport while lowering the costs for both government and businesses.

A very important aspect that must be considered is that in order to protect the entire transport chain, it is imperative to ensure that all parties involved in the supply chain operate in accordance with agreed-upon standards, since all stakeholders in the transport chain are interdependent. Otherwise, the traders that implement security measures and thus bear the associated costs will be at competitive disadvantage vis-á-vis other service providers who are not under an obligation to adopt such standards. To avoid such distortions of competition resulting from varying obligations and cost structures caused by implementation of different security requirements, there is a need for an international approach to security that applies to all service providers—ideally across all modes of transport and along the entire supply chain.

Although the approaches for all modes of transport should be comparable, there may be different security response based on necessity, proportionality, and the specificity of and exposure to risks characteristic of each transport operation, infrastructure, or equipment. Such measures need to be built on best available practices, with the aim of ensuring compatibility and fairness between modes. A viable approach to cross-modal harmonization would be to develop a common core of measures applicable to all modes of transport and then complete it with mode-specific rules that address modal specificities. Ideally, a set of measures would be applicable to all modes of transport and countries (what is called "vertical and horizontal harmonization") to prevent both security breaches and distortion of competition.

CONCLUSIONS

The security of air cargo has become one of the major global security concerns because of its recognized vulnerabilities, which make air cargo possibly the easiest target for terrorists. In recent years, a variety of national, regional, and international regulatory and policy initiatives have taken place in an attempt to counter the perceived risks and vulnerabilities in the aviation industry. Since it is agreed that screening of all cargo carried by air is not currently feasible due to limited technology and infrastructure, "flow of commerce" issues, and finite resources, the most practical security approach would involve a risk management technique that enables the authorities to identify high-risk shipments on which to concentrate their control. Several technology and operational measures have been identified to better address the threats to air cargo security. Among the procedural initiatives are the requirement for advance cargo information, expanding the use of "known shipper" and "regulated agent" mechanisms.

An internationally agreed-upon approach is necessary in order to adequately respond to the international nature of air cargo security risks and to avoid a patchwork of national and regional initiatives that may impede the flow of international trade. A viable international initiative should be based on best security practices identified by governments and international organizations and should aim at defining basic standard requirements for air cargo security and facilitation with the broadest geographical scope.

Solutions should be developed with due consideration for their impact upon air transport and trade. Future security measures should be effective and affordable and should be tested by practical experience. Only such measures, coupled with a workable authorized economic operator and a secure supply chain mechanisms can provide reliable guarantees of effective security in the air cargo system.

Setting up and implementing such a risk-managed approach would require close cooperation by all governmental authorities involved in international transport and trade. The use of automated risk-assessment systems, including mutual recognition of authorized economic operators, high standards of official and commercial integrity at all stages, and agreed-upon international security standards for all air cargo operations and related satisfactory methods of certifying and monitoring performance are essential requirements of such approaches.

NOTES

1. For the purposes of this work, "air cargo" takes the definition provided by the International Air Transport Association as being the equivalent of "goods," meaning

any property carried or to be carried on an aircraft except mail or other property carried under terms of an international postal convention, or baggage carried under a passenger ticket and baggage check, but includes baggage moving under an air waybill or shipment record. International Air Transport Association (IATA), "Glossary of IATA e-Freight Terms," http://www.iata.org/whatwedo/glossary_iata_e-freight.htm.

2. "Just-in-time" refers to a manufacturing and distribution system that relies on meeting immediate needs, as opposed to carrying large inventories "just in case." Boeing, *World Air Cargo Forecast* (WACF) 2006/2007, Boeing, http://www.boeing.com/commercial/cargo.

3. On Wednesday, September 21, 1988, Pan American Airways Flight 103, a Boeing 747–121, was destroyed by a bomb placed in its cargo compartment. The remains landed in and around the town of Lockerbie in southern Scotland. The aircraft was operating the London, Heathrow–New York, JFK route.

4. S. Rept. 108–38, *Air Cargo Security Improvement Act: Report of the Committee on Commerce, Science, and Transportation on S. 165*. United States Senate, 108th Congress, 1st Sess. (April 11, 2003).

5. Boeing, *World Air Cargo Forecast* (WACF) 2006/2007, Boeing, http://www.boeing.com/commercial/cargo.

6. For example, during fiscal year 2000, about 12.2 billion revenue ton miles of freight were transported in the United States by air. A revenue ton mile (RTM) is one ton of cargo transported one mile. U.S. Government Accountability Office (GAO), "Aviation Security. Federal Action Needed to Strengthen Domestic Air Cargo Security, GAO-06-76.

7. Boeing, *World Air Cargo Forecast* (WACF) 2006/2007, Boeing, http://www.boeing.com/commercial/cargo. Revenue ton kilometer (RTK) is one ton of cargo transported one kilometer.

8. Boeing, *World Air Cargo Forecast* (WACF) 2006/2007, Boeing, http://www.boeing.com/commercial/cargo.

9. *See* US Department of Transportation prognosis according to which air cargo (measured in revenue ton miles) carried by US commercial air carriers is expected to grow annually through 2013 by about one percentage point more than that forecasted for passenger travel (measured in revenue passenger miles). DOT data analyzed in U.S. Government Accountability Office (GAO), "Aviation Security. Federal Action Needed to Strengthen Domestic Air Cargo Security, GAO-06-76.

10. For example, in the United States, TSA inspectors have discovered numerous security violations made by air carries and freight forwarders during routine inspections of their facilities. U.S. Government Accountability Office (GAO), "Aviation Security. Federal Action Needed to Strengthen Domestic Air Cargo Security, GAO-06-76.

11. For example, the National Cargo Security Council estimates that cargo theft among all modes of transportation that occurs in such locations amounts to more than $10 billion losses in merchandise each year. Moreover, the FBI estimates that the majority of cargo theft in the United States occurs in cargo terminals, transfer facilities, and cargo-consolidation areas. U.S. Government Accountability Office (GAO), "Aviation Security. Federal Action Needed to Strengthen Domestic Air Cargo Security, GAO-06-76.

12. For example, the December 1988 crash of Pan Am flight 103 over Lockerbie, Scotland, was caused by an explosive device placed in a baggage container in the airplane hold, and the June 1985 crash of Air India flight 1982 off the coast of Ireland

showed evidence of an explosive device, most likely placed in checked baggage. Canadian Aviation Bureau Safety Board; Aviation Occurrence, Air India Boeing 747-237B VT-EFO, Cork, Ireland 110 Miles West, 23 June 1985.

13. National Commission on Terrorist Attacks upon the United States. *The 9/11 Commission Report* (New York, NY: W.W. Norton & Company, 2004).

14. Bart Elias, *CRS Report for Congress, Air Cargo Security* (updated July 30, 2007).

15. U.S. Government Accountability Office (GAO), "Aviation Security. Federal Action Needed to Strengthen Domestic Air Cargo Security, GAO-06-76.

16. U.S. Government Accountability Office (GAO), "Aviation Security. Federal Action Needed to Strengthen Domestic Air Cargo Security, GAO-06-76.

17. Bart Elias, CRS Report for Congress, Air Cargo Security (updated July 30, 2007), CRS-22.

18. U.S. Government Accounting Office, "Report to Congressional Requesters: Aviation Security. Vulnerabilities and Potential Improvements for the Air Cargo System," GAO-03-344 (December 2002).

19. U.S. Government Accounting Office, "Report to Congressional Requesters: Aviation Security. Vulnerabilities and Potential Improvements for the Air Cargo System," GAO-03-344 (December 2002).

20. U.S. Government Accounting Office, "Report to Congressional Requesters: Aviation Security. Vulnerabilities and Potential Improvements for the Air Cargo System," GAO-03-344 (December 2002).

21. Bart Elias, CRS Report for Congress, Air Cargo Security (updated July 30, 2007), CRS-18.

22. U.S. Government Accounting Office, Report to Congressional Requesters: Aviation Security. Vulnerabilities and Potential Improvements for the Air Cargo System, GAO-03-344 (December 2002) at 10, fn. 4.

23. U.S. Government Accounting Office, Report to Congressional Requesters: Aviation Security. Vulnerabilities and Potential Improvements for the Air Cargo System, GAO-03-344 (December 2002) at 11.

24. Bart Elias, CRS Report for Congress, Air Cargo Security (updated July 30, 2007), CRS-18.

25. U.S. Government Accountability Office (GAO), "Aviation Security. Federal Action Needed to Strengthen Domestic Air Cargo Security, GAO-06-76, Appendix VII.

26. *Convention on International Civil Aviation*, December 7, 1944, 15 U.N.T.S. 295, Annex 17, § 4.5.2.

27. The concept of "regulated agent" was introduced in Annex 17 by an amendment which became applicable in 1997.

28. *Convention on International Civil Aviation*, December 7, 1944, 15 U.N.T.S. 295, Annex 17, § 4.5.3.

29. *Convention on International Civil Aviation*, December 7, 1944, 15 U.N.T.S. 295, Ch. 1, Definitions.

30. P.L. 107–71.

31. U.S. Government Accountability Office (GAO), "Aviation Security. Federal Action Needed to Strengthen Domestic Air Cargo Security, GAO-06-76.

32. Jonty Bloom, "Air Cargo Security Gaps Exposed," BBC News (October 19, 2006).

33. Jonty Bloom, "Air Cargo Security Gaps Exposed," BBC News (October 19, 2006).

34. Jonty Bloom, "Air Cargo Security Gaps Exposed," BBC News (October 19, 2006).

35. UK Department of Transport, "Changes to the UK Air Cargo Security Regime", UK Department of Transport, http://www.dft.gov.uk/stellent/groups/dft_transsec/documents/page/dft_transsec_023330.hcsp.

36. UK Department of Transport, "Changes to the UK Air Cargo Security Regime", UK Department of Transport, http://www.dft.gov.uk/stellent/groups/dft_transsec/documents/page/dft_transsec_023330.hcsp. Each validation inspection costs _400 per site, plus the validator's travel expenses, whether it leads to a successful validation or not.

37. UK Department of Transport, "Changes to the UK Air Cargo Security Regime", UK Department of Transport, http://www.dft.gov.uk/stellent/groups/dft_transsec/documents/page/dft_transsec_023330.hcsp.

38. UK Department of Transport, "Changes to the UK Air Cargo Security Regime", UK Department of Transport, http://www.dft.gov.uk/stellent/groups/dft_transsec/documents/page/dft_transsec_023330.hcsp.

39. UK Department of Transport, "Changes to the UK Air Cargo Security Regime", UK Department of Transport, http://www.dft.gov.uk/stellent/groups/dft_transsec/documents/page/dft_transsec_023330.hcsp.

40. UK Department of Transport, "Changes to the UK Air Cargo Security Regime", UK Department of Transport, http://www.dft.gov.uk/stellent/groups/dft_transsec/documents/page/dft_transsec_023330.hcsp.

41. UK Department of Transport, "Changes to the UK Air Cargo Security Regime", UK Department of Transport, http://www.dft.gov.uk/stellent/groups/dft_transsec/documents/page/dft_transsec_023330.hcsp.

42. UK Department of Transport, "Changes to the UK Air Cargo Security Regime", UK Department of Transport, http://www.dft.gov.uk/stellent/groups/dft_transsec/documents/page/dft_transsec_023330.hcsp.

43. UK Department of Transport, "Changes to the UK Air Cargo Security Regime", UK Department of Transport, http://www.dft.gov.uk/stellent/groups/dft_transsec/documents/page/dft_transsec_023330.hcsp.

44. Transportation Security Administration, Statement of Admiral James M. Loy Administrator, Transportation Security Administration on Transportation Security before the Committee on Transportation and Infrastructure Subcommittee on Aviation, United States House of Representatives (October 16, 2003), Transportation Security Administration, http://www.tsa.gov/public/display?theme=47&content=0900051980063d1c.

45. Charles Piersall, "Taking Aboard All Players in Securing the Supply Chain," *ISO Focus* (January 2005) 10 at 10.

REFERENCES

Air Cargo Security Improvement Act: Report of the Committee on Commerce, Science, and Transportation. United States Senate, 108th Congress, 1st Session (April 11, 2003).

Boeing, World Air Cargo Forecast (WACF) 2006/2007, Boeing, http://www.boeing.com/commercial/cargo.

Canadian Aviation Bureau Safety Board, Aviation Occurrence, Air India Boeing 747-237B VT-EFO, June 23, 1985.

Convention on International Civil Aviation, December 7, 1944, Annex 17.

Elias, Bart. CRS Report for Congress, Air Cargo Security (updated July 30, 2007).

Jonty, Bloom. "Air Cargo Security Gaps Exposed," BBC News (October 19, 2006).

International Air Transport Association (IATA), "Glossary of IATA e-Freight Terms," IATA, http://www.iata.org/whatwedo/glossary_iata_e-freight.htm.

The 9/11 Commission Report: National Commission on Terrorist Attacks upon the United States (New York: W.W. Norton & Company, 2004).

Piersall, Charles. "Taking Aboard All Players in Securing the Supply Chain." ISO Focus (January 2005).

UK Department of Transport, "Changes to the UK Air Cargo Security Regime," UK Department of Transport, http://www.dft.gov.uk/stellent/groups/dft _transsec/documents/page/dft_transsec_023330.hcsp.

U.S. Government Accounting Office (GAO), "Report to Congressional Requesters: Aviation Security: Vulnerabilities and Potential Improvements for the Air Cargo System," GAO-03-344 (December 2002).

U.S. Government Accounting Office (GAO), "Aviation Security: Federal Action Needed to Strengthen Domestic Air Cargo Security," GAO-06-76 (2005).

CHAPTER 12

Commercial Vehicle Security

*U.S. Government Accountability Office**

BACKGROUND

Between 1997 and 2008 there were 510 terrorist-related commercial truck and bus bombing attacks worldwide, killing over 6,000 people, with 106 bombings occurring during 2007 alone, killing over 2,500 people. Of the 510 bombings since 1997, 364 have been bus bombings and 146 have been truck bombings; 156 have been in Iraq and 354 have been in other countries. In 2007, the use of truck bombs as a terrorist tactic more than tripled, resulting in 2,072 deaths. While trucks were involved in just 29 percent of the bombings since 1997, they accounted for 56 percent of the deaths.

Vehicle-borne improvised explosive devices (VBIEDs) are vehicles loaded with a range of explosive materials that are detonated when they reach their target. VBIEDs can also be used to explode flammable fuel trucks and disperse toxic substances. Terrorists have used a variety of trucks—rental, refrigerator, cement, dump, sewerage, gasoline tanker, trucks with chlorine and propane tanks, and fire engines—to attack a broad range of critical infrastructure, including police and military facilities, playgrounds, childcare centers, hotels, and bridges. Worldwide, commercial buses have also been attacked numerous times, including in Israel, England, Iraq, the Philippines, Lebanon, Sri Lanka, India, Russia, and Pakistan.

In the United States, terrorists used a commercial truck containing fertilizer-based explosives to attack the World Trade Center in 1993, killing

*Adapted from GAO Report GAO-09-85, "Commercial Vehicle Security: Risk-Based Approach Needed to Secure the Commercial Vehicle Sector."

six people and injuring 1,000. Two years later, a similar attack occurred at the Alfred P. Murrah Federal Building in Oklahoma City, Oklahoma, killing 168 people and injuring more than 800. Terrorists have also targeted overseas U.S. military personnel with commercial VBIEDs at the Marine barracks in Lebanon (1983), at the Khobar Towers in Saudi Arabia (1996), and at U.S. embassies in Kuwait (1983), Lebanon (1984), Kenya (1998), and Tanzania (1998).

THE U.S. COMMERCIAL TRUCK SECTOR

The Transportation Security Administration (TSA) estimates that there are approximately 1.2 million commercial trucking companies in the United States. Trucks transport the majority of freight shipped in the United States: by tonnage, 65 percent of total domestic freight; by revenue, 75 percent. According to TSA, 75 percent of U.S. communities depend solely on trucking to transport commodities. Trucks and buses have access to nearly four million miles of roadway in the United States. Trucking companies range in size from a single truck to several thousand trucks.

According to Department of Transportation 2004 data, which are the most current available, 87 percent of trucking companies operated six trucks or fewer, while 96 percent operated twenty or fewer. DOT estimates that about 40,000 new commercial trucking companies enter the industry annually. As of August 2008, nearly 11.9 million commercial trucks were registered with the DOT. Trucks come in a large variety of configurations and cargo body types to perform a wide range of tasks. Some trucks are used for local tasks such as construction, landscaping, or local package delivery, while others are used for transporting cargo over-the-road or for long hauls.

The trucking industry is diverse, involving several different sectors and including for-hire and private fleets, truckload and less-than-truckload carriers, bulk transport, hazardous materials, rental and leasing, and others. For-hire firms are those for whom trucking is the primary business, while private fleets are generally used to support another business activity, such as grocery chains and construction. According to a 2002 DOT survey, for-hire trucks represented 47 percent of the industry, while private fleets represented 53 percent.

While truckload carriers move loads from point to point, less-than-truckload carriers pick up smaller shipments and consolidate them at freight terminals. Bulk transport firms move bulk commodities such as gasoline, cement, and corn syrup in large trailers specifically designed for each type of commodity. Truck rental and leasing companies also are part of the commercial trucking industry. Consumer rental companies rent trucks to walk-in customers for short periods of time and represent 15 percent of the rental and leasing industry. Commercial rental and leasing companies generally lease trucks for a year or longer and account for the remaining 85 percent of the rental and leasing industry.

THE MOVEMENT OF HAZARDOUS MATERIALS

With respect to the transportation of hazardous materials, of an estimated 1.2 million commercial vehicle firms, 60,682 are registered as hazardous materials carriers, or about 5 percent of the commercial vehicle industry, and 1,778,833 drivers are licensed to transport hazardous materials. Hazardous materials are transported by truck almost 800,000 times a day, and 94 percent of hazardous material shipments are by trucks, which transport approximately 54 percent of hazardous materials volume (tons). DOT classifies hazardous materials under nine different classes of hazards. Most hazardous materials shipments by truck involve flammable liquids such as gasoline (81.8 percent), followed by gases (8.4 percent) and corrosive materials (4.4 percent). Class 6 toxic poisons, which include toxic inhalation hazards (TIH), comprise only 0.2 percent of hazardous materials transported by truck.

The shipment of security sensitive hazardous materials such as toxic inhalation hazards is of particular concern to TSA, although the agency estimates that they represent just 0.000058 percent of the commercial vehicle industry. Of the toxic inhalation hazards transported by truck, 81 percent is anhydrous ammonia and 10 percent is chlorine.

THE U.S. COMMERCIAL BUS SECTOR

Commercial bus companies represent less than 1 percent of the commercial vehicle industry, but according to TSA estimates, carry 775 million passengers annually. Intercity buses, or motor coaches, include buses with regularly scheduled routes, as well as tour and charter bus companies. In August 2008, DOT reported that there were 3,948 motor coach carriers, with 75,285 buses. Of these carriers, fewer than 100 are intercity bus companies, which transport passengers from city to city on scheduled routes, while the remaining carriers operate tour and charter buses. Most bus companies (95 percent) are small operators with fewer than twenty-five buses. Intercity buses, or motor coaches, serve all large metropolitan areas and travel in close proximity to some of the nation's most visible and populated sites, such as sporting events and arenas, major tourist attractions, and national landmarks.

A few intercity bus carriers also travel internationally to Canada and Mexico. According to a study commissioned by DOT, the accessibility and open nature of the motor coach industry make it difficult to protect these assets, and the level of security afforded to the infrastructure of the motor coach industry is relatively low compared to the commercial aviation sector, despite the fact that the motor coach industry handles more passengers a year.

U.S. PROGRAMS TO ENHANCE COMMERCIAL VEHICLE SECURITY

Federal Programs

A variety of federal programs have been implemented to enhance the security of the commercial vehicle sector. Several of these programs have been implemented by the TSA and other Department of Homeland Security components, others by the DOT, and several jointly by DHS and the DOT. Overall, these programs are designed to assess commercial vehicle industry security risks, develop guidance on how to prevent and deter attacks, improve security planning for an effective response to a potential terrorist attack, enhance cost-effective risk mitigation efforts, and support research on commercial vehicle security technology.

States, both individually and as members of transportation alliances with other states, have expanded their activities to secure the commercial vehicle sector as a part of broader homeland security activities. In addition, many commercial vehicle companies receive guidance on security awareness and best practices from industry associations.

According to the TSA's pilot study in Missouri, except for firms transporting hazardous materials, most commercial vehicle companies have implemented a limited number of security measures. In addition, the TSA and other DHS components have a number of programs underway designed to strengthen the security of commercial vehicles: the Truck Security Grant Program (TSP), the Intercity Bus Security Grant Program, security action items (SAIs), and the Hazardous Materials Driver Background Check Program.

The TSP provides grants that fund programs to train and support drivers, commercial vehicle firms, and other members of the commercial vehicle industry in how to detect and report security threats and how to avoid becoming a target of terrorist activity. TSP is administered by the Grant Programs Directorate of the DHS's Federal Emergency Management Agency (FEMA). For fiscal years 2004–2008, the principal activity funded by the TSP was the American Trucking Associations' Highway Watch Program, which provided drivers with security awareness training and support. In May 2008, however, a new grantee was selected.

DHS also established an Intercity Bus Security Grant Program to distribute grant money to eligible stakeholders for protecting intercity bus systems and the traveling public from terrorism. Current priorities focus on enhanced planning, passenger and baggage screening programs, facility security enhancements, vehicle and driver protection, and training and exercises.

In addition, TSA is consulting with industry stakeholders and the PHMSA to develop SAIs, or voluntary security practices and standards, intended to improve security for trucks carrying security-sensitive hazardous materials.

The SAIs are intended to allow TSA to communicate the key elements of effective transportation security to the industry as voluntary practices, and TSA will use CSRs to gauge whether voluntary practices are sufficient, or whether regulation is needed. TSA released its voluntary SAIs for hazardous materials carriers in June 2008. For example, it recommended using team drivers for shipments of the most security sensitive explosives, toxic inhalation hazards, poisons, and radioactive materials.

The USA PATRIOT Act passed in October 2001 prohibited states from issuing hazardous materials endorsements (HMEs) for a commercial driver's license to anyone not successfully completing a background check. In response, DHS developed rules regarding how the background checks will be conducted and implemented a hazardous materials driver background check assessment program to determine whether a driver poses a security risk. As of October 2008, the TSA had completed background checks for 990,961 out of approximately 2.7 million hazardous materials drivers, and 8,699 applicants have been denied HMEs since the beginning of the program.

In addition to DHS, at the federal level, the DOT has several commercial vehicle security programs underway: security contact reviews (SCRs), security sensitivity visits (SSVs), and the Hazardous Materials Safety Permit Program. SCRs, or compliance reviews, of commercial vehicle firms carrying hazardous materials are conducted. As of September 2008, 7,802 SCRs and 13,411 SSVs had been conducted since the inception of the programs. Federal law also directed the DOT to implement the Hazardous Materials Safety Permit Program to produce a safe and secure environment to transport certain types of hazardous materials. The Hazardous Materials Safety Permit Program requires certain motor carriers to maintain a security program and establish a system of en route communication.

In addition to CSRs, the TSA and the DOT also work collaboratively on several projects involving the security of commercial vehicles, including FMCSA and TSA research and development efforts for commercial vehicle security technologies. Both the FMCSA and the TSA have also completed pilot studies of tracking systems for commercial trucks carrying hazardous materials. Also, the TSA is testing tracking and identification systems, theft detection and alert systems, motor vehicle disabling systems, and systems to prevent unauthorized operation of trucks and unauthorized access to their cargos.

The 9/11 Commission Act requires that DHS provide a report to Congress by August 2008, that includes, among other things, assessments of (1) the economic impact that security upgrades of trucks, truck equipment, or truck facilities may have on the trucking industry, including independent owner–operators, (2) ongoing research by public and private entities and the need for additional research on truck security, and (3) the current status of secure truck parking.

The 9/11 Commission Act also had a number of mandates regarding the security of over-the-road buses, including that DHS issue regulations by February 2008 requiring all over-the-road bus operators to develop and implement security training programs for frontline employees, and requiring that DHS establish a security exercise program for over-the-road bus transportation. The 9/11 Commission Act further requires that DHS issue regulations by February 2009 requiring high-risk over-the-road bus operators to conduct vulnerability assessments and develop and implement security plans.

STATE ACTION

States are responsible for securing highway infrastructure, including highways, bridges, and tunnels, and for ensuring the security and safety of these roadways. State officials work on security issues within their individual states and with other states through several national associations. State transportation officials—through the American Association of State Highway and Transportation Officials (AASHTO)—and state law enforcement officials—through the Commercial Vehicle Safety Alliance (CVSA)—have worked collectively to strengthen the security of commercial vehicles and highway infrastructure through various expert committees and the implementation of joint initiatives with TSA and DOT.

AASHTO formed a Special Committee on Transportation Security that has sponsored highway and commercial vehicle security research at the National Academies of Science. AASHTO also conducts surveys of state DOT security efforts, priorities, and identified needs. AASHTO's August 2007 survey found that many state departments of transportation still needed basic training on integrating homeland security considerations in the planning process; detecting, deterring, and mitigating homeland security threats; and assessing transportation network homeland security vulnerabilities and risks. CVSA's state law enforcement members have also organized committees on transportation security, information systems, intelligent transportation systems, hazardous materials, passenger carriers, and training to pool and provide expertise to promote best practices, new programs, and the consistent application of regulations. For example, the purpose of the CVSA's Transportation Security Committee is to enhance homeland security by providing a forum to identify, develop, implement, and evaluate education, enforcement, and information-sharing strategies for enhancing commercial motor vehicle security.

CSR Pilot Study in Missouri

CVSA's Program Initiatives committee originated the idea of conducting a CSR pilot in Missouri. For this research, the U.S. GAO interviewed transportation, law enforcement, and homeland security officials responsible for commercial vehicle security from eight states to determine the nature and extent of their security efforts. These officials stated that they generally focused on law enforcement, protection of highway infrastructure, conducting inspections of commercial vehicles, and monitoring threats of all kinds.

Officials in each state stated that they understood the major transportation security risks in their state. For example, officials from one state that has numerous chemical plants expressed particular concern about the shipment of these chemicals, while officials from another state with extensive military bases expressed concern about shipments of nuclear weapons and waste. Officials from yet another state with numerous explosives plants were more concerned about the transportation of explosives. State and local authorities have also created fifty-eight fusion centers around the country to blend relevant law enforcement and intelligence information analysis and coordinate federal, state, and local security measures in order to reduce threats in local communities.

Although states have a number of security efforts involving the commercial vehicle sector, none of the state officials whom we interviewed (with the exception of those from Missouri) reported conducting formal vulnerability assessments of the commercial vehicle sector in their states.

Industry associations interviewed were actively assisting their members in strengthening the security of the commercial vehicle sector.

Twelve industry associations representing the commercial vehicle industry, including trucking, motor coaches, shipping, and unions, were also interviewed. Eight of these industry associations reported that they regularly provided federal officials with their industry's perspective on proposed regulations and legislation. Additionally, eight of the twelve associations reported that they were proactively providing security guidance to their members, which included guidance on security best practices, security awareness, and security self-assessments.

In addition, about a third of the associations reviewed reported providing training, security bulletins, and twenty-four-hour hotlines for their members. As discussed earlier in this report, the Missouri CSR pilot evaluation showed that firms carrying hazardous materials were complying with regulations and implementing more security measures to mitigate their risks than other commercial vehicle firms. In contrast, the study further found that truck companies not transporting hazardous materials were implementing few of TSA's best security practices. During site visits to twenty truck and six bus companies, ranging in size from the nation's largest commercial vehicle company with 27,453 trucks to an owner–operator with a single truck, it was found that most had some form of personnel security procedures and background checks in place, as well as terminal security, communications systems, and truck tracking systems.

Overall, the types of security practices among the commercial trucking companies visited were similar, but the prevalence and sophistication of these practices varied. The range of security practices that companies were using included requiring that drivers lock doors and inspect cargo, as well as requiring cargo seals; driver background checks; vehicle tracking technology;

terminal fencing, cameras, and gates; access controls, such as employee identification badges, sign-in and sign-out sheets or electronic key cards; en route security measures; and driver training. Large corporations and small one-truck owner–operators generally used differently scaled security approaches to the same problem.

For example, while a cell phone can suffice for the communications needs of a small operator, a large company may invest in integrated communications and tracking technologies. Conversely, where a large company may have a well-lit, gated terminal monitored by security cameras and guards, a small operator may lock the door of the vehicle and have a watch dog on the premises. In another example, small, independent owner–operator firms may rely solely on emergency responders such as 911 and state patrol hotlines, while larger firms may have dispatchers and in-house security specialists on duty twenty-four hours a day.

CONCLUSIONS

The nature, size, and complexity of the nation's commercial vehicle sector highlights the need for federal and state governments and the private sector to work together to secure this transportation sector. The importance of the nation's commercial trucking and motor coach industries and concerns about their security, coupled with finite homeland security resources, underscores the need to employ a risk management approach so that an appropriate balance between costs and security is obtained.

With fifty states and over a million diverse industry stakeholders, securing commercial vehicles can pose considerable communication challenges and lead to confusion about roles and responsibilities. Ultimately, the security of the industry is maintained by the companies themselves. Coordination and communications techniques that might work well in other transportation sectors may be insufficient for the larger, more complex commercial vehicle industry. The TSA has taken steps to coordinate with government and industry stakeholders, and has had some noteworthy successes, such as the Missouri CSR program. However, both industry and state officials who were interviewed stated that more needed to be done to enhance federal leadership and to better ensure that federal, state, and industry actions and investments designed to enhance security are properly focused and prioritized.

APPENDIX

In the interests of creating organizational memory, a listing of all worldwide terrorist truck and bus bombings from January 1997 through December 2008 is detailed here.

Date	Location	Description	Deaths
1/7/1997	Zugdidi, Georgia	Bus bombing	1
1/7/1997	Lagos, Nigeria	Bus bombing	2
1/7/1997	Algiers, Algeria	Car bomb hits bus	13
1/9/1997	Tel Aviv, Israel	Two bombs at bus station	0
1/21/1997	Algiers, Algeria	Car bomb hits bus	6
2/12/1997	Lagos, Nigeria	Bus bombing	0
2/25/1997	Urumqi, China	Bus bombing	3
3/7/1997	Beijing, China	Bus bombing	2
3/17/1997	Algiers, Algeria	Bus stop bombing	4
3/29/1997	Jammu and Kashmir, India	Bus station bombing	17
4/6/1997	Pathankot, India	Bus bombing	2
4/10/1997	Nablus, West Bank	Bus bombing	0
5/6/1997	Lagos, Nigeria	Army bus bombing	0
5/8/1997	Tirana, Albania (vicinity)	Bus bombing	3
5/12/1997	Shunde, China	Suicide bus bombing	5
6/1/1997	Algiers, Algeria	First of two bus bombings	14
6/6/1997	Pathankot, India	Bus bombing	7
6/17/1997	Bogota, Colombia	Truck bombing	8
6/30/1997	Sialkot, Pakistan	Bus bombing	8
7/9/1997	Jerusalem, Israel	Bus bombing	0
7/9/1997	Dagestan, Russian Federation	Bus bombing	9
7/14/1997	New Delhi, India	First of two bus bombings	0
7/14/1997	New Delhi, India	Second of two bus bombings	0
9/5/1997	Blida, Algeria	Bus bombing	4
9/18/1997	Cairo, Egypt	Bus incendiary bombing	10
10/15/1997	Colombo, Sri Lanka	Truck bombing	20
10/24/1997	Srinagar, India	Bus bombing	2
10/28/1997	Beirut, Lebanon	Bus station bombing	0
12/3/1997	Udumalpet, India	Bus stand bombing	3
12/28/1997	Galle, Sri Lanka	Truck bombing	3
12/30/1997	New Delhi, India	Bus bombing	4
1/20/1998	Algiers, Algeria	Bus bombing	1
1/24/1998	Algiers, Algeria	Bomb thrown from a bus	1
1/26/1998	Kandy, Sri Lanka	Suicide truck bombing of a temple	13
2/3/1998	Kosice, Slovakia	Bus station bombing	0
2/14/1998	Wuhan, China	Bus bombing	50
2/26/1998	Medea, Algeria	Bus hits a mine	10
2/27/1998	Gujranwala, Pakistan	Bus bombing	5
3/5/1998	Colombo, Sri Lanka	Suicide bus bombing	37
3/9/1998	Eravur, Sri Lanka	Truck bombing	6
4/6/1998	Sakrand, Pakistan	Bus bombing	6
4/22/1998	Sialkot, Pakistan	Bus bombing	0

Date	Location	Description	Deaths
7/29/1998	Sarajevo, Bosnia and Herzegovina	Bus bombing	0
7/30/1998	Algiers, Algeria	Bus bombing	2
8/7/1998	Dar es Salaam, Tanzania	Truck bombing of U.S. Embassy	12
8/7/1998	Nairobi, Kenya	Truck bombing of U.S. Embassy	246
9/11/1998	Kigali, Rwanda	Bus bombing	1
9/22/1998	Milan, Italy	Bus bombing	0
9/24/1998	Jerusalem, Israel	Bus stop bombing	0
10/7/1998	Ain Tagourait, Algeria	Bus bombing	1
10/7/1998	Barrancabermeja, Colombia	Truck bombing	0
10/11/1998	Halis, Iraq	Car bomb exploded near a bus	0
10/17/1998	Beersheva, Israel	Two grenades explode in a bus terminal	0
10/29/1998	Kfar Darom, Palestine	Car bombing of a bus	2
11/2/1998	Bacolod, Philippines	Bus terminal bombing	1
11/2/1998	Cagayan de Oro, Philippines	Bus terminal bombing	0
11/19/1998	Plaridel, Philippines	Bus terminal bombing	0
11/19/1998	Dipolog City, Philippines	Bus bombing	1
11/22/1998	Oued Atteli, Algeria	Bus bombing	0
11/25/1998	Kirikkale, Turkey	Bus bombing	4
12/24/1998	Van, Turkey	Suicide bus bombing	2
1/8/1999	Impasugong, Philippines	Bus bombing	1
1/12/1999	Davao, Philippines	First of two bus bombings	0
1/12/1999	Davao, Philippines	Second of two bus bombings	0
3/7/1999	Bursa, Turkey	Incendiary bombing of a bus	0
3/9/1999	Colombo, Sri Lanka	Bus station bombing	0
3/9/1999	Colombo, Sri Lanka	Bombing of bus and bus terminal	1
3/18/1999	Istanbul, Turkey	Bottled gas truck hit by grenade	0
3/26/1999	Istanbul, Turkey	Suicide bus bombing	1
6/9/1999	Baghdad, Iraq	Car bomb next to two buses	7
7/4/1999	Batman, Turkey	A tanker truck hit a land mine	1
7/8/1999	Esenler, Turkey	Time bomb on fuel tanker	0
7/12/1999	Istanbul, Turkey	Bus bombing	0
7/24/1999	Anantnag, India	Grenade attack on a bus stand	0
7/24/1999	Lusaka, Zambia	Grenade attack on a bus	0

Date	Location	Description	Deaths
7/27/1999	Rawalpindi, Pakistan	Bus bombing	11
8/14/1999	Dina, Pakistan	Bus bombing	6
8/16/1999	Suva, Fuji	Bus bombing	0
9/26/1999	Badulla, Sri Lanka	Bus bombing	1
11/14/1999	Cali, Colombia	Incendiary bomb attack on a bus stop	0
11/29/1999	Hyderabad, Pakistan	A bomb hidden under a bus seat	2
12/28/1999	Jammu, India	Bus terminal bombing	1
1/1/2000	Chittagong, Bangladesh	Bus stand bombing	0
2/3/2000	Kosocska Mitrovica, Serbia	Rocket fired at a UN bus	2
2/3/2000	Colombo, Sri Lanka	Bus bombing	0
2/25/2000	Ozamiz, Philippines	Bus bombing	44
3/15/2000	Kidapawan, Philippines	Bus bombing	2
3/15/2000	Matalan, Philippines	Bus bombing	0
4/4/2000	Kittuoothu, Sri Lanka	Bus hit a land mine	3
4/7/2000	Lahore, Pakistan	Bus station bombing	0
5/12/2000	Dzhaglarbi, Russia	Bus bombing	3
5/20/2000	Midsayap, Philippines	Bus terminal bombing	0
6/4/2000	Iligan City, Philippines	Bus depot bombing	1
6/6/2000	Vientiane, Laos	Bus terminal bombing	0
6/14/2000	Wattala, Sri Lanka	Suicide bus bombing	3
7/2/2000	Argun, Russia	Suicide truck bombing	50
7/2/2000	Gudermes, Russia	Two truck bomb suicide attacks	10
7/2/2000	Urus-Martan, Russia	Truck bombing	2
7/2/2000	Novogrozny, Russia	Suicide truck bombing	3
7/17/2000	Matalam, Philippines	Bus terminal bombing	0
7/24/2000	Jullundur, India	Bus bombing	7
9/3/2000	Lahore, Pakistan	Bus station bombing	3
9/12/2000	Grozny, Chechnya	Truck bombing	2
10/6/2000	Nevinnomyssk, Russia	Bus stop bombing	3
10/18/2000	Gaza, Palestinian Territories	Bus hit by grenades	0
11/20/2000	Kfar Darom, Palestine	Bus bombing	2
11/22/2000	Hadera, Israel	Car bombing of a bus	2
11/27/2000	Lahore, Pakistan	Bus bombing	0
11/27/2000	Burewala, Pakistan	Bus bombing	0
11/28/2000	Kebitigollew, Sri Lanka	Bus hits a land mine	7
12/8/2000	Gudermes, Russia	Truck bombing using a water tanker	3
12/25/2000	Hyderabad, Pakistan	Bus bombing	0
12/28/2000	Tel Aviv, Israel	Bus bombing	0
12/30/2000	Manila, Philippines	Bus terminal bombing	1
1/26/2001	Rishikesh, India	Bus bombing	2
2/5/2001	Grozny, Chechnya	Bus hits a mine	0
2/16/2001	Podujevo, Kosovo (vicinity)	Bus bombing	10

Date	Location	Description	Deaths
2/14/2001	Tel Aviv, Israel	Bus drove into crowded bus stop	8
3/2/2001	Umm al-Fahm, Israel	Bus bombing	1
3/7/2001	Jerusalem, Israel	Truck bomb using a garbage truck	0
3/7/2001	Grozny, Chechnya	Bus bombing	0
3/16/2001	Tovzeni, Russia	Bus bombing	7
4/1/2001	Dhaka, Bangladesh	Truck bombing	1
4/22/2001	Kfar Sava, Israel	Bus stop suicide bombing	2
5/25/2001	Hadera, Israel	Car bombing of a bus	2
6/25/2001	Maduvil, Sri Lanka	Bus hits land mine	6
7/20/2001	Karachi, Pakistan	Double bus bombing	2
9/6/2001	Digdol, India	Bus bombing	4
9/8/2001	Matan, India	Bus hits land mine	1
10/28/2001	Quetta, Pakistan	Bus bombing	2
10/29/2001	Belfast, Northern Ireland	Bus bombing	0
11/20/2001	Tafourah, Algeria	A bomb at bus station	0
1/25/2002	Tel Aviv, Israel	Suicide bombing of a bus station	1
1/26/2002	Bir Mourad Rais, Algeria	Bus stop bombing	0
2/3/2002	Bayt Immar, Israel	Incendiary bus bombing	0
2/19/2002	Mehola, Palestine (vicinity)	Suicide bus bombing	1
2/22/2002	Bhandara, Nepal	Incendiary bombing of a bus	5
3/5/2002	Afula, Israel	Suicide bus bombing	2
3/17/2002	Jerusalem, Israel	Suicide bus bombing	1
3/20/2002	Umm el-Fahm, Israel	Bus bombing	8
4/11/2002	Djerba, Tunisia	Truck bombing	20
4/11/2002	Haifa, Israel	Bus bombing	10
4/18/2002	Grozny, Chechnya	Truck bombing	17
4/25/2002	Jammu and Kashmir, India	Bus bombing	1
5/8/2002	Casanare, Colombia	Truck bombing of a bridge	0
5/8/2002	Karachi, Pakistan	Car bombing of a bus	14
5/14/2002	Calarca, Colombia	Bus bombing	0
5/20/2002	Ta'anachim, Israel	Suicide bus bombing	1
5/29/2002	Ahmedabad, India	One of three bus bombings	0
5/29/2002	Ahmedabad, India	One of three bus bombings	0
5/29/2002	Ahmedabad, India	One of three bus bombings	0
6/6/2002	Poso, Indonesia	Bus bombing	4
6/17/2002	Jerusalem, Israel	Suicide bus bombing	19
6/19/2002	Jerusalem, Israel	Suicide bomber attacked a bus stop	7

Date	Location	Description	Deaths
6/27/2002	Davao City, Philippines	Bus bombing	0
7/16/2002	Emmanuel, Israel (vicinity)	Bus attacked with grenades	7
8/13/2002	Shali, Russia	Bus hit a land mine	3
10/10/2002	Kidapawan, Philippines	Bus terminal bombing	8
10/10/2002	Tel Aviv, Israel	Suicide bombing of a bus	2
10/12/2002	Kuta, Bali	Bus bomb	101
10/18/2002	Quezon City, Philippines	Bus bombing	3
10/22/2002	Pardes Hanna, Israel	Suicide car bomb next to a bus	16
11/4/2002	Ganeshchowk, Nepal	Incendiary bombing of a bus	2
11/11/2002	Ramsu, Iraq	Bus hit a land mine	7
11/13/2002	Lasana, India	Bus bombing	0
11/14/2002	Malgobek, Russia	Hand grenade attack in a bus	4
11/14/2002	Charikot, Nepal	Bus hit a land mine	2
11/18/2002	Chintagudam, India	Bus bombed by remote detonation of land mine	14
11/21/2002	Jerusalem, Israel	Suicide bus bombing	12
11/23/2002	Munda, India	Army bus hit a land mine	12
11/25/2002	Mukinda, India	Grenades attack bus	0
12/2/2002	Mumbai, India	Bus bombing	2
12/27/2002	Chechnya, Russian Federation	Suicide truck bombing	57
1/5/2003	Jammu and Kashmir, India	Grenade attack on a bus stand	0
1/5/2003	Tel Aviv, Israel	Suicide bombing of a bus station	24
1/12/2003	Gaza, Palestinian Territories	Bus hit by grenades	2
1/14/2003	La Trinidad, Philippines	Bus bombing	0
1/19/2003	Kulgam, India	Grenade thrown at a bus	0
1/31/2003	Spin Boldak, Afghanistan	Bus on bridge hit a land mine	18
2/2/2003	Basaguda, India (vicinity)	Incendiary bombing of a bus	5
3/5/2003	Haifa, Israel	Suicide bus bombing	16
3/11/2003	Bogota, Colombia	Incendiary devices on buses	0
3/11/2003	Arauca, Colombia	Truck bombing	1
3/13/2003	Rajauri, India	Bus bombing at a bus terminal	4
3/16/2003	Bamungopha, India (vicinity)	Bus bombed by rebel triggered land mine	7
4/3/2003	Grozny, Chechnya	Bus bombing	8
4/8/2003	Gulu, Uganda	Grenades and bombs hit buses	10

Date	Location	Description	Deaths
4/12/2003	Qazigund, India	Grenade attack on a bus stop	1
4/12/2003	Kulgam, India	Grenade attack on a bus stand	0
4/23/2003	Carmen, Philippines	Bus hit a land mine and attacked by grenades	4
5/3/2003	Anantnag, India	Grenade attack on a bus stand	0
5/5/2003	Doda, India	Grenade attack on a bus stand	1
5/10/2003	Hyderabad, Pakistan	Bus bombing	0
5/18/2003	Jerusalem, Israel	Suicide bombing of a bus	8
5/23/2003	Netzarim, Israel (vicinity)	Bus bombing	0
5/30/2003	Grozny, Chechnya	Bus hit a land mine	0
5/31/2003	Hyderabad, Pakistan	Grenade attack on a bus	0
6/5/2003	Mozdok, Russia	Suicide bus bombing	20
6/11/2003	Jerusalem, Israel	Suicide bus bombing	17
6/23/2003	Shopian, India	Grenade attack on a bus station	2
7/12/2003	Kaloosa, India	Bus bombing	0
7/28/2003	Ghatkopar, India	Bus bombing	5
8/1/2003	Chechnya, Russia	Suicide truck bomb	50
8/4/2003	Vien-tiane, Laos	Bomb explodes at a bus station	0
8/13/2003	Helmand, Afghanistan	bomb wrecked a bus	15
8/19/2003	Jerusalem, Israel	Suicide bomber on a bus.	20
8/19/2003	Baghdad, Iraq	Truck bomb explosion	24
9/15/2003	Magas, Russian Federation	Truck bomb	2
9/23/2003	Tigzirt, Algeria	Truck bombing	0
9/24/2003	Baghdad, Iraq	Bus bombing	1
9/27/2003	Karachi, Pakistan	Bus bombing	0
10/12/2003	Irun, Spain	Two truck bombings	0
10/20/2003	Batmalloo, India	Grenade attack on a bus station	2
10/21/2003	Kulgam, India	Grenade attack on a bus stand.	0
11/12/2003	Nasiriyah, Iraq	Truck bombing	20
12/23/2003	Poso, Indonesia	Bus bombing	0
12/25/2003	Tel Aviv, Israel	Suicide bus bombing	5
1/4/2004	Medan, Indonesia	Bus terminal bombing	0
1/15/2004	Tikrit, Iraq	Bus hits a land mine	3
1/16/2004	Dhanakuta, Nepal	Bus bombing	4
1/28/2004	Baghdad, Iraq	Ambulance used as a truck bomb	3
1/29/2004	Jerusalem, Israel	Suicide bus bombing	11
2/10/2004	Iskandariya, Iraq	Truck bomb	50

Date	Location	Description	Deaths
2/12/2004	Bardibas, Nepal (vicinity)	Bus bombed crossing a bridge	6
3/29/2004	Tashkent, Uzbekistan	Suicide bombing of a bus stop	6
4/5/2004	Pulwama, India	Grenade attack on a bus station	8
5/23/2004	Woodsa, India	Bus bombing	28
5/30/2004	Kathmandu, Nepal	Bus bombed in a bus station	2
6/17/2004	Dagestan, Russian Federation	Truck bombing	0
6/24/2004	Guwahati, India	Bus bombing	5
6/24/2004	Istanbul, Turkey	Bus bombing	4
6/27/2004	Jalalabad, Afghanistan	Bus bombing	2
7/11/2004	San Francisco, Colombia	Bus bombing	2
7/11/2004	Tel Aviv, Israel	Bomb at a bus stop	1
7/19/2004	Baghdad, Iraq	Truck bombs hit police station	13
7/19/2004	Voronezh, Russia	Bomb at a bus stop	2
7/28/2004	Baqouba, Iraq	Suicide bus bombing	70
8/5/2004	Mozdok, Russia	Bomb attack on a bus stop	0
8/10/2004	Barkan, Israel	Bus bombing	0
8/25/2004	Guwahati, India	One of two bus bombings	1
8/25/2004	Gossaigaon, India	One of two bus bombings	0
10/7/2004	Taba, Egypt	Truck bombing of a hotel	34
11/13/2004	Poso, Indonesia	Bus bombing	6
12/24/2004	Baghdad, Iraq	Fuel tanker used as a truck bomb	12
1/2/2005	Balad, Iraq (vicinity)	Bus bombing	23
1/4/2005	Baghdad, Iraq	Truck bombing of a guard post	10
1/11/2005	Yussifiyah, Iraq	Bus bombing	7
1/14/2005	Karni, Gaza Strip	Border police truck bombed	7
1/19/2005	Baghdad, Iraq	Truck bomb attack on Australian Embassy	3
1/20/2005	Karamay, China	Suicide bus bombing	11
1/26/2005	Sinjar, Iraq	Truck bombing	15
1/30/2005	Abu Alwan, Iraq	Bus bombing	5
2/14/2005	Manila, Philippines	Bus bombing	3
2/14/2005	Davao, Philippines	Bus terminal bombing	1
2/14/2005	Beirut, Lebanon	Truck bombing	21
2/19/2005	Baghdad, Iraq	Bus bombing	18
3/9/2005	Baghdad, Iraq	Truck bomb hits hotel	4
4/1/2005	Mazar-e Sharif, Afghanistan	Tractor trailer truck bombing	2
4/5/2005	Srinagar, India	Bus bombing	0

Date	Location	Description	Deaths
4/5/2005	Tal Afar, Iraq	Bus bombing	3
4/30/2005	Cairo, Egypt	Bus station bombed	2
5/6/2005	Tikrit, Iraq	Iraqi police bus bombing	8
5/31/2005	Baquba, Iraq	Truck bombing	2
6/6/2005	Badarmude, Nepal	Bus bombing	38
6/10/2005	Narke, Nepal	Bus bombing	8
6/13/2005	Sungai Padi, Thailand	Garbage truck used as a truck bomb	1
6/13/2005	Groznyy, Chechnya	Bus stop bombing	0
6/25/2005	Srinagar, India	Car bomb attacks	9
7/7/2005	London, United Kingdom	Bus bombing	14
7/13/2005	Ofra, Israel	Bus bombing	0
7/16/2005	Kusadasi, Turkey	Bus bombing	5
7/21/2005	London, United Kingdom	Bus bombing	0
7/24/2005	Baghdad, Iraq	Truck bombing	40
8/10/2005	Karimnagar, India	Bus station bombed	0
8/17/2005	Baghdad, Iraq	Bus station bombed	25
8/28/2005	Beersheba, Israel	Bus station bombed	1
9/14/2005	Baghdad, Iraq	Suicide bus bombing	114
9/15/2005	Baghdad, Iraq	Bus bombing	3
9/23/2005	Baghdad, Iraq	Bus bombing	6
10/24/2005	Baghdad, Iraq	Cement truck used as a truck bomb	18
10/29/2005	Iraq	Date truck used as a truck bomb	30
11/14/2005	Jhalakati, Bangladesh	Bus bombing	2
11/14/2005	Ramadi, Iraq	Bus bombing	3
11/18/2005	Baghdad, Iraq	Truck bombing	6
11/19/2005	Beylikduzu, Turkey	Bus stop bombing	1
12/8/2005	Baghdad, Iraq	Bus bombing	32
12/12/2005	Baghdad, Iraq	Bus bombing near a hospital	3
1/4/2006	Ishaqi, Iraq	Bombing of a fuel tanker truck	0
2/5/2006	Quetta, Pakistan	Bus bombing	12
2/20/2006	Baghdad, Iraq	Bus bombing	12
2/26/2006	Hillah, Iraq	Bus bombing	0
3/2/2006	Baghdad, Iraq	Bus bombing	5
3/4/2006	Baghdad, Iraq	Bombing of trailer truck	0
3/4/2006	Baghdad, Iraq	Bus bombing	7
3/10/2006	Fallujah, Iraq	Truck bombing	7
3/10/2006	Rakhni, Pakistan	Truck hit a land mine	27
3/29/2006	Digos City, Philippines	Bus bombing	0
3/31/2006	Istanbul, Turkey	Bus bombing	1
4/1/2006	Istanbul, Turkey	Bombing of a bus stop	1
4/2/2006	Istanbul, Turkey	Bus bombing	3
4/3/2006	Baghdad, Iraq	Truck bombing near mosque	10

Date	Location	Description	Deaths
4/19/2006	Narathiwat, Thailand	Truck bombing	1
5/14/2006	Baghdad, Iraq	Bus bombing	5
5/20/2006	Baghdad, Iraq	Bus bombing	19
5/29/2006	Khalis, Iraq	Bus bombing	11
6/6/2006	Baqubah, Iraq	Bus stop bombing	1
6/8/2006	Mosul, Iraq (vicinity)	Fuel truck bombed	1
6/11/2006	Manila, Philippines	Bus bombing	0
6/15/2006	Kabithigollewa, Sri Lanka	Bus hit a land mine	62
6/15/2006	Kandahar, Afghanistan	Bus bombing	8
7/1/2006	Baghdad, Iraq	Suicide truck bombing	66
7/6/2006	Tiraspol, Moldova	Bus bombing	7
7/5/2006	Kabul, Afghanistan	Bus bombing	1
7/18/2006	Kufa, Iraq	Bus bombing	50
7/18/2006	Hawijah, Iraq	Roadside bomb near a bus station	9
7/31/2006	Trincaomalee, Sri Lanka	Roadside bomb exploded near a military truck	18
8/1/2006	Baiji, Iraq	Bus bombing	24
8/5/2006	Bangkok, Thailand	Bus bombing	0
8/6/2006	Samarra, Iraq	Truck bombing	9
8/15/2006	Mosul, Iraq	Truck bombing	5
8/27/2006	Marmaris, Turkey	Bus bombing	0
8/27/2006	Baghdad, Iraq	Bus bombing	9
8/30/2006	Kirkuk, Iraq	Bus bombing	3
9/12/2006	Diyarbakir, Turkey	Bus stop bombed	11
9/17/2006	Kirkuk, Iraq	Suicide truck bombing	18
9/20/2006	Baghdad, Iraq	Truck bomb attacks police	8
10/10/2006	Kabul, Afghanistan	Bus bombing	0
10/16/2006	Habarana, Sri Lanka	Truck bombing of bus terminal	67
10/17/2006	Baghdad, Iraq (vicinity)	Truck bombing	4
10/27/2006	Uruzgan Province, Afghanistan	Bus bombing	14
10/29/2006	Baghdad, Iraq	Bus bombing	1
10/30/2006	Algiers, Algeria	Truck bombing of a police station	3
11/13/2006	Baghdad, Iraq	Bus bombing	16
12/5/2006	Baghdad, Iraq	Car bomb hit bus	14
12/10/2006	Algiers, Algeria	Bus bombing	1
12/12/2006	Baghdad, Iraq	Car bomb hits bus	57
12/13/2006	Baghdad, Iraq	Car bombing of a bus stop	11
12/25/2006	Baghdad, Iraq	Bus bombing	2
12/31/2006	Bangkok, Thailand	Bus station bombed	1

Date	Location	Description	Deaths
1/5/2007	Nittambuwa, Sri Lanka	Suicide Bus	5
1/6/2007	Meetiyagoda, Sri Lanka	Suicide Bus	16
1/17/2007	Kirkuk, Iraq	Truck bombing	10
1/19/2007	Guwahati, India	Bus terminal bombed	2
1/28/2007	Najaf, Iraq	Bus bombing	1
1/28/2007	Ramadi, Iraq	Dump truck with chlorine	16
2/3/2007	Baghdad, Iraq	Truck bombing	135
2/12/2007	Baghdad, Iraq	Truck bombing	70
2/13/2007	Algiers, Algeria (vicinity)	Truck bombing	6
2/13/2007	Ain Alaq, Lebanon	Bus bombs	3
2/14/2007	Zahedan, Iran	Car bomb attack on a bus	11
2/19/2007	Baghdad, Iraq	Bus bombing	5
2/20/2007	Taji, Iraq	Chlorine gas tank trucks	9
2/21/2007	Baghdad, Iraq	Truck bombing using a chlorine gas tank truck	5
2/21/2007	Kirkuk, Iraq	Bombs at a bus depot	0
2/24/2007	Falluja, Iraq	Truck bombing	40
2/27/2007	Ramadi, Iraq	Truck bombing	19
3/11/2007	Baghdad, Iraq	Bus bombing	11
3/11/2007	Baghdad, Iraq	Car bomb hits truck	19
3/16/2007	Amiriyah, Iraq	Truck bombing using a chlorine gas tank truck	8
3/25/2007	Baghdad, Iraq	Truck bombing	20
3/25/2007	Hillah, Iraq	Truck bombing	20
3/27/2007	Tal Afar, Iraq	Truck bombing	152
3/29/2007	Fallujah, Iraq	Chlorine trucks	0
4/2/2007	Kirkuk, Iraq	Truck bombing	14
4/3/2007	Ampara, Sri Lanka	Bus bombing	16
4/6/2007	Ramadi, Iraq	Truck bombing	25
4/7/2007	Vavuniya, Sri Lanka	Bus bombing	7
4/12/2007	Baghdad, Iraq	Truck bombing	10
4/14/2007	Mosul, Iraq	Two oil trucks exploded	6
4/14/2007	Karbala, Iraq	Bombing of a bus station	43
4/15/2007	Baghdad, Iraq	Bus bombing	3
4/18/2007	Baghdad, Iraq	Bus bombing	127
4/18/2007	Rusafi, Iraq	Bus bombing	4
4/23/2007	Diyala Province, Iraq	Truck bombing	9
4/23/2007	Fallujah, Iraq	Truck bombing	3
4/24/2007	Ramadi, Iraq	Truck bombing	25
4/24/2007	Baghdad, Iraq	Chlorine truck bomb at military checkpoint	1
4/30/2007	Hit, Iraq	Chlorine tanker	10
5/9/2007	Irbil (Arbil), Iraq	Truck bombing	15
5/14/2007	Makhmour, Iraq	Truck bombing	50
5/15/2007	Diyala, Iraq	Truck bombing using a chlorine gas tank truck	45

Date	Location	Description	Deaths
5/18/2007	Cotabato City, Philippines	Bomb at bus terminal	3
5/20/2007	Ramadi, Iraq	Truck bomb with chlorine gas attacked a police checkpoint	11
5/24/2007	Colombo, Sri Lanka	Bus bombing	1
5/28/2007	Baghdad, Iraq	Truck bombing	24
6/5/2007	Fallujah, Iraq	Truck bombing	18
6/7/2007	Rabiyah, Iraq	Truck bomb at police headquarters	9
6/7/2007	Ramadi, Iraq	Truck bomb at police headquarters	3
6/7/2007	Abu Ghraib, Iraq	Truck bomb at Shiite mosque	3
6/8/2007	Qurnah, Iraq	Bus terminal bombing	18
6/10/2007	Albu-Ajeel, Iraq	Truck bombing	9
6/11/2007	Nairobi, Kenya	Bus stop bombing	2
6/15/2007	Bansalan, Philippines	Bus bombing	9
6/15/2007	Cotabato City, Philippines	Bus bombing	0
6/15/2007	Diyarbakir, Turkey	Bus station	0
6/17/2007	Kabul Afghanistan	Bus bombing	35
6/19/2007	Baghdad, Iraq	Truck bomb attacks a mosque	78
6/21/2007	Kirkuk, Iraq	Truck bombing	13
6/28/2007	Baghdad, Iraq	Car bombing of a bus station	25
7/1/2007	Ramadi, Iraq	Truck bomb	5
7/7/2007	Armil, Iraq	Truck bombing	150
7/12/2007	Lakhdaria, Algeria	Algerian solders attacked	8
7/16/2007	Kirkuk, Iraq	Truck bombing	85
7/18/2007	Tacurong City, Philippines	Bus bombing	0
7/26/2007	Baghdad, Iraq	Bus bombing	3
7/27/2007	Baghdad, Iraq	Truck bomb, Karada market	61
8/4/2007	Peshawar, Pakistan	Car bombing of a bus station	9
8/14/2007	Qahtaniya, Iraq	Four truck bombs attack village	500
8/14/2007	Northern Baghdad, Iraq	Bridge attacked again	10
8/17/2007	Christchurch, New Zealand	Bus bombing	0
8/22/2007	Baiji, Iraq	Truck bombing	50
8/22/2007	Taji, Iraq	Truck bombing	0
8/22/2007	Baiji, Iraq	Police station bombing with truck	23

Date	Location	Description	Deaths
8/26/2007	Baghdad, Iraq	Bus bombing	3
9/1/2007	Afisyoone, Somalia	Bus bombing	1
9/5/2007	Rawalpindi, Pakistan	Army bus bombing	24
9/10/2007	Northern Iraq	Truck bombing	10
9/14/2007	Beiji, Iraq	Truck bombing of police checkpoint	4
9/16/2007	Parwanipur, Nepal	Bus bombing	1
9/16/2007	Jaffna, Sri Lanka	Bus bombing	2
9/21/2007	Trincomalee, Sri Lanka	Bus bombing	2
9/24/2007	Tal Afar, Iraq	Truck bombing	6
9/29/2007	Kabul, Afghanistan	Military bus bombing	30
10/2/2007	Kabul, Afghanistan	Bus bombing	13
10/11/2007	Kirkuk, Iraq	Truck bomb exploded at a market	7
10/16/2007	Mosul, Iraq	Truck bombing	16
10/19/2007	Karachi, Pakistan	Truck bomb near Bhutto	136
10/20/2007	Dera Bugti, Pakistan	Bus bombing	7
10/23/2007	Mogadishu, Somalia	Bus bombing	7
10/25/2007	Mingora, Pakistan	Truck bombing	20
10/31/2007	Togliatti, Russia	Bus bombing	8
11/22/2007	North Ossetia and Kabardino-Balkaria, Russia (vicinity)	Bus bombing	5
11/23/3007	Mosul, Iraq	Truck bomb on bridge	0
11/24/2007	Rawalpindi, Pakistan	Bus bombing	19
12/5/2007	Baquba, Iraq	Bus station bombed	5
12/9/2007	Baghdad, Iraq	Truck bombing	8
12/9/2007	Algiers, Algeria	Bus bombing	12
12/9/2007	Nevinnomysk, Russia	School bus bombing	2
12/10/2007	Kamra, Pakistan	School bus bombing	0
12/11/2007	Algiers, Algeria	Multiple truck bombs	37
12/12/2007	Tambon Bang Khoo, Thailand	Bus bombing	0
12/17/2007	Mosul, Iraq	Truck bombing on dam	1
12/24/2007	Baghdad, Iraq	Bus bomb	2
12/25/2007	Baghdad, Iraq	Truck bomb	25
1/2/2008	Colombo, Sri Lanka	Bus bombing	4
1/3/2008	Diyarbakir, Turkey	Bus bombing	5
1/16/2008	Buttala, Sri Lanka	Bus bombing	23
1/29/2008	Colombo, Sri Lanka	Bus bombing	18
2/1/2008	Kabul, Afghanistan	Bus bombing	1
2/2/2008	Dambulla, Sri Lanka	Bus bombing	20
2/3/2008	Mogadishu, Somali	Bus bombing	5
2/5/2008	Weli-Oya, Sri Lanka	Bus bombing	13
2/12/2008	Beirut, Lebonon	Truck bomb	1
2/22/2008	Pakistan	Truck bomb	12
2/24/2008	Colombo, Sri Lanka	Bus bombing	0

Date	Location	Description	Deaths
2/26/2008	Tall Afar, Iraq	Bus bombing	8
3/2/2008	Diyala, Iraq	Bus bombing	5
3/4/2008	Lahore, Pakistan	Truck bomb	7
3/11/2008	Nassiriya, Iraq	Bus bombing	14
3/12/2008	Between Basra and Nasiriya Iraq	Bus bombing	16
3/12/2008	Mosul, Iraq	Truck bomb	0
3/12/2008	Samarra, Iraq	Truck bomb	3
3/14/2008	Humera, Ethiopia	Bus bombing	7
3/24/2008	Pakistan/Afghanistan border	Truck bomb	0
4/5/2008	Baghdad, Iraq	Bus bombing	3
4/14/2008	Mosul, Iraq	Truck bomb	12
4/22/2008	Ramadi, Iraq	Truck bomb	12
4/25/2008	Piliyandala, Sri Lanka	Bus bombing	23
5/9/2008	Midsayap, North Cotabato	Bus bombing	0
5/15/2008	Legutiano, Spain	Truck bomb	1
5/22/2008	Erez crossing between Israel and the Gaza Strip	Truck bomb	1
5/28/2008	Farah province, Afghanistan	Bus bombing	8
6/5/2008	Baghdad, Iraq	Truck bomb	15
6/6/2008	Columbo, Sri Lanka	Bus bombing	21
6/11/2008	Baghdad, Iraq	Bus bombing	5
6/13/2008	Kandahar, Afghanistan	Truck bomb	9
6/14/2008	Baghdad, Iraq	Bus bombing	2
6/18/2008	Baghdad, Iraq	Bus bombing	63
7/1/2008	Gayarah, Iraq	Truck bomb	1
7/21/2008	Kunming, China	Bus bombing	2
7/24/2008	Philippines	Bus bombing	0
7/25/2008	Bangalore, India	Bus bombing	20
8/3/2008	Baghdad, Iraq	Truck bomb	12
8/10/2008	Baghdad, Iraq	Bus bombing	4
8/12/2008	Peshawar, Pakistan	Bus bombing	13
8/13/2008	Tripoli, Lebanon	Bus bombing	18
8/20/2008	Bouira, Algeria	Bus bombing	12
8/23/2008	Kandahar, Afghanistan	Bus bombing	10
8/28/2008	Bannu, Pakistan	Bus bombing	8
8/30/2008	Columbo, Sri Lanka	Bus bombing	12
9/1/2008	Manila, Philippines	Bus bombing	6
9/2/2008	Mosul, Iraq	Bus bombing	4
9/20/2008	Islamabad, Pakistan	Truck bomb	60
11/4/2008	Baghdad, Iraq	Bus bombing	11
9/30/2008	Tripoli, Lebanon	Bus bombing	5
10/1/2008	Agartala, India	Bus bombing	2
10/20/2008	Baghdad, Iraq	Bus bombing	4

Date	Location	Description	Deaths
10/29/2008	Hargeisa, Somalia	Truck bomb	21
11/2/2008	South Waziristan tribal region, Pakistan	Truck bomb	8
11/10/2008	Baghdad, Iraq	Bus bombing	28
11/12/2008	Baghdad, Iraq	Bus bombing	12
11/12/2008	Kandahar, Afghanistan	Truck bomb	7
11/24/2008	Baghdad, Iraq	Bus bombing	11
12/4/2008	Falluja, Iraq	Truck bomb	13
12/6/2008	Baghdad, Iraq	Truck bomb	1
12/15/2008	Khan Dhari, Iraq	Truck bomb	9
12/24/2008	Lahore, Pakistan	Truck bomb	1
12/28/2008	Afghanistan	Truck bomb	14

Source: U.S. Government Accounting Office.

CHAPTER 13

Distribution/Network/ Configuration: A Photo Essay on Operating Control

Ross Rudesch Harley

Contemporary distribution stands or falls on the steps taken to securely move and store products, from the manufacturing phase to the customer phase of the supply chain. The global supply chain links together a complex network of organizations, people, technology, logistics, information, and resources needed to safely move products from the supplier stage to the customer stage of the process.

The configuration of this mobile network optimizes distribution by tracking and moving things as efficiently as possible from place to place. The guarantee of their secure arrival underscores the financial viability of the transportation industry.

In the 1980s, the term supply chain management (SCM) was developed to express the need to integrate the key business processes, from end user through to original suppliers. The basic idea behind SCM is that businesses cooperatively involve themselves in a supply chain by exchanging information regarding market fluctuations and production capabilities. Today's supply chain security combines SCM with state-of-the-art networked security requirements of the system, which are driven by perceived threats such as terrorism, piracy, and theft.

The supply chain network constitutes one of the world's largest industries. This global sector mobilizes resources that range from trucks to airplanes, trains, ships, barges, pipelines, warehouses, and logistics services. During 2008, the total value of the U.S. transportation industry was about $1.8 trillion. The supply chain, in its many facets and sectors, is estimated to employ about 4.5 million Americans. Recent improvements in credentialing, screening and validating of products, advance notification systems, locks and tamper-proof seals, perimeter checks, and surveillance systems provide the security that is essential to today's SCM.

Speed is a central component of SCM. Despite this, the sequencing and scheduling of inventory often appears immobile, locked away in containers, sitting on docks and lying inert. Velocity is measured not so much by land speed as it is by response time (the time between when a customer places an order and when the customer receives delivery of the order). This is a key determinant in differentiating the provision of services by competing firms.

Product variety (the number of different products available in the system) is guaranteed by standardized processing that calculates information inputs and outputs. Thus, information management provides the configurations that a customer desires from the distribution network. In a complex series of sourcing, manufacturing, and delivery of products, SCM networks privilege the concept of "availability" above all else (the probability of having a product in stock when a customer order arrives).

According to the principles of SCM, if all relevant information is accessible to all companies, everyone in the supply chain has the possibility of optimizing the entire supply chain (rather than making it less efficient based on local self-interest). SCM suggests that this will lead to better planning of production and distribution, which cuts costs and provides a better overall product. However, none of these efficiencies can be attained if the security of the supply chain cannot be guaranteed.

The wide acceptance of SCM has given rise to a new kind of competition in the global market. Competitive edge is no longer based on one company versus another, but rather takes place on a supply chain versus supply chain basis. For this reason, standardized data models have been implemented by the World Customs Organization in an effort to improve operational capacity while maintaining security of the overall system.

The WCO's Framework of Standards to Secure and Facilitate Global Trade, known as the "SAFE Framework" underscores the manner in which SCM approaches have influenced security management. The Container Security Initiative (initiated in 2002 by the U.S. Bureau of Customs and Border Protection under the auspices of the Department of Homeland Security) extends the zone of security outwards to reciprocal participant countries. Such initiatives seek to reduce the reporting burden of industry through the elimination of duplicated data entry and by maximizing the reuse of information across regulatory agencies.

Several distinct problems for SCM security have arisen in the wake of the global financial crisis of 2008–2009. As retail and business-to-business sales have fallen, worldwide purchasers and importers of goods have implemented inventory reduction to better position themselves for the recession. Because of this, orders to manufacturers have plummeted, and therefore the need to ship goods has plummeted as well. Much of the global distribution network currently lies idle, and security vulnerabilities do not have the same priority as economic fundamentals.

The global credit crisis has made it extremely difficult (sometimes impossible) to get the vital trade financing that has historically funded the flow of global shipments. In global capitalism, circulation (of all kinds) is crucial to the operation of the economy. However, firms that operate the container ships that traverse the world have seen a dramatic reduction in business. Intense competition and empty ships have created a fall in shipping prices. Ports are suffering a large decline in arrivals.

In early March 2009, the number of massive container ships sitting idle globally was estimated at an all-time high of 453 vessels. Container shipping prices had fallen by more than 90 percent at one point in early 2009.

Air cargo has seen substantially changes, with a global drop of 23 percent in January 2009. According to business reports, firms such as UPS, DHL, and FedEx are experiencing a significant slowdown in the movement of products via their global networks.

The recent downturn in global distribution needs to be seen in a broader historical context. According to World Trade Organization statistics through 2005,

- World merchandise exports have risen from $157 billion in 1963 to $10.159 trillion (in 2005).
- The nations of the European Union lead the world in merchandise exports, accounting for $4.0 trillion in 2004 and representing 39 percent of all global merchandise exports. The United States accounted for $904 billion, representing 8.7 percent of all global exports; China for $762 billion, representing 7.3 percent; and Japan for $595 billion, representing 5.7 percent of all global exports.

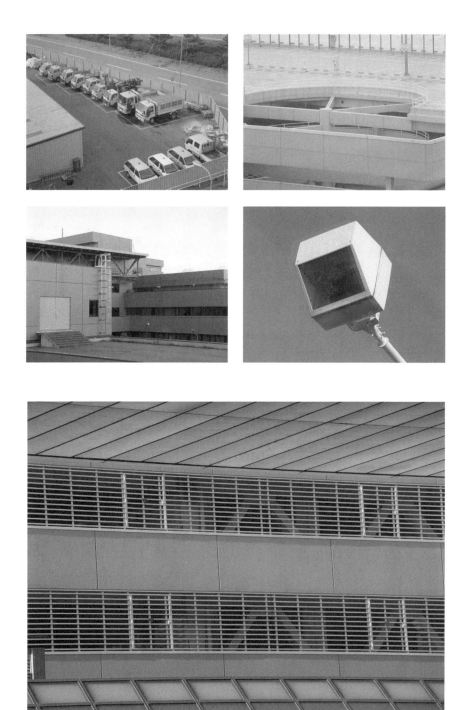

Index

About the Editor and Contributors

ANDREW R. THOMAS is Assistant Professor of International Business at the University of Akron. A bestselling business writer, he is author, coauthor, or editor of more than a dozen books, including *Direct Marketing in Action*, which was a finalist for the American Marketing Association's Berry Award for the Best Marketing Book of 2008.

Professor Thomas writes, consults, and speaks extensively on building the sustainable global enterprise, from supply chain security, production, and operations to marketing, sales, and distribution. His research has appeared in *The Wall Street Journal*, the *MIT Sloan Management Review*, and *Business Horizons*.

A successful entrepreneur, Dr. Thomas has traveled to and conducted business in more than 120 countries on every continent. He also serves on the visiting faculties of the International School of Management and Emmanuel University in Oradea, Romania. Andrew is founding editor-in-chief of the *Journal of Transportation Security* and a regularly featured media analyst for MSNBC, CNN, BBC, and FOX NEWS.

JARRET BRACHMAN is an internationally recognized counterterrorism specialist. He currently directs the Center for Transportation Security at the Upper Great Plains Transportation Institute, housed at North Dakota State University. From 2004 to 2008, he served as the director of research at the Combating Terrorism Center, West Point. Brachman routinely advises on counterterrorism and homeland security issues for the U.S. military, intelligence, homeland, and law enforcement agencies. Brachman has testified before the House Armed Services Committee and spoken before the British House of Lords, and his research is regularly cited in international press. His book, *Global Jihadism: Theory and Practice*, was published in 2008 by Routledge Press.

MARIA BUZDUGAN, Ph.D. is an associate with Milbank Tweed Hadley and McCloy LLP International Law Firm in New York City and Triant Flouris, Ph.D. is dean of the School of Aviation Sciences at Daniel Webster College, Nashua, New Hampshire. They have a combined expertise in the regulation and management of international civil aviation and extensive working experience in industry and academic settings.

FRANCES L. EDWARDS, Ph.D., C.E.M., is deputy director of the Department of Homeland Security's National Transportation Security Center of Excellence in the Mineta Transportation Institute and the director of the Master of Public Administration program and associate professor of political science at San José State University. She is a subject matter expert for the Department of Homeland Security and a site visitor for the National Science Foundation. She is past chair of the American Society for Public Administration (ASPA) Section on Emergency and Crisis Management. She is coauthor, with Friedrich Steinhausler, of two books in the NATO Science Series on terrorism threats and the author of a monograph with Brian Jenkins on 9/11, a monograph with Dan Goodrich on campus emergency planning, and numerous chapters for textbooks and professional books, most recently the ICMA's *Emergency Management: Principles and Practice for Local Government*, with Goodrich. She has written over thirty-five professional journal articles, most recently on disaster communications in *American Journal of Disaster Medicine* and on federal homeland security grants in *State and Local Government Review*. Dr. Edwards was director of the Office of Emergency Services in San José, California—America's tenth largest city—for fourteen years, including service as director of San José's Metropolitan Medical Task Force (MMTF) and head of the San Jose Urban Area Security Initiative. She has a Ph.D. and M.U.P. from New York University, an M.A. (international relations) from Drew University; and a Certificate in Hazardous Materials Management from University of California, Irvine.

A. O. ABD EL HALIM is currently the Chair of the Civil and Environmental Engineering Department and a Full Professor at Carleton University. He has been the Director of the Centre for Geosynthetics Research Information and Development. He has lectured and consulted in Canada, U.S.A., U.K., Egypt, Australia, Holland, Belgium, Norway, UAE, China, Pakistan, Japan, and Jamaica. He is the inventor of the new asphalt roller AMIR that is expected to revolutionize the field of pavement construction. Dr. Halim was selected the 1999 Top Newsmaker by the USA magazine, *Engineering News Record*. Also, he won the NOVA award by the *Construction Innovation Forum*, the Nobel Prize for construction innovation, making him the first civil engineer to receive both awards in the same year. Dr. Halim is the recipient of the 2005 Sanford Fleming Award for outstanding contributions to the development and practice of transportation engineering in Canada. He is a Fellow of the CSCE and has served as co-chair of the 4th International Rilem Conference on Reflective Cracking in Pavements. He recently led the establishment of two new programs that will start in 2009. The first is a "Master of Infrastructure Protection and International Security" which is a joint graduate program with the School of International Affairs and the second is a joint undergraduate program with the school of Architecture on conservation and engineering sustainability. Finally, Dr. Halim was appointed a member of the Executive Editorial Board of the Journal of Transportation Security.

MOHAMED ELSHAFEY has obtained his Master and Ph.D. from Carleton University and is currently a Post Doctor Fellow at the same university. Dr. Elshafey completed his Master's degree on the safety and security of airport passengers following the events of September 11, 2001. He continued his Ph.D. program in a challenging research area which dealt with the complexities associated with the fields of blast loading, use of numerical simulation to provide protection for transporting dangerous materials and the security and safety of the Canadian citizens. His work in both the Master and Ph.D. programs produced thirteen technical papers with three in peer reviewed Journals and ten in international conferences proceedings.

RICHARD FLOOD has a BBA in quantitative methods from Indiana University and a Ph.D. in management science from the University of Florida. He currently teaches statistics and economics at the College of William and Mary. His research and consulting interests are in the fields of decision making under uncertainty and applied quantitative methods.

TRIANT FLOURIS, Ph.D. is dean of the School of Aviation Sciences at Daniel Webster College, Nashua, New Hampshire, and Maria Buzdagan, Ph.D. is an associate with Milbank Tweed Hadley and McCloy LLP International Law Firm in New York City. They have a combined expertise in the regulation and management of international civil aviation and extensive working experience in industry and academic settings.

G. TOM GEHANI is a senior business analyst at Target Corporation in its supply chain operations center at Target's headquarters in Minneapolis, Minnesota. He played a leading role in Target's pioneering initiative to develop and roll out a national supply network for frozen foods. He majored in economics at the University of Michigan at Ann Arbor, MI.

R. RAY GEHANI is the director of graduate programs in management of technology and innovation at the University of Akron. He is a fellow of the

Fitzgerald Institute of Entrepreneurship and a fellow of the Center for Intellectual Property in its School of Law. His research and teaching interests are in global innovation strategies, and he has taught executive, graduate, and undergraduate classes in global supply chain management, production and operations management, strategic management, management of technology and innovation, and more. Dr. Gehani has earned two doctorate degrees: one in polymer science and technology from the Tokyo Institute in Japan and the other in business from the Graduate Center of the City University of New York. His seminal book on *Management of Technology and Operations* was published in 1998 by John Wiley & Sons.

DANIEL C. GOODRICH, M.P.A., C.E.M. is an emergency management coordinator for Lockheed Martin Space Systems and an instructor and Research Associate for the Mineta Transportation Institute at San José State University. He was a 2006 Fellow of the Foundation for Defence of Democracies. He has been the director for eight exercises for the San José Metropolitan Medical Task Force, where he created facilitated exercises, from which Harvard University's Kennedy School of Government created a case study. He served in the U.S. Marine Corps for ten years, including leadership positions in security forces, and in the Army Reserve as a small arms instructor. He is a consultant to the California Department of Transportation and has trained NASA/Ames Research Center staff in emergency management. His most recent publications are a monograph on campus emergency planning and the chapter "Organizing for Emergency Management," in the ICMA Green Book *Emergency Management, 2nd edition*, both coauthored with Frances Edwards, and three entries on nuclear topics in *The WMD Encyclopedia*. Mr. Goodrich has a master's degree in public administration from San José State University.

HECTOR GUERRERO is an associate professor and former director of the M.B.A. program at the College of William and Mary School of Business in Williamsburg, Virginia. He teaches in the decision making, statistics, information systems, general management, and business quantitative methods. He has previously taught at the Amos Tuck School of Business at Dartmouth College and the College of Business at the University of Notre Dame. Professionally he is active in the areas of operations management and information systems. He has published scholarly articles on the topics of logistics, catastrophic planning, intelligent systems, forecasting, supply chain management, product design, and demand management. Prior to entering academia, he worked as a power systems engineer for Dow Chemical Company, as a design and reliability engineer for Lockheed Missiles and Space Co., and as a consultant to Economic and Engineering Services, Inc. Professor Guerrero has thirty-five years' consulting experience with a wide variety of clients. Some of his clients include IBM, Newport News Shipbuilding, Northrop Grumman, Arthur Andersen, Miles Laboratories, Sterling Drugs, Lockheed, Digital Equipment, Welsh Oil, Trout

Trading Co., Müller Martini Manufacturing Corp., IRIS, U.S. Department of Labor, Virginia Dept. of Planning and Budget, Virginia Port Authority, U.S. Department of Justice, Transportation Security Administration, Hamburg Sud, and Maersk Lines Limited, among others.

ROSS RUDESCH HARLEY is an award-winning artist and writer. His video and sound work has been presented at the Pompidou Centre in Paris, New York MoMA, Ars Electronica in Austria, and at the Sydney Opera House. He is also well known for directing audio and visuals for the Cardoso Flea Circus videos and for live performances with Colombian-born artist Maria Fernanda Cardoso. Recent work includes *Aviopolis* (with Gillian Fuller), a multimedia project and book about airports (Black Dog Publications, London; Busface, a photo-media installation with the Ejecutivo Colectivo exhibited at ArtBasel, Miami; and the DVD installation *Cloudscope* in collaboration with Durbach Block architects at Elizabeth Bay House, Sydney. He is a former editor of the journal *Art + Text* and has written regular columns on design and popular culture for *Rolling Stone* and *The Australian*. He has edited a number of anthologies, including *New Media Technologies* (1993), *Artists in Cyberculture* (1993), *Before and after Cinema* (1999), and *Parallel Histories in the Intermedia Age* (2000).

In 1992, he was the director of the influential International Symposium on Electronic Art (ISEA). He is professor and head of the School of Media Arts, College of Fine Arts at the University of New South Wales, Sydney, Australia.

O. B. ISGOR is associate professor in the Department of Civil and Environmental Engineering at Carleton University. He carries out leading-edge research in durability of structures (natural or forced deterioration mechanisms), computational materials science (finite element method, boundary element method, computational fluid dynamics, and ab initio techniques), corrosion science, and nondestructive testing of concrete structures.

MOHAMMAD KARIMBOCUS has degrees in mathematics and transport and has been an active air traffic controller for over twenty years. He is presently in the management team of the Air Traffic Management Unit of the Department of Civil Aviation of Mauritius. Mohammad is involved in research in the fields of airport management and aviation human factors and contributed to *Aviation Safety Management*, edited by Dr. Andrew Thomas.

PANAYOTA MORAITI holds a degree in civil engineering and a master's of science in environmental engineering from Imperial College of Science, Technology and Medicine. Since 2005, she has joined NTUA as a research associate, developing research and consultancy studies in the field of transport planning and management, freight transport, transport modeling, transport security, and evaluation of transport projects. She is the coauthor of papers in scientific journals and conferences.

DAVID MURRAY holds a Ph.D. from the University of Michigan and an M.B.A. and B.Sc. (mathematics) from Concordia University, Montreal. Dr. Murray is assistant dean for information technology and a clinical professor of business administration. He teaches in the area of information technology at the M.B.A. and undergraduate levels. Prior to joining the William and Mary faculty, he taught at the University of Michigan Business School. His research interests are focused on the role that information technology plays in manufacturing and supply chain design and analysis, with emphasis on the ways that information technology can be used to improve the coordination of value-adding activities among firms in the supply chain. Dr. Murray has over thirty-five years' experience in the information systems field. He has held executive-level positions within large organizations in systems programming, operations and systems development, marketing, and strategic planning and has extensive experience in modeling, logistics system design, and operation. His consulting clients include the Department of Homeland Security, Amazon.com, Nissan, General Motors, Philip Morris, Sunoco, Trinova, Whirlpool, Avon, Andersen Consulting, Aspen Technologies, the Commonwealth of Virginia, the Departments of Justice of North and South Carolina, CANAC Consulting, Canadian National Railways, Indian Railways, Brazilian Railways, and the Kowloon Canton Railway.

YUKO J. NAKANISHI is founder and principal of Nakanishi Research and Consulting, LLC, a transportation security expert, technology researcher, consultant, and educator based in New York City. For the last fifteen years, she has been championing both technology and training to make transportation systems safe, secure, and efficient.

Dr. Nakanishi is the vice president of ITS-NY and has been actively involved in technology planning and management, security awareness efforts, and performance management and measurement. Dr. Nakanishi has published numerous technical and policy papers and reports. She is also the author of three books. Dr. Nakanishi is also a longstanding board member of ITS-NY, and chair of the Transportation Research Board Committee on Critical Transportation Infrastructure Protection's Subcommittee on Training, Education, and Technology Transfer, regularly participating as a panel member on Cooperative Research Program project panels. In 2006, she received the Transportation Research Board Excellence Award for Service. Dr. Nakanishi has published numerous technical and policy papers and reports. Dr. Nakanishi holds a Ph.D. in transportation planning and engineering from the Polytechnic Institute of New York University.

MARY F. SCHIAVO. Throughout her distinguished career in law and public service, Mary Schiavo has held corporations, institutions, and the government accountable for their obligation to protect the safety and security of the traveling public. From 1990 to 1996, Schiavo served as the inspector general of the U.S. Department of Transportation. She is the author of the *New York*

Times bestseller *Flying Blind, Flying Safe*, which exposed the poor safety and security practices of airlines and the failures of the federal government to properly police aviation. She also served as a professor of aviation and public administration at the Ohio State University, prosecuted federal cases for the U.S. Department of Justice as an assistant U.S. attorney, and served as a prosecutor in the Organized Crime and Racketeering Strike Force. She is a cum laude graduate of Harvard University and earned a master's degree in public administration from Ohio State University, where she was a university fellow. Schiavo earned a juris doctorate from New York University and was a Root–Tilden Public Interest Law Scholar. After leaving the Transportation Department, Schiavo joined the international plaintiffs' law firm, Motley Rice, where she leads the aviation team. She has represented passenger and crew families in nearly every major U.S. air crash and in many foreign crashes. Recognized by television audiences worldwide, Schiavo was a consultant for NBC and ABC News and frequently appears on NBC, ABC, CBS, CNN, Fox News, the History and Discovery Channels, the BBC, and Canadian Broadcasting. Schiavo was also a White House Fellow, assistant secretary of the U.S. Department of Labor, and Special Assistant to the U.S. Attorney General.

DIMITRIOS TSAMBOULAS is a professor at the Department of Transportation Planning and Engineering, Faculty of Civil Engineering, at the National Technical University of Athens (NTUA). Currently, he is the chairman of the board of directors of the Athens Urban Transport Organisation and member of the board of directors at the Athens International Airport. He has more than thirty-five years of professional experience. He has been involved in more than 150 research and consultancy projects both in Greece and internationally. He holds a diploma as a civil engineer from the National Technical University of Athens, Greece (1973), Master of Science (1975) and Civil Engineer's degrees (1981) from the Massachusetts Institute of Technology, and a Ph.D. from the University of Massachusetts (1983). He is the author of three books, chapters in twelve international books in the field of transportation, and more than 250 papers in scientific journals and conferences, with more than 300 citations.

Also by Andrew R. Thomas

Aviation Security Management: A Three-Volume Set

The Handbook of Supply Chain Security

Aviation Insecurity: The New Challenges of Air Travel

Air Rage: Crisis in the Skies

The Distribution Trap: Keeping Your Innovations from Becoming Commodities (with Timothy Wilkinson)

Direct Marketing in Action: Proven Strategies for Finding and Keeping the Best Customers (with Dale Lewison, William Hauser, and Linda Foley)

Defining the Really Great Boss (with M. David Dealy)

Global Manifest Destiny: Growing Your Business in a Borderless Economy (with John Caslione)

Managing by Accountability: What Every Leader Needs to Know About Responsibility, Integrity . . . and Results (with M. David Dealy)

The Rise of Women Entrepreneurs: People, Processes, and Global Trends (with Jeanne Halladay-Coughlin)

The New World Marketing, Volume 3 of *Marketing in the 21st Century* (with Timothy Wilkinson)

Growing Your Business in Emerging Markets: Promise and Perils (with John Caslione)

Change or Die! How to Transform Your Organization from the Inside Out (with M. David Dealy)

The Greatest Thing Ever Built: The Saturn V Spaceship (with Paul Thomarios)